Praise for *Heart to Heart*

"The brightest insights, the most powerful wisdom, and the most getgoing thoughts in network marketing are contained in this brilliant book."
—MARK VICTOR HANSEN, coauthor of *Chicken Soup for the Soul*® series

"Living a successful life is based on the connections you make with others. *Heart to Heart* shows how to do just that."
—JIM McCANN, president of 1-800-FLOWERS

"Everyone who is interested in making money should read this book."
—ROCKY H. AOKI, founder of Benihana Restaurants

"Few people outside network marketing have the understanding to bring the field to life like these two highly talented authors. *Heart to Heart* is a tour de force."
—PAUL ZANE PILZER, author, entrepreneur, economist

"Finally, a book that unveils the mystique and true benefits of network marketing while capturing the emotion and passion at the heart of this unique method of distribution."
—MITCHELL SCHLIMER, chairman of Let's Talk Business Network

"Wonderful stories—especially about the women who are succeeding and loving life in a field that sets no limits on achievement."
—CAROL ANDERSON TABER,
former publisher of *Working Woman* and *Working Mother* magazines

"Both entrepreneurs and CEOs will find this book a roadmap to success through the greatest profession of all—selling."

—JOSEPH MANCUSO, founder of the Chief Executive Officers Club

"This book will fill you with visions of free enterprise."

—DOTTIE WALTERS, author of *Speak and Grow Rich,* publisher of *Sharing Ideas* magazine, and president of Walters International Speakers Bureau

"You'll read about an incredible variety of people all living lifestyles that were once beyond their wildest imaginations."

—LINDA CHANDLER, author, inspirational speaker

"Doctors, ministers, single mothers, retired grandparents, regular families—all living unimaginably successful lifestyles. This book tells how anyone willing to work hard has a fair shot at joining them."

—PATTI DeMATTEO, president and CEO of JMW Group, Inc.

"The companies in this book have found ways to energize, motivate, and empower people that are innovative and cutting edge. We all can learn from these excellent company examples and practices."

—BOB NELSON, president of Nelson Motivation, Inc., and author of *1001 Ways to Reward Employees* and *1001 Ways to Energize Employees*

"Here are the principles and strategies you need for winning in the most revolutionary field of marketing."

—GERALD A. MICHAELSON, author of *Sun Tzu: The Art of War for Managers*

"What a wealth of valuable information! What a treasure chest of subtle, profound, and wealth-producing insights! My heart-to-heart advice to everyone is to read this book and feel your life being transformed."

—CYNTHIA KERSEY, speaker and author of *Unstoppable: 45 Stories of Perseverance and Triumph from People Just Like You*

Scott DeGarmo and Louis A. Tartaglia, M.D.

Heart to Heart

The Real Power
of Network Marketing

Prima Publishing

PRIMA PUBLISHING and colophon are registered trademarks of Prima Communications, Inc.

Library of Congress Cataloging-in-Publication Data
DeGarmo, Scott.
    Heart to heart : the real power of network marketing / Scott DeGarmo, Louis Tartaglia.
      p.   cm.
    Includes index.
    ISBN 0-7615-1759-6
    1. Multilevel marketing.   I. Tartaglia, Louis   II. Title.
HF5415.126.D34   1999
658.8'4—dc21   99-15073
                                                                CIP

99 00 01 02 03 04 05 BB 10 9 8 7 6 5 4 3 2 1
Printed in the United States of America

How to Order
Single copies may be ordered from Prima Publishing, P.O. Box 1260BK, Rocklin, CA 95677; telephone (916) 632-4400. Quantity discounts are also available. On your letterhead, include information concerning the intended use of the books and the number of copies you wish to purchase.

Visit us online at www.primalifestyles.com

Contents

Foreword

A GREAT CHANGE IS coming over the world. You will not read about this change in the headlines, nor hear it bandied about on cable talk shows. It was never foretold by John Naisbitt or Alvin Toffler or by any other brand-name trendspotter.

But the change is coming, nonetheless. It will strike without fanfare or warning. It will turn work and commerce upside down. No life in its path will be left untouched. In the wake of this change, millions of people around the world will find themselves freer, happier, and wealthier than they could ever have imagined.

Heart to Heart presents the clearest vision that I have yet seen of this coming change. Through a series of true-life success stories, Scott DeGarmo and Dr. Louis Tartaglia show us a world in which people no longer slave for corporate taskmasters. They introduce us to a new breed of entrepreneur: men and women who work for themselves, in the comfort of their homes, surrounded by their loving families—all through the magic of network marketing.

That's right. I said *network marketing*. Otherwise known as multi-level marketing or MLM. Only a few short years ago, it was hardly possible to utter these phrases without arousing snickers and grimaces. Network marketing was equated with chain letters and pyramid schemes. Its practitioners were envisioned as fast-talking hucksters in plaid suits and patent leather shoes.

But those days are gone. In the five-year period ending in 1998, the number one stock on the American Stock Exchange, in terms of profit growth, was a network marketing firm called Pre-Paid Legal Services. The largest financial services company in the world, Citigroup, uses an MLM subsidiary called Primerica to sell life insurance and mutual funds. MCI uses Amway to sell long-distance service. IBM offers Internet training programs through a third-party multilevel company called Big Planet.

The list goes on. In the last few years, network marketing has taken its place as an indispensable arm of corporate America. And it has emerged as a fantastically powerful industry in its own right.

Multilevel companies today do $90 billion per year in business, through 27 million self-employed networkers worldwide. In 1988, only 25 percent of the Direct Selling Association's member companies used multilevel compensation plans. Now nearly 80 percent of DSA companies use network marketing—allowing sales reps to recruit other sales reps and earn commissions from the sales of their recruits. Recent converts to MLM include the 113-year-old, $5.2 billion-dollar direct sales giant, Avon Products.

You would hardly know any of this from reading the business press. The MLM revolution remains, to this day, one of the great untold stories of American commerce. But it's a story that is not going to go away.

Scott DeGarmo and Louis Tartaglia, M.D., have set out to tell a big part of this story in *Heart to Heart*. That they have succeeded so brilliantly should hardly surprise anyone. No two authors could possibly be better qualified for the task.

It has been my privilege to call Scott DeGarmo my mentor for more than ten years. Along with the late Allen Ginsberg, Scott is one of two teachers whom I would credit with making me the writer that I am today. When I studied with Ginsberg at Naropa Institute, in 1981, the great poet taught me to write with clear, concrete images, with honesty and passion. But it was Scott DeGarmo who taught me how to inspire others and, through my writing, to bestow the gift of success.

Scott is a hard-boiled journalist who made his bones as a newsman and editor for wire services and newspapers, including *United Press International,* the *St. Petersburg Times,* and the *Philadelphia In-*

quirer. He later became editor of the 13-million circulation *Family Weekly* and of *Science Digest.* But it was in his most recent role as editor-in-chief of *Success* (1984–1997) that Scott truly made his mark.

When Scott took the job, *Success* was an obscure motivational magazine with a paid circulation of less than 200,000 and without a single page of national advertising. By the time Scott left, it had acquired 1.4 million readers, with every issue chock-full of blue-chip ads. Under Scott's leadership (both as editor and publisher), *Success* was cited repeatedly as one of the best-performing magazines in the country in growth in newsstand sales. It became a nationally recognized brand name, alongside *Forbes* and *Fortune.* As an example, during one six-month period in 1995, *Success* outsold *Forbes* and *Fortune* on the newsstand by nearly 100 percent.

How did Scott do it?

His secret was to combine two great traditions. Scott took the wisdom of writers like Napoleon Hill, Dale Carnegie, Norman Vincent Peale, and W. Clement Stone and married it successfully to the sort of hard-nosed business reportage exemplified by *Fortune, Forbes,* and the *Wall Street Journal.*

Under Scott's direction, a new way of writing about business evolved. It was packed with exhilarating human drama. But the tales were delivered in a levelheaded journalistic voice, brimming with sophisticated knowledge about sales, marketing, finance, and management theory.

Scott showed that inspirational writing was not just for the starry-eyed wannabe who goes home each night to gaze dreamily at the latest infomercial promising millions in real estate. Scott understood that small business owners, CEOs, and multimillionaire entrepreneurs all hunger for principles, concepts, and insights that will guide and motivate them in bringing their dreams to fruition. *Success* gave it to them, in a form that perfectly fit their sophisticated needs.

For all these reasons, the *Success* magazine that Scott DeGarmo created became the perfect vehicle for what would ultimately be its most lasting achievement—the championing of network marketing as a legitimate, mainstream business. In this endeavor, I was privileged to play a small but crucial role.

It all began innocently enough. One of my jobs, as senior editor of *Success,* was to write a backpage column each month, in which I predicted future trends. In May 1990, I wrote a column about a new method of word-of-mouth marketing that had recently come to my attention. The story was headlined, "Network Marketing: The Most Powerful Way to Reach Consumers in the '90s."

What I did not realize was that I had broken a time-honored journalistic taboo. It was simply not acceptable among "responsible" journalists, in 1990, to write positive articles about network marketing. When MLM appeared in print at all, it was virtually always in the context of some lurid exposé.

In recent years, I have been praised for the supposed "courage" that I showed in writing that first article. But my boldness came from ignorance, not bravery. I simply was not aware that the subject was controversial.

Scott DeGarmo, however, was keenly aware of this fact. By permitting me to do the story, he exposed his magazine and himself personally to tremendous criticism. Scott could have killed the story the first time I pitched it to him. But, instead, he gave me the green light, not only for that first column, but for a subsequent cover story on MLM that I edited. Scott's genuine courage in making these decisions is chiefly responsible for all the wondrous developments that followed.

Success readers, quite simply, went crazy. Phones rang off the hook. Faxes rolled unendingly. Letters to the editor gathered in heaps. And the message was invariably the same: Thank you, *Success!* Thank you for finally writing the truth about a great industry.

How long ago those days seem. Today, the industry has its own national magazine called *Network Marketing Lifestyles.* Positive pieces on MLM companies have appeared in *Inc., Forbes,* the *New York Times,* and the *Wall Street Journal.* But *Success* will always have a place in networkers' hearts, because it was the first to step up to the plate.

Long after I left *Success*—which I did in 1992—Scott DeGarmo and his Senior Editor Duncan Anderson (now editorial director of *Network Marketing Lifestyles* magazine) kept *Success* in the forefront of MLM coverage, providing the industry with what, for many years, was its only access to national media.

I went on to write MLM books such as *Wave 3* and *The Wave 3 Way*. Nearly half a million copies of the "Wave" books have been sold. At one point, in November 1996, both books appeared simultaneously on the *BusinessWeek* bestseller list, occupying the ninth and second positions, respectively. *The Wave 3 Way* appeared on the *New York Times* business bestseller list in the same month. Even so, not a single national publication chose to review either book. None but *Success* that is.

This is the kind of service that Scott DeGarmo and *Success* magazine have rendered for this industry through the long, dark years when MLM remained a taboo subject. And that is why it is uniquely fitting that Scott should emerge as the coauthor of one of the most important books on MLM ever written.

I have never met Dr. Louis Tartaglia but, of course, I know him by reputation. The inimitable "Dr. T."—a psychiatrist turned personal development coach—has delighted and edified readers for years with such inspirational classics as *Flawless!* and *The Great Wing*. Tartaglia's personal knowledge of network marketing (his in-laws transformed their lives through MLM) makes him keenly sensitive to the human drama of suffering, redemption, and ultimate triumph that characterizes so many of the stories in *Heart to Heart*.

The personality of each author is imprinted on every page. From Dr. T., the book acquires warmth, empathy, and a deep moral perspective. From Scott, it gains journalistic rigor, exuberant writing, and penetrating insight into the financial, sociological, and strategic aspects of MLM. Anyone who has ever worked for Scott can recite from memory a famous quote from the historian Macauley: "What is written without effort," Scott would admonish us ceaselessly at *Success,* "is read without pleasure." The pleasure that greets readers on each page of *Heart to Heart* testifies to the in-depth reportage, profound thought, and meticulous craftsmanship that characterize the book.

Heart to Heart brings the triumph of network marketing home to the general reader. For the experienced networker, it offers boundless inspiration and role models galore. It gives us a "slice of life" look at a great and growing industry and helps us understand why that industry is destined to play an ever larger role in our world. Most important of all, *Heart to Heart* shows us a new way to build wealth and security for our families, in one of the most turbulent and uncertain eras of economic history. It is a simple method, but an overwhelmingly powerful one, a method that proceeds one prospect at a time, eyeball to eyeball, face to face, and heart to heart.

Richard Poe
Author of *Wave 3* and *The Wave 3 Way*

Preface

WHAT IS THE real power of network marketing? The people in these pages have all discovered it. Before entering this new field they spent their lives as doctors, lawyers, nurses, military officers, housewives, students, ministers, entrepreneurs, executives, farmers, laborers, schoolteachers, athletes, policemen, clerks, computer technicians, welfare mothers, pilots, and college professors. Today, they hold the following truths about network marketing to be self-evident:

It's an exciting, energizing, uplifting way of life. You're in constant contact with positive people who are your friends, mentors, and coaches. They help you undergo empowering personal transformations that remove the obstacles to your success.

It's a new form of entrepreneurship open to all. You don't need a lot of resources to get started. You don't need to call on hundreds of investors or raise millions of dollars. You can use your own money to launch your own dream, and there's no limit to how big that dream can be.

Sophisticated business experts endorse the heart-to-heart method of selling. Financial analysts, corporate executives, marketing consultants, and even medical doctors—all quoted in these pages—have found that the personal testimonials used in network marketing are the most effective way to spread the word and distribute products.

You can create the lifestyle you want. Rather than becoming a tool of the business, you shape your work to the way you and your family want to live. You can travel, move abroad, or live in multiple locations. You can make the choice to live a life that's emotionally fulfilling.

You're surrounded by people who genuinely want you to succeed. Network marketing fosters true cooperation. Colleagues are profoundly motivated to help one another, both because they are bound in close relationships and because their success depends on mutual support.

Some people will never be happy working in a corporation. Sadly, many wrongly blame themselves, as if their unsuitability for corporate life were a personal failure. They spend their years trying to adjust or to find the perfect job. Yet many of these same individuals might find enormous satisfaction working in a home-based business. As a 25-year-old woman in chapter 14 says after getting a taste of being a wage earner and concluding it would be a waste to live that way: "You only get one chance to go through this life."

Competition is not the way. Traditional organizations will always be rife with internal competition. We often try to hide this fact from ourselves and then feel shocked or betrayed when it becomes obvious what game is really being played. Workers and managers compete among themselves for pay, status, recognition, advancement, and job security. Network marketing, by contrast, is structured in such a way as to render all this contention pointless.

There's room for everyone. Being disadvantaged, ill, disabled, unemployable, or saddled with past failures is no bar to prospering in network marketing. Some of the most successful individuals in the field suffer from chronic ailments and terminal illnesses. Top distributors include single mothers who have never been in the workforce, people whose health problems prevent them from holding a steady job, plus all sorts of workers who were fired, downsized, or saw their businesses go under.

Your mind is opened to unlimited possibilities. Ingrained skepticism often leaves people incapable of imagining themselves wealthy. Such was the case with a former journalist profiled in these pages. After seeing dozens of examples of network marketers who had achieved what he thought impossible, he overcame his self-imposed limitations and became a millionaire.

Personal growth equals business success. You have access to a limitless supply of the world's best ideas, mentors, and trainers in the fields of self-help and self-development. The people around you help you identify and deal with your problems and concentrate on achieving your objectives. The barriers to your success, such as problems with self-esteem, melt away, and as they do, your dreams come true.

You form powerful bonds that last a lifetime. Bonding with others to pursue worthwhile goals fulfills a deep need and is an elemental part of being human. While the business world is a poor breeding ground for strong, trusting relationships, in network marketing they are the norm.

Résumés and credentials mean little or nothing. People come from every walk of life. Past experience is seen in a whole new light. What's important is not what you have done, but how willing you are to learn and how well you adapt what you know to the new tasks at hand. The housewife, student, and day laborer find themselves on equal footing with the former executive, salesman, and entrepreneur. One woman who earns more than $1 million per year attributes all her success to what she learned as a mother.

People come first. In regular companies such statements represent noble intentions or just plain rhetoric. Those organizations could not stay in business for long if they really placed the needs of workers before those of the company. But in network marketing that's literally the way it works.

You'll be boss-free. Having a boss—good or bad—can be a mentally, physically, and emotionally unhealthy experience for many people. Being subjected to powerlessness, frustration, and unfriendly bio-chemicals that eat away at your system day after day is no way to spend your life. Even the most capable bosses can take the joy out of life in a system where people do not come first.

You enhance your own life and the lives of others. As one family puts it, you work part-time and live full time. You discover your "why" and live with passion, whether that means helping the poor in Latin America, building hospitals in Africa, or going salmon fishing in Alaska. As with the people in these pages, the choice is yours.

You can be there for your family when they need you. From attending soccer games to lending emotional support at the bedside of an ailing spouse, you can be wherever you need to be. Turning your attention away from the business does not stop the flow of residual income.

You share your success with your family. The conflict between work and home dissolves. Instead of being pulled in two directions, your life takes on a unity of purpose. Spouses and children can see how the business works and become a part of it.

Network marketing children are its most enthusiastic proponents. From day schoolers to college graduates, the kids of people in the business know they are special. It's no wonder that they so often choose to enter the business themselves.

It's easy for your children to step into the business. There will always be plenty of positions for your offspring in your organization, and you'll be able to allow them whatever degree of independence they desire.

The business brings families together. Siblings can freely share and cooperate with no apprehension that they will ever face the bitter rivalry that so often strikes family businesses. Mom and Dad need feel no pressure to step aside because everyone can have his or her own independent business within the family organization.

You can stop postponing the enjoyment of life. Having fun is the way business gets done. Cruises, trips, vacations, parties, and conventions—often in exotic locales—are plentiful. Some decide to travel the world with friends and families. And that doesn't just mean two-week vacations. It may mean six months abroad. People begin doing things and going places they never imagined possible.

You learn to dream bigger dreams—and you get help in fulfilling those dreams. The supportive individuals around you teach you how to dream dreams that matter—and then they help you make those dreams come true.

No other form of business grows as fast as a network marketing company. When nurtured and tended to in the proper fashion, an MLM business can undergo an astonishing explosion of growth. It's the best way to introduce a product and achieve rapid market penetration, as many fortunate distributors have found.

Much of the criticism of MLM is wrong. Press coverage tends to be inaccurate, misleading, and incomplete. MLM companies are radically different from traditional businesses, and are notoriously misunderstood by the media.

People find close friendships, emotional support—even romance and marriage. Meeting someone aboard a cruise ship, then falling in love and getting married at a wedding in front of hundreds of people in your organization, may seem too fortuitous to merit examination. But in fact it happens a lot. Within are the stories of various romances and how the couples were "set up" by fellow distributors who knew them, cared about them, and conspired to connect them.

You are part of a new wave of home-based businesses. Ever since the beginning of the Industrial Revolution, work has been taking men and women out of their homes and shaping their lives—always with the battle cries of Centralize, Mechanize, and Standardize. Corporations have dictated when we worked, where we lived, and the income we earned. Now, for the first time since we began streaming into the factories some 200 years ago, the trend is reversing. We are returning to our homes in great numbers—and many of us are discovering that it feels like the right place to be.

Introduction

I F ANYONE CAN come up with a better phrasing of the old saying, "Two heads are better than one," I'd be delighted to hear from you. The phrase is timeworn, but it expresses precisely what I think about this book.

For example, without two heads (that is, if I had written the book alone) it might have ended up being a manual—entitled *Eye to Eye,* or *Face to Face,* or even *Belly to Belly*—about the power of one-on-one selling. It would have been useful, but incomplete—heartless, so to speak—just like most business writing about network marketing. My coauthor, Louis Tartaglia, M.D., a psychiatrist and prominent author, made the difference.

For my part, I have written or published hundreds of magazine articles on the subject of network marketing—as well as thousands of pieces on business in general. In the past, in evaluating the success of a company or an individual, I had stuck to business criteria. My big question was always the same: Did the person or company achieve long-term financial success? I avoided the issue of psychic rewards—or psychic punishments, for that matter. If a person attained his or her material goals, then I considered such a person successful.

Whether their strivings had left them and their families happy and fulfilled, or wreaked the emotional equivalent of bankruptcy on their lives, was a matter I considered subjective and outside the realm of my inquiry. After all, I was experienced at verifying factors such as revenues and expenses, but I had no way of quantifying personal fulfillment, satisfaction, or happiness.

I even felt it could be misleading to make too much of anything as elusive and "unreal" as feelings when I was trying to demonstrate how network marketing was a valid economic opportunity. Yet as I stuck to this conventional path, I knew I was bypassing much of what was worthwhile about network marketing. I was exploring a country by driving on the interstates because I didn't know the back roads and byways.

I made do with techniques like assigning dollar values to the cornucopia of rewards network marketing made possible, such as free time and company-paid trips and vacations. But even the most financially successful network marketers I interviewed tended to put the highest value on intangibles such as friendships, relationships, spending time with their families, and personal growth. "How do you calculate dollar values for those?" I asked, dismissing the task altogether. They also talked about the profound sense of freedom they experienced, and the thrill of working with their spouses or being part of a team.

In a standard business story, relationships and teamwork are treated simply as means to an end—that is, a way of generating profits. But for network marketers, these were genuine payoffs, treasured for their own sake, and part of an entire way of life.

Beyond that, what was I to make of such cases as the following: A woman who had been abused as a child had suffered a lifetime of pain, depression, and low self-esteem, which therapy did little to alleviate. Upon joining a network marketing organization, however, her emotional life began to blossom. She found new friends and colleagues who genuinely cared about her, including successful women who acted as role models and even mother figures. Unlike the typical corporate employee, she had no reason to fear revealing her weaknesses and seeking help. Even her therapist was amazed after attending a meeting where her client gave a speech before a large audience—something she would never have been able to do before becoming a network marketer.

To my comment that the emotional details of this woman's recovery had nothing to do with business, my coauthor replied that such examples had everything to do with the quality of one's life, which was in fact our subject matter. I present this anecdote so that readers of this book can share the gratitude I feel toward Dr. Tartaglia for zooming in on exactly what I was insisting we ignore. In so doing he opened up our inquiry to layers of depth and humanity that I previously had omitted.

In the case of the woman in question, further thought on both the part of Dr. Tartaglia and myself led us to realize with renewed clarity that stories like hers were much more than inspiring anecdotes; they were central to the main point we had set out to make: That is, the supportive culture of network marketing, with its emphasis on personal growth, is precisely what gives it its unique power to change lives, develop businesses, and create wealth.

Dr. Tartaglia's insights into network marketing draw on his personal experience. His wife's parents, Joanne and Ralph Cline, have been involved in network marketing for nearly three decades. They entered the field after Ralph, a lieutenant in the Toledo fire department, became disabled while fighting a blaze. In the 1970s the Clines traveled the country in a custom-made motor home as distributors with Shaklee—a network marketing company founded in 1956—and later turned their business over to their son Daniel.

In the 1990s, "Dr. T."—friends also call him Lou—was there to watch the Clines build their current Shaklee business. Their success made an impression on Lou. He saw them driving the car they had earned. He heard about the annual conventions and the trips to England, Austria, Japan, and Hawaii. He learned from his wife, Barbara, what it means to be part of a network marketing family. In just the past year, he saw the Clines' income leap when the company's compensation plan was improved. He also saw their pride flower when six new individuals in their group climbed to the level of supervisor. Lou also used his trained eye to diagnose and discern just what made it all work for the Clines. "The key ingredient in their success was their belief in the business and what it could provide," says Lou. Today, Ralph, now in his seventies, says, "Where else can you go to build an income to whatever you want in spite of your age?"

Like the other success stories we recount, that one is a reminder of what first brought Lou and me together—namely, our mutual appreciation for Napoleon Hill, the great motivator and author of *Think and Grow Rich,* the bestselling business book of all time. We are both so steeped in Hill's principles of entrepreneurial success that we can assure the reader they are infused into every page. Yet here as well the "Two heads are better than one" rule holds true. I leaned toward presenting role models who were examples of such Hill principles as goal-setting, persistence, and self-discipline. Fortunately, Lou was on hand to make sure we did not shortchange his favorite Hill precepts, including applied faith, a positive mental attitude, and the power of the subconscious mind. Together, we covered the Napoleon Hill waterfront, profiling people who are all immensely uplifting examples of vision, energy, and enthusiasm.

One final note on this score: You may have wondered whether a psychiatrist's clinical and medical training robs him of his natural warmhearted responses to others. I can now report that the interviews we conducted revealed the answer to that question again and again. For example, after hearing one powerful though lengthy story of struggle and triumph, Lou looked at me and said, "Boy, did that pack an emotional wallop." Noting the symptoms he was suddenly displaying—red, watery eyes and an unsteady voice, which he sought vainly to conceal—I suggested he make a self-diagnosis. After a moment of reflection the doctor noted the cause as "Prolonged exposure to a gripping, heartwarming human drama."

"What about our readers?" I wondered out loud. "We'll be exposing them to this material. Will they be similarly affected?"

On this point Dr. T. was definitive: "The emotional content is intensely inspiring. It's inevitable that normal people will have a strong positive reaction."

Then Dr. T. added, in layman's terms: "It's going to grab them by the gut and knock their socks off."

So there you have it—a product warning of sorts.

Read the book, then watch out for what you're likely to achieve.

Like the people you'll be reading about, you may amaze everyone—including yourself.

Scott DeGarmo

Out of the Box

SEVERAL HUNDRED PEOPLE from around the country converged on the Orlando Airport Marriott in September 1998 for what was billed as the launch of a new company. In fact, it was a preliminary launch, in preparation for the full rollout in early 1999. The occasion was nonetheless remarkable. One reason was that the new company, Legacy USA, had descended from two of America's largest corporations, DuPont and ConAgra. Another reason centered on the revolutionary product the company would be marketing: BioChoice Immune Support.

A Radical Decision

THE PRODUCT APPEARED to have the power to change the lives of its users, both healthy people and those who suffered from disease. A dietary supplement, it had been in development for many years, taken millions of dollars to create, and had yielded more than a hundred worldwide patents. But what made the event worth noting was the method of selling and distribution the company planned to use. No new company with such impressive backing had ever made such a decision. The decision was unconventional—definitely "out of the box."

Simple, Powerful, Personal Stories

BioChoice Immune Support would not be sold in drugstores, or grocery stores, or via prescriptions—though all those approaches and more had been considered. It would be sold via distributors, who would be users themselves, and who would explain the benefits of the product in person—face to face and heart to heart. The efficacy of that method had just been demonstrated by a group of men and women on stage. As the applause subsided, a listener in the first row leaned over to her colleague and whispered, "You'd have to be a cold fish for that story not to pull at your heartstrings." Her companion whispered back, "All of the stories pulled my heartstrings. They were so simple, and personal, and powerful." Clearly, judging from the enthusiastic response, the rest of the audience thought so also.

Heart-to-Heart Testimonials

The brief testimonials from the handful of men and women on stage had been delivered without notes, or lecterns, or slides. They came from everyday people who had stepped forward, grabbed a microphone, and spoke with sincerity about problems that had plagued them for years. One woman had suffered from an intractable case of candida, a yeast infection that strikes people whose immune systems are weak. Next, a man told how he had endured a lifetime of distress from attention deficit disorder. Perhaps the most affecting story was from a young woman who told with dignity and frankness of being tormented by irritable bowel syndrome. Flare-ups of the condition had ambushed her to the point that she and her husband could no longer make firm social commitments. The attacks had mangled her social life, burdened her family, and undermined her self-confidence. When she, like her companions on stage, expressed her gratitude for the product that had apparently given her relief, her voice cracked with emotion.

"This Is Really Going to Work!"

As the group stepped off the stage, the strong, sustained applause seemed to signify several things at once. First, it was a compassionate reaction, expressing the audience's delight with the good fortune of each of the speakers. Second, it was a show of appreciation for their having appeared and told their stories. Third, the applause was a burst of approval for the sheer effectiveness of the testimonials—plaudits aimed not at the speakers themselves but at the decision makers behind the event. And, finally—if an explosion of clapping can be parsed this finely—the ovation was given by a highly self-satisfied group of men and women congratulating themselves and saying, "We made the right decision. By God, this is really going to work."

A Major Decision

"Why network marketing?" asked the next speaker. The decision to use it was momentous, he noted. But why did a company with the awesome resources of this one—formerly DuPont/ConAgra Visions, now an independent entity called DCV—choose to sell its product through the distribution method known as network marketing, or multilevel marketing, or MLM? It was a system in which anyone could sign up as a distributor and sell products and at the same time sponsor other distributors and earn commissions off their sales.

The Pluses of Network Marketing

Unlike the people delivering their testimonials, Neal Kane bore the earmarks of upper-level corporate America. His words, like his suit, were carefully chosen and well-tailored, though delivered in a friendly and enthusiastic fashion. Kane, a vice president of DCV, described himself as something of a latecomer and an outsider to network marketing. As he learned about it, he said, he had been won over by its many pluses.

One clear advantage, he noted, had just been demonstrated by the men and women on stage. As they had shown so well, the heart-to-heart selling that is part of network marketing "has the ability to deliver a complex sales message." In addition, he said, "You have the ability to tailor the message to the audience." Indeed, it would be hard to imagine a paid advertisement or commercial conveying even a fraction of the credibility, sincerity, and passion that had come across in the testimonials just heard.

Kane also noted that "network marketing has a demonstrated ability to develop new markets," and he pointed out that "vitamin sales today would be half of what they are without network marketing." He also noted that network marketing when done effectively provided "a faster route to market" for products. Such rapid penetration would enable the new company to outpace competitors and quickly achieve dominance. Kane also liked the fact that "you get rapid feedback on the success of new products." Yet another virtue was that "you create a potential route to market for other company products"—and in fact, he revealed, such new products would be forthcoming.

Finally, Kane acknowledged the presence of the corporate executives in the room by noting that network marketing boasted a "short cash-flow cycle time" with low inventories and low accounts receivable.

Why Create a Company?

Having made the case for using network marketing, Kane then addressed the question of why the parent company, DuPont/ConAgra Visions, chose to launch its own company, Legacy USA. It could, after all, have sold or licensed its product to any one of dozens of existing network marketing companies.

Kane crisply ticked off the reasons: "You can design the company and the product together. You can be closer to the customers. You can have quality control end to end. You have the ability to add new products with a cost that is a factor of ten smaller. You can unify the message and the marketing."

Other obvious reasons were that having your own company helps you ensure your product doesn't get overlooked in the product mix of other companies. It also helps ensure that you are not putting your fate in the hands of a potential competitor.

A less obvious reason surely existed in Kane's mind, though it would have been impolitic of him to mention it in a room filled with people who had been distributors for other companies. That reason was related to the prestigious origins of DuPont/ConAgra Visions as compared to the pedigree, or lack thereof, of the typical network marketing company.

Two Corporate Giants

The DuPont half of DCV's parentage derives from the venerable and still vital E. I. du Pont de Nemours & Company, a diversified chemicals, energy, and specialty products corporation with sales of more than $45 billion. ConAgra is the country's number two leading diversified food company (behind Philip Morris) with annual sales of $24 billion.

If the name ConAgra does not ring a bell as quickly as does DuPont, ConAgra's overwhelming presence in American life is confirmed by a stroll down the supermarket aisle past an ever-expanding array of brands that includes Swift's Healthy Choice, Hunt's, Peter Pan, Hebrew National, La Choy, Armour, Parkay, Butterball, Marie Callender's, and Swiss Miss. ConAgra ranks number one in U.S. frozen foods as well as in U.S. flour milling, and distributes fertilizers, seeds, food ingredients, and grain-based products worldwide.

The combined technology and know-how of these corporate giants had gone into BioChoice Immune Support, the product that was now being brought to market.

By contrast, Kane had learned, many network marketing companies were formed before they even had a product to sell. While he did not give voice to his thoughts on stage, he considered the field "cursed" by companies that were "nothing more than money games." Such disreputable organizations, he was sure, had kept the field of network marketing from growing. As a chemical engineer with extensive business responsibility during his thirty years at DuPont, Kane says he was "shocked" upon learning the way many network marketing companies operated. "Perhaps I was naïve," he says.

Family and People

But Kane withheld such thoughts on stage. Instead, he emphasized the positive aspects of network marketing. "You've got to start with the best people. I hadn't appreciated that," he admitted. "It's family and people." With his next remark Kane's gaze shifted to a man in the front row, the president and founder of Legacy, Ted Elias. "Ted has brought with him a lot of good people," Kane said, referring to the room full of veteran network marketers. However, only a handful of the people there understood just how lengthy a journey Ted Elias had traveled.

The Ted Elias Story

"IT'S NOT EVERY day that a billionaire asks you to come visit him," said Ted Elias to himself in June 1991 as his passenger plane lifted off a Florida runway and turned toward its destination in Cincinnati. Elias knew that the man he was flying to meet, the eighty-seven-year-old tycoon who had asked to see him, was an interesting character. "A billionaire," thought Elias. A millionaire himself, Elias wondered how they'd get along.

His host's name was Ralph J. Stolle. While few individuals outside of Ohio knew his name, one of the products Stolle had developed was a ubiquitous part of daily life in America. At almost the very moment Elias was thinking that, the flight attendant handed him a soft drink. He pulled back the tab and heard the familiar "fzzz-chnnk" sound as it opened. "The father of the 'pop-top,'" smiled Elias. Every time anybody anywhere did what he just did—and millions did it every day— Stolle earned a royalty. Well, if nothing else, one thing the two men would have in common was their appreciation for residual income.

Elias also knew the old guy was a visionary and a humanitarian with a special interest in health-related research that could benefit mankind. Of course, the products from that research could also be immensely profitable. That's where Elias came in. He knew how to get products into the hands of millions in record time.

If you asked all the experts, they'd tell you Ted Elias was the ideal person for the challenge Stolle had in mind. Stolle, of course, had indeed asked people. He would have done his homework, or had others do it for him, Elias knew. And what he would have heard is that Ted Elias had accomplished feats in marketing that few others had.

Sell it face to face, heart to heart. Ted Elias convinced others he knew the most effective way to bring a leading-edge product to market.

An Icon of Free Enterprise

Other passengers on the plane didn't recognize Elias. The only business magazines ever to run his picture were those geared to entrepreneurs. Yet for hundreds or even thousands of people, Ted Elias was and is a more meaningful icon of American free enterprise than the likes of John D. Rockefeller, Thomas Edison, or Bill Gates. That may sound like an exaggeration—a wild, even preposterous exaggeration—so it bears repeating, explaining, and underscoring.

The Making of a Hero

As a number of very sober, conventional corporate executives would eventually come to realize—and as Stolle himself had been informed—Elias really was a hero to many. He was a hero because all kinds of people who could never imagine themselves trampling competitors, or inventing lightbulbs, or creating software were able to identify with the accomplishments of Ted Elias.

A magazine story on Elias published in 1985 provided some insight. A picture with the article showed him sitting at the wheel of his custom-made Zimmer Golden Spirit, a metallic silver car with a huge 24-karat gold eagle on its hood. Elias had had the massive car custom-made, and it occupied space in the garage of his Boca Raton mansion along with assorted other cars ranging from Fords to Porsches to Cadillacs. His firm, Elias Enterprises, was then pulling in yearly revenues in the $650 million range, partly through real estate transactions and yacht sales. But land and boats were not the basis of Elias's wealth. Had he been just another rich real estate developer, Ralph Stolle would have had little use for him in June 1991. What had brought the fifty-two-year-old Elias to Ralph Stolle's attention were the same accomplishments that made Elias a hero to so many. The central fact was that the foundation of Elias's fortune had been laid twenty years earlier when he worked as a distributor for Amway.

"Come Back and See Us When You're Rich"

"Come back and see us when you're driving your Cadillac," someone shouted at Ted Elias as he walked out the factory door. "Ha, ha, ha," they all laughed. It was loud, scornful, mocking laughter. "Come back when you're a millionaire. Ha, ha, ha, ha." It was 1964, and Elias lived in Newark, Ohio, beside a dirt road in a trailer with freezing pipes. He'd just gotten married. His full-time job was as an unglamorous, hands-on worker in a Minute Man missile factory. He'd taken that job after a three-and-a-half year stint in the Air Force, which he'd joined after dropping out of school at age sixteen. His part-time occupation, which he had just begun, was as an Amway distributor—and he had just received his first monthly check. It was for $3.09. Up to that point—with the exception of the enforced egalitarianism of the military—much of Ted Elias's life seems to have been an experience in genuine deprivation.

Spinning tales about their threadbare origins is almost an art form among American businesspeople. But most of the stories of Elias's childhood don't fit into the I-walked-five-miles-to-school variety of anecdote that people tell their children and recall with a mixture of pride and nostalgia. In contrast to such heartwarming tales, the stories from Elias's past—especially as told by members of his family—tend to be heart-wrenching and heartbreaking. They are recollections of a family befallen by tragedy, where things were often desperately, terribly wrong. For public consumption, Ted skims the surface of these memories, turning them into humorous or self-deprecating sound bites. Those closest to him know the details. His sister, Thea DiNardo, believes that the pain Ted endured is what gave him his drive and turned him into a leader capable of empathizing with others. "Along the way Ted has had so many hurts. I think that's what gave him his amazing ability to communicate with people in that special heart-to-heart way of his," says Thea.

A Hardscrabble Existence

Thea remembers all too vividly the moment that their safe, secure childhood was blasted to tatters, exposing her and Ted to a cold and often ugly world. "My father died suddenly when we were toddlers. Ted was four, and this left him the man of the family. Mom had to go to work." Ted's younger half-sister, Linda Tuttle, says, "Mom was not well educated. She's a full-blooded Italian who grew up in an era when Italians were often looked down on and ridiculed, so she got out of school as soon as she could." Linda remembers stretches when "it was very difficult for everybody," episodes when "things were horrible." Her memory of life in the projects in Utica, New York, is that it was "appalling"—a hardscrabble existence in "houses with one person on top of another."

Of the years when Linda's father was married to Ted's mother, "it's the bad parts I remember so vividly, the worst things that stick out in my mind," she says. Her father's alcoholic rages made life both sad and scary. During the "years and years of struggle," their mother waitressed and worked on an assembly line making baseballs. But Linda especially recalls the dismal world of welfare, the bleakness of poverty, and the constant dread of having "a mom who was always sick, who once spent a whole summer in the hospital with hepatitis."

Heart to Heart Testimonial

Below is an actual example of the kind of personal testimonial that the makers of BioChoice realized would be a powerful marketing tool under the network marketing system of distribution:

> I [want] to relay the great success I have been having with your product BioChoice. I am an active, forty-nine-year-old male suffering with arthritis pain and stiffness. My back, neck, shoulders, and fingers are affected most, and I have pain and swelling in both knees. . . .
>
> I began taking one pack of BioChoice just before dinner about six weeks ago. After seven days, much of the mobility I had lost began to return. My back and neck became more flexible and the sharp pain I had been experiencing in my left

Linda Tuttle is now a happy, attractive, well-adjusted woman who's had a successful career, but talking about her childhood quickly causes tears to well up in her eyes. To be sure, not everything was gloomy. There were strong bonds of affection and loyalty among mother and children and siblings and grandparents. "We had so much love," remembers Linda. "My mother adored my brother. He was like her saving grace, her protector, who would take care of us all."

Teddy in Action

What stands out most brightly is the picture of "Teddy" Elias in action—working, hustling, and maneuvering with the speed of a shoulder subsided. I am an avid and aggressive racquetball and squash player and have noticed that my grip has become much better and that I am much faster on the court. Most important, much of the overall joint pain I had is beginning to subside. This has improved my life tremendously, and I feel energized with a general sense of well-being. . . . [My] psoriasis is improving as well, with some of the skin cracks, breaks, and bleeds completely disappearing. . . .

BioChoice has changed my life, and I am hopeful that others suffering from the disabilities of arthritis will obtain some of the relief I have experienced. I greatly appreciate having my energy and mobility back, which has improved both my work and home life tremendously. . . .

Yours Sincerely,

P.K.

demon to fulfill the role of breadwinner: Teddy shoveling snow with socks on his hands instead of mittens. Teddy mowing lawns. Teddy walking or running everywhere "because he refused to spend the money on bus fare." Teddy delivering papers and finishing in a blur so he could race to the diner and wash dishes. Teddy coming home at night with his pockets full of bread and discarded vegetables and the ends of salamis and putting them on the table.

Perhaps most telling of all is Linda's comment: "I will never forget the one time I saw my brother actually playing. I will never forget that day." It's not a cheerful story. Teddy had come across a stray dog, a German shepherd–type, and was walking home with it. Something had clicked between them, and they had become instant friends. On the way they passed a game of sandlot baseball and Teddy responded to the players' cries to join them. He knew he shouldn't, that he had more important things to do. He had a family to feed. He wasn't supposed to forget that. But Teddy pushed aside his concerns and stepped onto the field. As if in swift, divine retribution for this act of frivolity and defiance, the dog was struck by an accidentally flung bat and died in Teddy's arms. "Teddy was so, so upset. I'll never forget it," says Linda. "After that he worked even harder."

"Someday He'll Return"

When Teddy was in high school, Linda recalls, "my mom married my stepfather, her third husband," and the family moved to a farm and what Linda calls "a tarpaper shack with three or four rooms" near Rome, New York. The transition was also "the beginning of the end of Teddy being around. I saw him a few more times. Then he was gone." While Teddy made his way in the world, Linda began a life of long hours in the fields of the family plot, hoeing, watering, and harvesting, even getting up at midnight to plant thousands of peppers, then feeding the chickens before school. "Have you ever driven through a poor rural area and looked out and seen those little raggedy kids?" she asks. "That was me." While she worked, Linda often thought of the big brother she worshiped. She knew that someday he would return as a millionaire. She was absolutely sure of it. "He was my big brother, and he had promised."

They All Signed Up

Despite their gibes, Ted's coworkers at the Minute Man facility in Ohio—a windowless place Elias remembers as "a cross between a factory and an insane asylum"—eventually all signed up with Amway. After seven months, Elias quit work at the factory because he was making four times more in Amway than he was in his full-time job. When he left, he had twenty people under him in the factory who had attained the significant level of "Direct Distributor."

They Were Buying Like Crazy

Among the people Ted Elias met around this time was Charlie Marsh, a policeman in Rome, New York, where Ted's mother and half-sister Linda still lived. Marsh had used an Amway product called Shoe Glow and had become excited about it. He wrote Amway to obtain more product and information. Because Elias had customers in the Rome area, the lead was sent to him. Elias was now making frequent trips back home. As Linda recalls, "The first thing Ted wanted to do was get our family involved." Elias met with Marsh and signed him up as a distributor, putting him under Elias's mother. Soon, "policemen were buying Shoe Glow like crazy," remembers Linda. Then Marsh began signing up distributors as well as customers.

The Hottest of Hotbeds

Before long, the obscure and lackluster city of Rome, New York, population about 40,000, became the hottest of hotbeds of Amway activity. "All out of that little town," says Elias. "All were looking for a way out, and I was rolling." Among the distributors Marsh signed up was a truck driver named Dexter Yager. Today Yager's organization regularly holds rallies attended by crowds with several times the number of people who currently live in Rome.

Meanwhile Elias saw to it that his growing success precipitated a shower of gifts and benefits upon his family, one that continues to this day. The first "neat thing" Linda remembers as a teenager was driving Ted's Lincoln. From there the largess grew ever more bountiful. "He shared with all of us. He was able to give my mother everything she could have wanted." In an unending stream came living room furniture, television sets, new cars, refrigerators, stoves, washers and dryers, plane tickets and vacations, and much, much more. For his part, Elias remembers that success "just kept on snowballing." In the first year after reaching the level of Direct Distributor, he did over $1 million of business. "Amway itself did only $500,000 in its first year, and Amway had a head start because it grew out of another company," says Elias, referring to Nutrilite, Amway's predecessor.

Elias was Amway's youngest, fastest-growing distributor, able to retire after just seven years. Years later he returned and created a second successful Amway business. He became the only individual to attain the level of Diamond Distributor twice in two entirely different efforts.

A Billionaire's Passion

TED ELIAS HAD found his host at that first momentous meeting in Cincinnati to be "very cordial, and bright, and interesting. I was quite taken with him. He was a wise old man."

Up until his nineties, Ralph Stolle had continued to be vigorous and active. People who saw him at his offices in Cincinnati or at his farm in nearby Lebanon talked with wonderment about his energy. Elias recalls spending a whole day with him in meetings "and at the end of the day I was pretty much exhausted. He was still pumping."

Stolle himself had no doubts about the source of his prodigious energy. It was the direct result of the scientific research he had been doing on his farm for thirty years. The research was aimed at helping the human immune system fight illness; it had resulted in a number of U.S. patents for producing hyperimmune animals. It had also resulted in products created by injecting farm animals with human ailments so their immune systems would create antibodies useful to humans. One product was called Stolle Immune Milk. Ralph Stolle "was the living example of his own research," recalls Elias. "At ninety-one years old, he was running twenty-five companies, working fourteen hours a day, and loving every minute of it," he adds. "His friends were benefiting too," recalls Elias. "He had all these elderly friends and all were incredibly dynamic and on the go. Stolle had told them about the amazing impact Stolle Immune Milk had had on him personally, and now they all were taking it and telling others about its benefits. People joked that it was some sort of youth serum," says Elias.

Getting some form of his "youth serum" to market in the United States had become one of Stolle's passions. As Elias observed, Stolle "had wanted to do this for years. He was a humanitarian. He felt this could improve the quality of life for millions. He didn't need the money. He was a billionaire. He wanted to get the product out to the public."

Sell It Like Amway

As Stolle traveled about the world and ran his companies as if he were a nonstop dynamo, he told people about his product's remarkable benefits. His sincere, heart-to-heart testimonials were especially moving when he revealed that he himself was dying of cancer. His special product, he explained, gave him an energy he would not otherwise have.

From what Ted Elias could tell, Ralph Stolle seemed to have grasped a fact that had eluded many: For the kind of rapid, large-scale market penetration he wanted, there could be no more powerful means of distributing a product like his than by telling people about it face to face, one person at a time—just like was done at Amway and the other network marketing companies. Stolle and his associates had heard the case for network marketing, and Stolle had wanted action. "He was getting frustrated. He knew time was running out for him," said Elias. But the people in Stolle's company could not agree on the direction needed. Network marketing was too big and radical a step for some of them to imagine taking. Ralph Stolle died in January 1996 without realizing his dream of bringing Stolle's Immune Milk to market.

Without Stolle's support, what had seemed like a unique opportunity for Elias—a chance to sell a remarkable health product by network marketing—slipped away. The likelihood of his picking up the pieces seemed remote. It would have been a golden chance for Elias to demonstrate the efficacy of network marketing and build upon his past career.

A Quiet Man, Another Pinnacle

THE ROUTE THAT Ted Elias took to the pinnacle of success could not be more unlike the path taken by Dr. Örn Adalsteinsson, a science prodigy from Reykjavík, Iceland, who came to America as an undergraduate in 1969. He was recognized as one of the top ten chemical engineers in the country upon graduating from college. He then earned a Ph.D. at the Massachusetts Institute of Technology, where he was deeply impressed by the complexity of the human body's chemical interactions. Where Elias became a hero by recruiting distributors and living lavishly, the quiet, low-key Adalsteinsson ascended the austere and forbidding hierarchy of scientific achievement by illuminating the mysteries of molecules and securing valuable patents for his employers. By his early twenties, Adalsteinsson had risen high enough on the scientific pyramid to be on familiar terms with the luminaries at the very peak. In 1979, attracted by the company's technological prowess, he joined DuPont.

On Fire with a Mission

Despite his unassuming manner, since 1992, Adalsteinsson has been a man on fire with a mission. As vice president of DCV, he is the person most closely associated with BioChoice for the longest period of time. In spearheading its development, he had to overcome major scientific and technological obstacles.

As a DuPont employee, Adalsteinsson had traveled to Ohio to meet billionaire Ralph Stolle and evaluate the Stolle organization's work in creating products to support the human immune system. Adalsteinsson got to know Stolle. He admired his energy and vision. "I was fascinated by his love for science and his belief in hyperimmune products," he says. For Stolle, that belief included drinking daily doses of antibody-packed milk taken from cows that had been inoculated with human pathogens. "Stolle was a pioneer in the domain of hyperimmune products—in spite of not being trained in science," says Adalsteinsson.

Victory signing. A triumphant moment for research into the benefits of DCV's breakthrough product occurred in September 1998. Örn Adalsteinsson, seated, and Neal Kane, fifth from left in back, won a prestigious agreement—for extensive testing of the active ingredient in BioChoice—with the Department of the Army, signed by Col. David M. Penetar.

Rescuing the Technology

But even the wealth and willpower of a self-made billionaire were not enough to get Stolle's product out of the floundering stage it was in and make it suitable for manufacture and sale in the United States. That step required the takeover of the Stolle technology by the joint venture that came to be known as DuPont ConAgra Visions, or DCV.

Adalsteinsson knew Stolle's antibody-laden milk helped its users in the same way that mother's milk provides immune protection to a newborn baby. But Adalsteinsson proposed a more powerful solution than cow's milk. "People at first thought I was sort of nuts," he says. He knew that chicken eggs have almost twenty times more antibodies for their weight than cow's milk. In addition, egg antibodies are more effective than milk antibodies in eliminating infection.

Dr. Hellen Greenblatt, DCV's vice president for product development, recalls "the whole new way of thinking" she encountered when Adalsteinsson told her about an egg-based technology. "Extremely skeptical" at first, she too came to see that the egg was a powerful biological package precisely "because it is the chicken's only chance" to pass on immunity and nutrients to its offspring. Eggs could also be produced in huge quantities; they could be easily converted into powder form; and they could be economically packaged for convenient consumption. With DCV's egg technology, hyperimmune products soared from being a product used only by a billionaire and his small coterie of privileged friends to one that was available to the world at large.

Taking that step required tapping into Adalsteinsson's vast network of contacts in the scientific world. He knew that modern scientific progress relied on the work and knowledge of highly specialized individuals and teams. As he had seen all too clearly, in complex areas like biotechnology, maverick geniuses and independent scientific gurus rarely had the intellectual or financial capital to make important advances. What had made Adalsteinsson's new product possible was the immense resources of two giant corporations, DuPont and ConAgra. In describing the way modern science works, Adalsteinsson likes to quote a saying in his native Icelandic: "An individual alone is only half; with others he is more than himself."

Adalsteinsson had easy access to these "others" as a result of his brilliant scientific career. As if in preparation for his work at DCV, he had learned of the importance of "reaching out to others" to pursue multidisciplinary solutions. Working in collaboration with DCV, the U.S. Army did two clinical studies with BioChoice, and researchers at two leading clinics in Boston and New York—Beth Israel/Harvard and New York Hospital—are also doing studies. "I think that in many ways discoveries are based on exposure, breadth, and training, and the ability to integrate all the pieces," Adalsteinsson says.

The Marketing Challenge

NOW A NEW challenge faced Adalsteinsson. It perplexed him in a way that the science had not. Unfamiliar up to that point with network marketing, he and his company could not decide how to communicate accurately to the consumer the extensive benefits of their twenty-first century technology. One problem was that their new product was both more powerful and more subtle than the pharmaceutical and medical solutions previously offered to the public.

A New Approach to Health

For example, BioChoice was a natural product aimed at keeping people healthy rather than pumping them full of drugs and medicines after they became ill. Adalsteinsson knew consumers were rejecting the old approach to health. That approach often involved injecting the body with chemicals—with their deleterious side effects. Antibiotics killed not only the harmful, disease-causing invaders in your body, they wiped out many beneficial organisms as well. And their widespread use had led to the growth of superorganisms that resisted all treatment.

BioChoice, by contrast, worked to complement and support the consumer's own immune system, helping people heal themselves. It was packed with antibodies that zeroed in on specific harmful antigens: viruses, bacteria, toxins, parasites, fungi, and other organisms. It presaged an enormous boon to people with autoimmune diseases such as arthritis and lupus. In the view of Hellen Greenblatt, it was also a product that enabled users to go beyond the old standard of simply "not being sick" and allowed them to improve the quality of their lives. Greenblatt and the others on the DCV team began speaking of BioChoice as having the power to usher in "a new golden age" of health and well-being. Insiders at DuPont and ConAgra had even begun boldly comparing the product's benefits to the development of vaccines and antibiotics and to the discovery of vitamins. Adalsteinsson believed that its benefits might continue to be discovered for years to come.

How to Tell Consumers

The benefits, in fact, were so numerous that no conventional method of telling consumers about it would be suitable. It was a product with sixty major ingredients, plus subcategories of those substances. Its multivalent vaccine included antibody protection against diseases ranging from salmonella to *E. coli* to the organisms that cause tooth decay. Even a glance at the links on the DCV Web site shows the huge variety of potential users, including people suffering from or seeking information on arthritis, lupus, spondylitis, cancer, AIDS, bowel dysfunction, fibromyalgia, Crohn's disease, diabetes, and kidney disease. The DCV Web site also links to sites on preventive medicine and sexual health.

Perfect for One-on-One Selling

DCV vice president Neal Kane describes the marketing opportunity this way: "This product is perfectly tailored for one-on-one selling. In one case you'll be talking about flexible healthy joints. In another, about how it helps you maintain cardiovascular functioning. If you ran a conventional ad or commercial and put all those statements together, it would sound a bit strange and unbelievable. But when you hear from a friend about their personal experience, it's easy to believe."

Kane speaks enthusiastically today of heart-to-heart marketing. But the road he traveled down to accept multilevel marketing, or MLM, was not a smooth or easy one. In his own words, "I forced myself to look at it." Several factors impelled him in that direction. The first was Ted Elias. When DCV assumed control of the Stolle operation, Elias might well have been left out in the cold. Neither Adalsteinsson nor Kane had met him. Nor did either of them know much about network marketing. Moreover, what they did know struck them as negative. But Elias's legendary reputation kept surfacing. When Kane started doing background checks on Elias, he came across people who said things like, "Ted Elias? He was my hero."

Adalsteinsson, for his part, vividly recalls his first meeting with Elias. It took place in 1995 in DCV headquarters in Wilmington, Delaware. "I was totally intrigued with him," recalls Adalsteinsson. "He was well dressed. He presented himself nicely. He told me of his success in Amway and what he had done. I was impressed by his downline," he says, adding: "For me it was a challenge to get to know Ted, to find out what made him tick. I decided: 'He is an individual we should listen to.' I also thought, 'I would love to get this guy on board.' It took me a while to do so. We weren't ready then. We needed more data."

Debating the Routes to Market

Adalsteinsson invited Ted Elias to a positioning meeting at the DuPont Country Club in Wilmington. The gathering included heavyweight marketing people from DuPont and ConAgra as well as outside consultants in the areas of pharmaceuticals, retail distribution, and ingredients. Each expert had been invited to shed light on introducing BioChoice into the intensely competitive field of health-related products, a field that included overlapping categories such as neutraceuticals, functional foods, and dietary supplements.

Sitting around tables in groups of eight to ten, they discussed the various "routes to market" for the product. Attendees recall Elias as gingerly avoiding the role of being a blatant advocate for network marketing; instead, he presented the case for it in a restrained fashion that intrigued and enticed those around him. "He stayed objective about it," recalls one attendee. "He presented the pros and cons."

In retrospect, however, Neal Kane now says that from the moment Elias entered the picture he used all his persuasive powers to proselytize on behalf of network marketing. "One attribute to effective selling is that you never go away, you never give up," says Kane, noting that Elias was persistent and unrelenting. At the same time, Adalsteinsson was expending every breath on building support for BioChoice. He was campaigning single-mindedly "to get buy-ins from others, to get people on the team, to do internal selling, to get others on board." His campaign included sending BioChoice to corporate personnel, including a key executive at ConAgra and his secretary, both of whom suffered from arthritis. The executive quickly found relief from the stiffness in his neck and was able to resume his passion for hunting. His secretary felt so much better she was able to put off her planned retirement and work for several more years.

With such reinforcement, the stock of BioChoice rose internally. Anecdotes about such dramatic results became part of the unofficial lore of the company, cited at meetings as proof of the power of personal testimonials.

Nothing Beats Hearing from a Friend

The suitability of network marketing was again underscored in a series of focus group sessions held over a two-day period in 1995. The sessions "confirmed the importance of hearing about a product from someone you know personally, especially from a friend," says Kane.

Held at an agency in Philadelphia, the sessions consisted of eight or so potential product users around a table with a facilitator guiding their discussion. Observing from behind a mirror was a crowd of executives, plus representatives from the company's public relations firm and ad agency, and technical people from DuPont's regulatory affairs department. Whispering among themselves in the darkened room, they munched on free shrimp and listened intently for insights. "It became clear," says Kane, "that hearing a personal story told with emotion was a powerful way of marketing."

The event marked Kane's first step toward acceptance of network marketing. "I would never have thought about network marketing," he says. "Having it come up in that focus group session got me to think about it." Kane came to realize that "an attribute of network marketing is that you feel the passion. You feel the nonmonetary reinforcement of meeting with somebody you have personally helped," he says, adding, "Nothing is better for your ego than being looked upon as a deliverer."

Needed: Passion

IRONICALLY, THE CORPORATE and scientific backgrounds of Neal Kane and Örn Adalsteinsson would be of limited use in attracting men and women with the passion needed to merge their personal stories and identities with that of BioChoice. For that mission, you needed people outside the corporate fold, people who could get excited and commit themselves, people who could see this new product as a vehicle for their own success and independence.

They are the kind of people who look naturally to Ted Elias, seeing him as a hero, a soulmate, and another "real person" like themselves. They're the kind of people who flock to network marketing.

2

Real People

I WAS WARMLY AND totally accepted with open arms, and valued for who I was. I'd never experienced that at work before," said the enthusiastic networker. One of the "highs" of network marketing is knowing you can be yourself within a culture where differences are valued, not suppressed. By contrast, today's corporate workplace thrives on divisions and abounds in stereotypes. Employees often become reflections of their jobs, occupations, and companies to a degree that seems almost alarming. One corporation hires executives only if they are tough-minded and hard-nosed. You can recognize them by their speech, dress, neighborhoods, cars, and choice of Scotch, not to mention their children's schools, their breed of dogs, and their values (if you want to call them that).

Another firm is known for being dominated by engineering types; they are utterly different from the executives just described, though equally predictable. Yet another company favors arrogant MBAs; everyone who works there fits the mold. Law firms often select their new associates and partners with a scrutiny and concern for personal minutiae akin to animal breeders weeding out the non-pedigreed creatures who have the wrong coats, the wrong gaits, or the wrong bloodlines. Some call it all dehumanizing. Others call it ridiculous. Whichever, it's a world from which network marketing provides a breathtaking liberation.

Here, diversity rules, individuality reigns, and people mold their work to suit themselves, rather than vice versa. Network marketers come from anywhere and everywhere—including the corporations and law firms from which they've escaped or been expelled.

They enter a world in which they can always feel at home with their colleagues, a realm where no one ever gets demoted or passed over for having an unacceptable idea or for presenting the wrong image. It's a domain that has long embraced Les Brown, with his genuine, wholehearted enthusiasm, as well as folks like the other "real people" you'll meet in this chapter.

Les Brown

THE SPEAKER IS a dynamo whose words resound with hope and promise:

"Network marketing is a training ground for people to literally reinvent themselves," he is saying. It's a captivating message of self-improvement.

But can you trust him? Can you believe him?

You can, and you do—because he is Les Brown. You do because his story is so powerfully, overwhelmingly, hands-down convincing. If anyone knows about self-development, he does.

If anyone is speaking from the heart, he is.

He's One of the World's Great Energizers

Les Brown was born in abject poverty and abandoned as a baby. In school he was mistakenly labeled retarded, and was repeatedly scorned, shunned, and humiliated. He fought for years to overcome the stigma. Despite repeated kicks in the teeth, he scrapped and schemed and seized opportunities until he had a leg up on the world.

He went on to a life of enviable success, becoming an elected state representative, the host of numerous PBS specials, the creator of the *Les Brown Show,* as well as a bestselling author. By all accounts he is one of the world's greatest public speakers.

When he steps on stage and lets loose with his passionate delivery, you're in for one of the most energizing self-help stories ever told. Skeptics open their minds. Cynics open their hearts. And the whole crowd rollicks with laughter until their sides hurt.

Heart to heart means personal loyalty and a supportive culture based on personal growth. Speaker Les Brown has conveyed that message more effectively than anyone.

Why Network Marketing Is Special

Les Brown speaks before every kind of audience, from educators to civic groups. But there's a special place in his heart for network marketing engagements, he says. Why? One reason is simple: "Speaking for them is exhilarating. Where I leave off with a regular organization is where I have to come in with them," he says, referring to how pumped up he gets before he starts speaking with MLMers (multi-level marketers). "They push you to have energy, fervor, drive, and commitment. I love it."

Beyond the opportunity it gives him to rise to his best as a speaker, there's another reason he relates so strongly to these audiences: It was network marketing that launched his own career as an entrepreneur. The ill-fated soap company he joined went bust; the experience was, all told, a disaster, so you might wonder how it could leave such fond memories. The answer lies in all that MLM can do for you as a person. For Les, it awakened his entrepreneurial spirit. It helped him realize his dream of being a speaker. And it provided a powerful episode in personal growth that created within him a desire to have more, to be more, and to achieve more.

Change Your Habits

Les Brown has done training for most of the major MLM companies. Companies love him because he brings to life the transformation that people can undergo when they enter network marketing. It happens—as it did with him personally—when people change their habits and day-to-day behaviors and undergo an "internal paradigm shift."

Now, it's one thing to hear a slick former salesman—say of insurance or stocks and bonds—try to pump you up into believing you'll never be the same again. It's one thing to hear a smug writer or academic theorize about transformation from the comfort of a middle-class perspective. But Les Brown is a fighter who saw the worst of black poverty, who endured firings, rejections, and repossessions. Yet through it all he kept on going without ever losing his sense of humor or the decency and morality imbued in him by his beloved Mama, who adopted him as an infant.

He's not a guru with a super-secret success formula. He's a real person who's climbed the ladder by being conscientious, dedicated, and hardworking. In one book, *It's Not Over Until You Win,* he shares some of the painful, embarrassing moments that accompanied the failure of one of his recent ventures. The stories reveal a sincere guy who continues struggling to improve himself even to this day. With faith, optimism, and energy—lots of energy—you too can do what he promises in the title of his first book: *Live Your Dreams!*

Achieve a Personal Breakthrough

One legitimate question this all may raise is "Can I really stoke my inner fires until they burn with the white-hot desire Les Brown says I need?" You can indeed, promises Les. "I have seen it repeatedly over the years," he says, adding, "That kind of achievement has fascinated me." He marvels at how often MLM has been the launching pad for a shy or introverted person to achieve a personal breakthrough—and in the process ascend from making $30,000 a year while working a dreary job to earning $60,000 a month and living the lifestyle of his or her dreams.

Watch the Others, and Believe

It all sounds impossible, says Les, until you see others around you doing it. That's what opens up people's minds. They then say to themselves, "If that guy or gal can do it, I can too." In network marketing you see examples all around you, and you are empowered to dream. As a matter of fact, he points out, it was network marketing that caused him to dream of becoming a motivational speaker. After being part of a network marketing company, "I was never the same," he says. "I am a living example of what happens as a result of getting involved in network marketing."

In MLM you take your mind off what is merely likely to happen, and instead start concentrating on your unlimited potential. Les calls it focusing on your possibilities rather than your probabilities. Paraphrasing Ralph Waldo Emerson, he says MLM "helps people become architects of their own futures." That is exactly what successful entrepreneurs do. But becoming an entrepreneur on your own is full of pitfalls and perils. It often requires a heavy investment of time and money, and it has a high rate of failure.

You Get a Major Helping Hand

Network marketing sets you onto the path of entrepreneurship by giving you a major helping hand. Good MLM companies help you grow to meet your new challenges because they realize that your personal development is the key to their own bottom line.

More than any other vehicle in our society, says Les, MLM is a breeding ground for entrepreneurs. It prepares people for this role by requiring that they take a serious look at themselves. "They must ask what they have to give up or change about themselves. That's awesome!" In MLM, part of the individual's path of personal development involves casting off the old employee mindset and replacing it with a new independent mentality. You learn the habits of self-reliance needed for success as an entrepreneur. You are "forced to take yourself to another level. You become a person who accepts responsibilities and learns how to communicate with others." In short, it is a business that builds better people as a means of building bigger organizations.

Learn from Entrepreneurs

You must learn to be tough, says Les. Become a relentless talent scout for people. Choose those who passionately want more out of life. Find individuals with your same values, honesty, and willingness to work. Like entrepreneurs, network marketers are relentless in the pursuit of their dreams. They are committed to their goals and full of drive. MLMers are also much like entrepreneurs in being masters at building and maintaining long-term personal relationships. In one area, however, the industry is unique—and that's in the loyalty that people have to one another. "Making the transition from a job to being in business for yourself is never easy. But in network marketing you are never in business by yourself," he says.

MLM's Culture of Self-Development

"People are helping other people live their dreams," says Les. Only in MLM do you find that. Network marketing is also distinct in the strength of its culture of self-development. It is the glue that holds large organizations together. In the most sophisticated organizations, members listen to tapes each week They have book-of-the-month clubs. They provide support and training on a regular basis. When it comes to creating such a culture, Les believes Dexter Yager, a famed Amway Crown Ambassador whom we mentioned in chapter 1, has set the standard for others to reach. Les puts it this way: "As you grow, so shall your organization." It will grow along with your ability to recruit people and your capacity to help them share your vision and be a part of your dream. MLM "allows an individual to go from receiving a check to writing his own check. It allows the average person to become an entrepreneur."

Everyone Needs Multiple Sources of Income

The MLM explosion is happening at the best time possible for America, says Les—a time when job security no longer exists for anyone. New jobs and new industries are being created faster than ever before, and this means old businesses are being displaced at a faster rate than ever. Over six million people lost their jobs in the last ten years. For now, even if you plan on staying in your job, you can give yourself another option by beginning to build a network marketing business. "It's a poor rat that only has one hole to get some cheese out of," he says with a deep laugh. Eventually, says Les, everyone will learn they must have multiple sources of income.

Turning Your Dreams into Reality

During the two decades Les has been a motivator to the industry, he has watched it evolve. He has seen it become more sophisticated and also more user friendly. He's seen the creation of an array of new tools that makes communicating with your upline—those above you in the sponsorship chain—and your company easier than ever. "But what hasn't changed," he notes, "is that you still get in life what you are. Only if you are willing to do the internal work as well as the external work can you make your dreams become a reality."

To make sure your dreams are on track, says Les, start examining yourself. Ask yourself these questions about your desires and intentions:

- What are the goals I want to achieve?

- What is important to me?

- What is it that I want in life? The dream home? Free time?

- What is it that is driving me?

- Can I maintain my passion and bring it into the market?

- What kind of person do I have to become to achieve the results I want?

- Can I keep my commitment to my commitment?

In addition, he says, ask these questions about the company you are choosing:

- Have I found a product and organization I believe in?

- Is the compensation plan one I can live with?

- Does the organization have credibility?

- Is it financially sound?

- Will it continue to be strong in the coming years?

He'd Broken Away—Forever

As for Les's first misadventure in MLM, he was one of the early players in a failed business. He fondly recalls buying $3,000 worth of soap and bringing it all into his living room. A friend warned him that the floor would cave in from what looked like two tons of product. But while his floor did not collapse, the business did. By that time, though, he knew he'd never go back to pulling down a paycheck and walking the tightrope between "working hard enough to keep them from firing you while earning just enough to keep from quitting." He had broken away. For the rest of his life he would be an entrepreneur.

Looking back, he is filled with gratitude for the whole experience and all it taught him about being independent. Just thinking about his good fortune makes him humble, makes him fall to his knees and say, "Thank you Lord."

Pam Lewko

PAM LEWKO HAS accomplished a lot. You could call her a case study in spunk, energy, and stick-to-it-iveness. The scenes of Pam in round-the-clock action at home while building her business could be cut from a movie about a mom who for a limited time became a marvel of single-mindedness. But Pam always reminds you, "I couldn't have done it without my support system—my family."

Pam is also a superb example of how much pleasure one can get from setting a clear, specific goal and attaining it.

The Desire to Change

Today lots of little things remind Pam of how pleased she is with her achievements. For example, when baby Abbigail rolled over for the first time, it happened in the office right where Pam and her assistant were sitting.

As Pam recalls the event, her voice resonates with happiness, fulfillment, and satisfaction about the decision she made in 1995 to become a distributor for New Vision International, a company with nutritional, personal care, skin care, and sports supplement products.

Had she not made that momentous decision, "I would have missed seeing her roll over," she said. "It really hit home how thankful I was that I can be here—right here when my older son gets home in the afternoon, here when the middle one gets out of preschool."

These days, her approach is to "work really hard in the morning, and leave the rest of the day open." It's a big contrast to the nonstop effort she put in when she started.

Looking for a Better Way

The decision that changed her life came after she had "reached a point where I was sick and tired of the freeway, of missing soccer games, of missing award ceremonies." It was a state of mind that has been called

Pam Lewko found a company to "pour my heart and soul into"—and rapidly succeeded. L. to R.: Abbigail, husband Stan, Taylor, and Jason.

"inspirational dissatisfaction." Fueling Pam's desire for change was the fact that "I couldn't miss work, of course, and I was seeing a lot more of my co-workers and the freeway than my own family." There were days when she said to her son, "Please, please, please don't get sick. I can't miss work," she recalls. "I had gotten to where I was thinking, 'There's got to be another way.'" She realized she was not building anything for herself and her family, and she had no freedom.

Pam had had her second child, Taylor, in 1994. She was determined "not to compromise my family time. I had done that for way too long. I wasn't willing to miss out on anything with my second child."

It was at that time when a friend, Bill Jerrils, came to her with New Vision. After learning about the company, Pam told him, "Let me talk to my family." That night at dinner she outlined for her husband, Stan, and son Jason, then fourteen, what she saw as the pros and cons.

Stan was a top salesperson in commission sales. While some months his earnings were great, there was a long sales cycle, and months of uncertainty could go by when "it would get scary." Adding to the concern was the fact that just months before Pam learned of New Vision, Stan's company had fired its president. "If they could fire the president, I knew my husband was not invulnerable. We had one income, and that one income was very volatile. I was wondering if New Vision could possibly provide us the vehicle to really have consistency in our finances."

"You've Just Gotta Try It"

Her enthusiasm for the opportunity must have been shining through whatever doubts she had. In any case, Pam clearly remembers Jason urging her to seize the opportunity. "We were cleaning up, and Jason said, 'Mom, you've just gotta try it.'"

Pam called her friend back the next morning and explained her plan: She had to be making money within six months or she would drop out. "As we began working our list and telling people about the opportunity, I got really excited. I started calling everyone I knew. I realized quickly that I had found a company that I could pour my heart and soul into." Within months Pam had established a system that would allow her to use every minute of the day to maximum efficiency.

In the morning, she would do "all the regular mom stuff—get my older son off to school, get my husband off to work. Then I would put the baby down for a nap and run across the hall."

Pam would phone prospects while Taylor was sleeping, "and I would do nothing but phone during that period. I would not organize the office, I would not write letters. Doing those things doesn't bring people into your group." Those tasks would be saved for later in the day and evening—and sometimes far into the night.

At times the routine was grueling. "But I had talked with my family and we had an agreement that I would work really hard for two years, and that life might be crazy but that all of us were going to have to pull together and chip in." Pam stayed motivated by keeping her mind focused on the payoff.

Each day she scrambled to fit her work in between the rhythms of family life. At first Taylor was taking three naps, then two, then one. As her phone time got squeezed, Pam began using a cordless headset. "And so there I would be out in the sandbox or pushing him on the swing or walking around making phone calls. For quite a while he didn't know I was talking on the phone—he thought I was talking to him. So I played with him and watched him as I was conducting business."

Before long the calls plus the follow-up meant Pam was getting no more than three to four hours of sleep a night. Her husband was at

Heart to Heart **Wisdom**

Pam Lewko, New Vision International:

"Network marketing is real people impacting real lives. It is about changing people's lives, and changing their futures. Our products and businesses have saved lives, helped people with their health challenges, and saved them when they couldn't make house payments and buy food and groceries. So please remember it is those stories that sell and change the directions of people's lives."

"It is really a business where you are able to inspire others."

"I don't know anybody who has ever signed up off the cold hard facts. People need stories."

"I always ask people how has this business changed your life and how have the products changed your life. I can pull out stories."

"If the focus is too much on yourself, you don't get anywhere. Put the focus on other people. If you help enough people get what they want, then you'll be able to get what you want."

"It is all about teamwork, about helping people achieve their goals and their dreams. You need to ask people, 'How can I help you?'"

"A lot of salespeople don't do well at first in network marketing. They are used to selling facts to a president or vice president who is trying to make a strictly rational decision."

"I always keep this handy fact sheet about the business right next to the telephone. There are thinkers who need facts to help make their decision."

"When you introduce the product first, then it can be hard to segue into the opportunity. But it is easy to segue into the products after presenting the opportunity."

"You need to just keep in touch, to keep 'dripping on people' and sharing stories."

"There's magic on those three-way calls. It's the power of three, the blend of different personalities. When you're new you don't have all the answers yourself. But two of you will come up with the answer. It takes the pressure off and relaxes you and you have more fun. There's something magical that happens."

"Another magical thing about a three-way call is the access to a different story bank."

"People get stuck thinking, 'I don't know a lot of people.' But it is not about who you know, but who they know."

"I don't see any problem with telling friends. If a friend owned a grocery store you'd be buying groceries there, or you'd be buying insurance from a friend. People get stuck on that, but it need not be a problem."

"This business is an opportunity to manage, to listen, to help people, to share blessings."

that time a real morning person; his company's home office was on the East Coast, and that pulled him out of bed early. At the same time, Pam was pulled in both directions, taking advantage of the nights "to put packs together and stuff envelopes and write letters and label tapes and think of whom could I call in Hawaii or Alaska."

"There were times when I was going to bed at two or three or four in the morning as my husband was getting up," she remembers.

Looking Back with Pride

Today Pam and her family look back at that time with a mixture of pride and nostalgia. "Over the weekend we laughed about what we had done," she said. "Stan said to me, 'I don't know how you survived that period.' But when you look at it," notes Pam, "two years is such a short time. I doubled his income last year, which was really cool. My first goal with New Vision was to make the house payment. My third check was over $1,200, so I could almost make it. I made it by the fourth check. Then the next goal was to replace my husband's income. During my first full year in New Vision, I did replace his income—$100,000 per year. Last year I doubled his income," says Pam, who is now an Executive Diamond in New Vision.

Fortunately, Stan's income soared in 1998, but the hit it took in 1997 still makes Pam say, "Thank God for New Vision." She's reminded how glad she is she put in the effort.

"So just for a very short time—for two years—I worked my rear off and survived on very little sleep. Now we have a consistent income. We are able to send our son to a private school, which would not have been an option before, and he can choose to go to a private college."

One of the activities that especially pleases Pam is her ongoing financial contributions to two San Diego area missionary families, one in Papua, New Guinea, and the other in South Africa. Thanks in part to her donations, New Guinea will be getting a new airstrip for receiving supplies, and the family in South Africa was recently able to buy a new car to replace the broken-down one they were using.

"People who go out on a mission in the field and risk their lives to share the Word are the ultimate example of selflessness. I have a real place in my heart for people who make that their calling and passion." Pam eagerly reads the letters from the families—letters that describe the challenges and physical dangers of living in the bush, as well as the hardships and deprivations of the natives. By comparison, whatever difficulties she and her family may be facing always appear to her as trivial.

Despite the immense work, looking back now Pam calls the whole experience "a pretty fun journey."

Rocking Abbigail in her arms, Pam sympathizes with "my friends who have tough choices to make. I don't want to leave my baby. I am so thankful I did not have to do that. I don't have to make that tough decision."

And then she adds, "I'm so, so thankful I can work at home."

Paul Stevens

ON HIS WAY to building a personal fortune in Amway, Paul Stevens collected enough entertaining stories from around the world to fill several large volumes. One anecdote in particular paints a colorful vignette of some delightfully ambitious women in a village in Panama.

Little Soldiers in the Revolution

Stevens knows, however, that the account of their antics and hustle-bustle energy is much more than just an amusing tale. Some would call it a sympathetic story of simple people and their humble dreams. That description is not too far off the mark, except that it surely conveys an untruth in suggesting that the dreams of poor people in thatched huts are any different, at bottom, from the dreams, hopes, and aspirations that we all have for ourselves and our families.

Worldwide Appeal

When introduced to network marketing in 1983, Stevens quickly foresaw its worldwide appeal and looked forward to taking it to foreign markets. Born in Puerto Rico, Stevens lived in Miami and worked in communications, theater, TV, and film, selling his bicultural expertise to ad agencies that produced commercials in Spanish. As such, he was the perfect person to build MLM organizations in the Hispanic community in the United States as well as to export MLM to Latin countries. He also understood the many nuances of the Latino cultures and how they differed from one Hispanic country to another.

Taking network marketing to other cultures, Paul Stevens moved swiftly. Before long he had signed up Chefita, or "Wonder Woman."

One of the first stereotypes Stevens had to combat among U.S. distributors was their view that going into Latin America meant dealing only with prospects with limited ambition who would put off everything until *mañana*. "We would go into a new country and deal with the middle class," he notes. Some of the prospects "were yuppies who had gone to Wharton, watched CNN, and made a good living," Stevens adds. His Yankee compatriots "didn't understand that right away." But Stevens did, and for that reason took the Latin opportunity seriously. In Panama, for example, his keen appreciation of the marketplace allowed Stevens to put one thousand distributors into his group within ten days after Amway opened the country.

Breaking the Cycle of Poverty

On the other hand, not all his distributors came from affluent classes. Indeed, one of the miracles of network marketing in general and of Amway in particular has been its ability to give people from low-income economies a way to put themselves on an entirely new economic footing. Without the ability to accumulate a small stake of capital, poor families can be forced to continue in a hand-to-mouth struggle for years. No matter how hard they work, they're unable to climb out of the backbreaking cycle of poverty. For such people, the rewards of network marketing have proven to be more abundant than all the false promises of all of this century's bloody revolutions combined.

In any case, even with his cultural sensitivity, Stevens wasn't always ready for the "diversity" that faced him. Following up on a referral that originated with a man in Oklahoma, Stevens drove for two and a half hours out to a dry province in central Panama to show the Amway plan to a lady named Chefita.

"It was the classic example of a referral," says Stevens. "Chefita told me that if her brother-in-law in Oklahoma said, 'Do it,' then she was in, whatever it was." Here Stevens digresses to weave into his anecdote some pointers on what he considers the most important success factor in network marketing—the power of getting the recommendation of a trusted friend. "If you are looking to enter into a close relationship you don't go to a phone book. The core of the MLM concept is one friend talking to another."

Chefita's Big Dreams

Though Chefita appeared to be an unlikely candidate, Paul started making the lengthy trips out to her village to help her. He recalls, "She had no car, rode a bicycle, and had to practically beg for work. But she did whatever she could to take care of her family."

Chefita had dreams, big dreams, to own her own property. She needed $300 to get a plot of land so that she could build a house. Her first month in the business she earned $90. That was more than she had ever earned in one month. In her second month she earned $300. "I told her she could buy her land now," says Stevens. "But now she had a bigger dream, for a bigger piece of land. So she bought a motorcycle instead. It gave her status and helped her go beyond the village and sell product. People began to call her La Mujer Maravilla—Wonder Woman."

It was at about that time that Amway began selling its cosmetic line in Panama. Stevens drove out to do a meeting for a distributor in his group. He found his way through the countryside to a group of houses with thatched roofs. The walls were made of quincha, a reed that is used in making huts in Central America. As was the custom, the reeds stopped short of the roof of the hut, leaving a gap. "Get the picture," says Stevens, clearly enjoying his retelling of the story. "There were two rooms—a kitchen–living room combo and a bedroom. I set up my white board to do the meeting. Three ladies were present, and there was Mama in the kitchen area. She had a chicken tied by a piece of twine. It was pecking at the floor as I started my presentation. As I get rolling with the plan, Mama spins the chicken around and wrings its neck."

Showing the Plan

Paul Stevens has witnessed some pretty unusual reactions to the Amway sales and marketing plan, but that was the most unexpected.

"Next thing I know she is dipping the bird in boiling water and then pulling the feathers off, throwing them on the floor," he recalls. "It didn't seem to faze anyone there, so I kept going. I showed them the new cosmetics and then gave the ladies a form that showed them what to buy, based on skin type."

The first woman picked out about $230 dollars worth of cosmetics. He was shocked. Next the other two made their $200 selections.

"Then they started asking me about the color cosmetics, the eye shadow and lipsticks," says Stevens. He tried to be polite and patient, wondering what he was doing there. Still somewhat unconvinced about their ability to follow through, he became more concerned about the two-and-a-half-hour drive in the dark that lay ahead. By then the chicken had become part of a fricassee.

Moving into the Middle Class

"When I was finished, the woman whose thatched hut I was in asked what the total price would be for everything. I told her it would cost about $1,200—and then I explained that they could order a little at a time," he remembers. What happened next was the clincher: "She gets up, rolls up the mattress, and pulls out a tin can. Then she counts out $1,200 and says, 'When can I have it?'" As for Chefita, within a couple of years, she had become a Direct Distributor and she and her family had made the transition into the middle class.

To Stevens, who retired from Amway in 1994, being part of success stories like that of Chefita give him a lifelong satisfaction about being in the business. "She got a totally new lease on life from network marketing. She had always wanted to be important and to be respected. Every time I saw her she would become teary eyed with gratitude that she had actually been able to fulfill her dreams. She was overwhelmed with emotion," says Stevens, his voice starting to waver a little at the memory—"and to tell the truth, so was I."

Ruby Miller-Lyman

NETWORK MARKETING ATTRACTS some of the most energetic, colorful, can-do people in the world—adventurous souls who love life's challenges and dream big dreams.

All the Way to Shangri-La
Ruby Miller-Lyman learned as a girl that you can make your dreams come true. She grew up in a family with ten children on a farm where "everybody worked hard." Ruby picked beans. She butchered beef. She worked as a soda jerk. Starting at age thirteen, she cut the hair of everyone in the family. Full of energy, she also was a cheerleader, drum major, and winter carnival queen at her high school. She lived in little Ogilvie, Minnesota, but she dreamed of conquering the world.

Right out of high school, Ruby entered direct sales in the early 1950s with a hair-care products company called Radelle, which later became an MLM. The experience fired her ambition and taught her how to turn dreams into clear, achievable objectives. At the time Ruby had three dreams for which she was willing to work and sacrifice. The first dream

A forever-young adventurer. Ruby Miller-Lyman, in 1988, in fabled Hunza, or Shangri-La, with Begum, 89, and her mother, Nara, 120.

was to earn enough money to get her teeth fixed—an unaffordable luxury for her family. Her second dream was to get a new red and white Olds Delta 88. For eight months she kept pictures of that Olds 88 all around her: on the dash of her car, on the rearview mirror, on the mirror where she put on her makeup, on her appointment book— everywhere. At the age of eighteen, Ruby walked in and paid cash for the car. The third goal was to make a down payment on her first house. She was nineteen when she accomplished it. Those three goals got her started.

Willing to Pay the Price

"I began to believe in this business. I started believing that I could have anything I wanted if I was willing to pay the price—that I could write the figures on my own check. It was simple. The harder I worked, the more I made."

Selling Radelle's hair-care products gave Ruby the experience and knowledge to launch other entrepreneurial ventures. She moved to Fargo, North Dakota, soon opened eight beauty salons, and then purchased a modeling studio. She began handling a skin care line for another direct selling company whose products were a great match for her salons and hair-care business. She continued to add products and soon had full-service beauty salons that did everything from custom-fitting bras to offering nutritional items for weight loss.

Ever in tune with her customers' needs, Ruby was driven by a desire to help women look and feel better. She knew that even when a customer took the pounds and inches off, inside there was often still a fat woman. To provide support and motivation to customers, she developed the concept of weight-loss clubs. In a few years she had over 150 clubs in the upper Midwest, stretching from North and South Dakota through Minnesota, Iowa, and Wisconsin. She also involved her customers in her own TV and radio shows, a venture she used to promote the nutritional products of another direct selling company called NutriMetics. Her innovative promotional gambits soon made her the number one distributor in the company. That eventually led to a career as a full-time national director of training for a health and weight-loss club concept she had developed for NutriMetics. In 1988, after eight and a half years of travel plus the responsibilities of raising her three now-grown children, says Ruby, "I was free and ready for some adventure." Ruby realized that holding a salaried job—no matter how glamorous—could never be adventurous enough for her. Not compared to her start as an entrepreneur and network marketer.

A Desire for Romance and Adventure

What now aroused her thirst for adventure was the opportunity for yet more travel—a chance to visit Hunza, one of the most beautiful and inaccessible spots in the world and supposedly the inspiration for the fabled Shangri-La in James Hilton's classic novel, *Lost Horizon*. For romance and legend, few destinations can beat this quaint, fabled labyrinth of a village set in a stunning valley encircled by snow-capped mountains.

The trip had been planned by Renee Taylor—a fellow health enthusiast and friend of many years—who invited Ruby to accompany her. An expert on longevity who herself was nearing ninety, Taylor had made eight trips to study the local population of Hunza, the rosy-cheeked Hunzakuts, who often live past the age of a hundred.

Free of the Corporate World

"I had read her books on Shangri-La. I really wanted to go to the land of the forever young," Ruby says. When her boss refused to give her one month off, she resigned. "Once you've tasted the freedom of network marketing," says Ruby, "you're never going to let a boss cancel your dreams. Taking this trip was fulfilling an important dream for me." Thrilled at being free of the corporate world, Ruby set off with Renee. They traveled to India, then to Islamabad, where they boarded a propeller-driven plane to Gilgit, a small principality in the Himalayas. From there they headed out on the old Silk Route that Marco Polo took on his journeys. It is one of the highest and most beautiful routes in the world—as well as one of the most harrowing—and along the way they were routinely delayed by rock slides.

At one point the guide gave them each a large plastic cup and led them down a steep path. Walking upon huge rocks they came to a magnificent gushing glacial waterfall etched thousands of feet high into the valley wall. Says Ruby, "We took the glasses and filled them with water to make a toast. I looked into the glass and saw crystals of gold and silver glistening in the water. It was what they called 'mountain milk,' rich in the essential minerals we all need. Just before we drank it, I said to my friend Renee, 'We can't drink this, it's all filled with sparkly stuff.'" Then Renee explained that the minerals Ruby saw were thought to be one reason for the great health of the Hunzakuts.

The Magic of Hunza

Around the next bend, almost close enough to touch, they saw Mount Rakaposhi—an awesome glacial mountain sparkling like a trillion diamonds dancing in the sun—and then journeyed on to Hunza. They were picked up by a fleet of Jeeps that spurted madly off to the palace. Ruby held on with white knuckles, barely daring to peer into ravines thousands of feet deep as the drivers dodged wandering cattle in an insane race up the mountain road. Far up the mountain was the Royal Palace, overlooking the entire country.

Ruby was invited to a private audience in the palace with the Rani, or Queen of Hunza. The high matter of state prompting the invitation was the Rani's desire for a complete, custom makeover—a gift Ruby happily bestowed inside the Queen Mother's boudoir.

Like visitors for centuries, Ruby was amazed by the vigor and health of the population. She recalls one eighty-nine-year-old woman who cut the grass on the palace grounds each day with a scythe from a squatting position, displaying the energy of someone fifty years younger. She then carried the fresh-cut grass to feed her cattle. Ruby chatted with her and her mother—who at 120 years of age was a true senior citizen in Hunza.

A writer who recently visited Hunza said of the natives, "Their strength and ruggedness is belied by their gentle, warm and hospitable character." The writer's recommendation was one that Ruby and her companion tried to follow: "Stay a while! Delight in the local cuisine—fruits such as apricots, apples, plums, grapes, walnuts, cherries, and peaches—and tune into the feeling of change taking place within yourself!" Ruby and Renee sampled the vast array of herbs and exquisite fruits and wondered about the health secrets of this land where such maladies as heart disease, high blood pressure, cancer, and diabetes are all but unknown.

Dreams Reawakened

For Ruby, one enormous change caused by the trip was the powerful reawakening of her dreams. She realized "it was time to get back into network marketing." In 1988, she joined Matol Botanicals, and still takes its herb drink. The second big change was her delighted re-entry into the state of marriage, after she and Ted Lyman met through Matol. "He's a tall handsome dude," laughs this sixty-five-year-old grandmother of seven and great-grandmother of three. Together she and Ted travel all over the world, revisiting some of Ruby's favorite places, such as the Holy Land, Rome, and the Isle of Capri.

"Home Again" in Network Marketing

About two and a half years ago Ruby and Ted joined Essentially Yours Industries, a Canadian company that sells nearly half its volume of health and nutritional products to health practitioners. Ruby says she was drawn to the company because of its weight-management product.

On discovering the company she says, "I felt I was home again." Today her group makes up about 20 percent of all the distributors of Essentially Yours.

Ruby Miller-Lyman believes that network marketing is meant for big dreamers. She uses herself as an example. Referring to her recent trip to Thailand—where more than 23,000 people signed up with her group in the first six months—she raised the challenge to her downline: "If I can get from North Dakota all the way to Thailand, then how far can you go if you dream big?" Essentially Yours will enable Ruby to spread her message of health in markets around the world. As the *Bangkok Post* reported in May 1998, the firm "decided to enter Thailand because of the growing awareness among the middle class about health care." Noting its tenfold growth in exports to the United States between 1996 and 1997, the paper reported the company's plans to enter the Philippines, Taiwan, Singapore, and eventually Malaysia and Indonesia.

A Personal Mission to Help Others

Ruby embraces the company mission. She also has no doubt of her personal mission in life: It's to help others achieve optimum health and wealth by using herself as an example of what is possible when you dream big. She feels a powerful bond with those she meets in network marketing, and uses the following poem to express her feelings:

> *There is a destiny that makes us brothers.*
> *No one goes too far alone.*
> *All that we put into the lives of others*
> *Comes back again into our own.*

The words say what she has always believed, and what she considers the essence of network marketing: "How you use the talents God has given you is in direct proportion to how He prospers and benefits your life." Ruby says, "God gave me everything I need to be the most successful person I can be." One of her gifts, she says, is that "I have always been the leader and peacemaker—even as a child."

Go Where the Fish Are

Ruby uses the words of the Bible when she teaches her network marketers to become "fishers of men." To be a fisher of men for your MLM you have to:

1. Go where the fish are. In network marketing go where the people are, and that's everywhere.

2. Use the right bait to catch the fish—your sales aids, literature, videos, and an armada of audiotapes. "Your audiotapes never make a mistake, never get tired, and they are always ready to go to work to tell the story."

3. Keep your line in the water and keep on fishing. "You've got to continuously be prospecting and bringing in the new. Sponsoring and prospecting is the lifeblood of our industry."

Ruby says her passion is to get the professional homemaker back into the home raising her own children. "Because the one-paycheck family is almost extinct, I want to work with homemakers to help them meet and exceed their current paychecks with a home-based business—and a dream."

But be warned. Once you start dreaming, you may find yourself in some exotic place like Thailand—or even Shangri-La. That's what happened to this gal from Ogilvie and Fargo who refused to put a limit on how big her dreams would be, or how far they might take her.

3

Descendants

"You're the only guy I know who takes notes in church," said Debra Victor.

Ron Victor looked at the three-by-five cards he was holding and smiled. "It's another thing I picked up from Dad," he said to his wife.

Over a lifetime of self-improvement, Ron's father, Joe Victor, had seized every opportunity to learn. Ron was forever in awe of the practical wisdom Joe had acquired. It was as if Joe had distilled the brilliance of the world's greatest motivators, the most successful strategists, the best generals, the top marketers, and the wisest sages and spiritual leaders. Joe had combined it all with his own originality and humanity, and turned it into a philosophy for building a network marketing business that everyone could understand—if only they listened.

Ron Victor had listened well. He considered himself the most fortunate person on Earth for having his father as "my best friend and my mentor at the same time." Ron cherished the hours they spent together. They were hours in which Ron learned the self-help philosophy that had helped

Ron Victor, here with wife Debra, became Amway's youngest Direct Distributor at nineteen and later took over his father's organization.

Joe build one of the biggest and most successful Amway organizations in the world.

Ron considered himself blessed that he had "spent more time with Joe Victor than anybody else," he noted with pride and gratitude. "Everything I have learned," said Ron, "I have learned from him. I am just an extension of Joe Victor." Whenever Ron speaks of his father it is with great energy, enthusiasm, and clarity about Joe's ideas. Above all, he speaks with respect.

"My father was one of the great teachers and builders. He had a special power to talk to you, to uplift you. It is the most special power in the world."

Touching People One by One

WHAT IS THE real power of network marketing?

Ron Victor's older brother, Jody, knows the answer as clearly as any man or woman on Earth. It's the same power the Victors used to build organizations that extend into eighty-three countries with more members than some nation-states have citizens. It's the most valuable secret Jody's ever known, the most priceless gift he's ever shared.

Nothing reveals the power better than what happened one day in November 1995.

Jody Victor was walking through the Akron airport that morning. Hurriedly, he bought a newspaper, not knowing it contained a story that would change his life and echo around the world and across the generations.

Jody had not intended to get distracted. He was on his way to Florida for a cruise with a group of top distributors in his downline. A few hours later, he had already stepped on board the boat and was pulling away from the dock when he spotted a column written about a bright four-and-a-half-year-old girl named Miranda Robinson. The story quickly moved him to action.

Miranda had been born with cerebral palsy. She was unable to walk. But experts thought she might learn and be helped in other ways with special therapy at the world famous Peto Institute in Hungary. Miranda's mother, Monica Robinson, was about to leave work to travel with Miranda to Budapest and stay with her there.

Jody was struck by "this single mother packing her bags and flying to Budapest, where she didn't know anybody, with just a credit card and a wing and a prayer." In fact, as he would learn, the need for action was urgent if the therapy was to help Miranda.

The column ended with the words, "This little girl needs help, and that's where you come in, dear readers." Jody knew instantly that he had to answer that plea.

He began by calling the writer of the story, columnist Jewel Cardwell of the *Akron Beacon Journal*. From Cardwell he got Monica Robinson's phone number.

Jody believed strongly in service to others. For his entire life, his parents, Joe and Helyne Victor, had hammered into him the importance of doing something good for the world. Of all the gifts he had received from his remarkable parents, "I treasured above all my father's and mother's ability to be of service to others," says Jody.

Connected to the Past

Joe and Helyne were two of the country's pioneers in network marketing. In 1951 they had started out in Nutrilite, a predecessor to Amway. They joined Amway when it was founded in 1959.

Jody's parents taught him that success and leadership meant "certain standards and demands were placed upon you." As the cruise ship headed out to sea, Jody took action.

"I called Monica Robinson up and said, 'Hi, my name is Jody Victor.'" To his amazement, Monica replied, "Miranda and I were praying you would call."

How could she have expected his call?

"Don't you know who I am?" said Monica Robinson. "My mother was Helen Prbanick."

Jody was stunned. Monica was the daughter of one of Joe and Helyne's first distributors.

As Jody stood holding the phone, the years flashed through his mind. He recalled his father's constant reminders that "What you do today has an impact far into the future—even on the lives of people not yet born." The Victors called it "thinking generationally."

Jody remembered Monica playing in his yard when they were both children. He also remembered her mother. Helen Prbanick could hardly have imagined when she joined Amway that Joe Victor's son might someday play a crucial role in the lives of her daughter and granddaughter. Jody was even more surprised when Monica said she had just sent him a fax that he had not yet seen.

> "I've been involved in the business from the time I was very little. My father always made the children feel we were a part of it. It was natural to decide that this is what we want to do."
>
> —Terri Sue Victor Fraumann

A Ray of Hope

Monica told Jody her story. Miranda's father had abandoned the family soon after learning his daughter had cerebral palsy and would need twenty-four-hour care.

Despite her lively intelligence, Miranda Robinson was helpless and had spent most of her life on the floor. But Monica had learned of a therapy with remarkable results in treating cerebral palsy and other neurological conditions. Based on the research of Dr. Andras Peto of Hungary, the system was called "conductive education." Using Peto's methods, Miranda might be able to train the healthy part of her brain to take over tasks that the damaged areas were unable to perform.

The method could not cure Miranda's cerebral palsy. But patients could improve their bodily movements. They also could gain more confidence to develop emotionally and intellectually.

Conductive education relies on one highly trained teacher per student, instead of the standard approach in the United States that fragments the treatment into individual therapies. Also unlike the American approach, therapy is done in a group, so children can motivate and encourage

Kathy and Jody Victor, parents of the bride, at daughter Terri Sue's wedding to Greg Fraumann, the son of Amway Diamonds.

each other with songs and rhymes. But children are able to obtain the lifelong benefits of the Peto method only if they are treated early in life. Miranda had been moved up on the waiting list but needed to enter training by the age of five.

Swinging into Action

As Jody heard Monica's story he was making plans. He was someone who was used to making things happen—big things, when the need arose. He could easily pull strings in other parts of the world, including Eastern Europe.

Jody called Beverly Sallee, an Amway distributor in Texas. She called Jim Dornan in California, also in Amway though not in her line of sponsorship. Dornan called Janus Demetter—an ice skater and Olympic gold medalist. Janus and his wife Rachel are Amway Diamonds in Budapest.

When Monica and Miranda Robinson stepped off the plane in Budapest they were greeted by a party headed by the Demetters. The

Amway folks also rented an apartment for mother and daughter, and got them a car and a phone. They received funds from distributors near and far, and Miranda began her therapy on schedule. The big question was whether the exercises done each day to the rhythms of children's songs would actually be able to help Miranda. Dr. Peto had developed his method in 1945, though some experts in the United States continued to dismiss the approach as a hopeless waste of time, energy, and money. But the little girl who had spent her life as a lovable but helpless bundle on the floor brimmed with optimism as she filled her days and weeks with routines she hoped would lead to her being able to stand, eat, dress, and walk.

Huge Accomplishments—and Loss

For Jody Victor 1998 was filled with both phenomenal success and deep sadness.

Jody maintained his nonstop travel schedule, and Amway continued its booming growth around the world, opening up new markets at a breakneck pace. In the new frontier of Eastern Europe, the best workers—men and women who once considered it reward enough to have their names printed in the Socialist Bulletin—now saw the benefits of a fat residual check. In Poland, which Jody had come to call "my adopted homeland," the number of distributors in his network was climbing toward the hundred thousand mark. A report prepared by the U.S. Embassy in Budapest in July 1996 noted that network marketing had become "a very powerful channel in the Hungarian market" with Amway at the forefront. In the Czech Republic, in Romania, and elsewhere around the region and the world, families were seizing upon network marketing as the fastest way to step out of one era and into another. Joe Victor was pleased but not surprised. He had foreseen it all years earlier.

The power of Joe Victor's words and ideas was strikingly fresh and alive. He had always told his children to "dream bigger dreams." He had urged them "to get passionate about your dreams." But now as their dreams were being fulfilled, Joe was failing physically.

"You've Got to See Who's Here!"

On March 30, 1998, Joe Victor died. Saddened and grief-stricken, Joe's family and friends mourned his death. People hugged and consoled one another as they arrived at the funeral home during the calling hours. Then Kathy Victor, Jody's wife, walked up to her husband and said, "Jody, you've got to see who's here."

Into the room came a young girl very different from the one who had gone to Budapest—a girl who was doing something extraordinary. She was walking. As she walked up to Jody Victor, nothing could hide her bubbly enthusiasm. "I'm walking now," she said mischievously—"and it's all your fault."

Helyne and Joe Victor were pioneer distributors in the American Way Association, which became Amway. Joe died in 1998.

Little Miranda Robinson then turned to Kathy Victor and said, "I've lived such a wonderful life."

At that moment, and as Miranda's words were passed on and repeated, the entire Victor family was inspired and uplifted. Miranda's presence reminded them all of Joe's dedication to helping others.

Pure Joy

Every year Jody Victor's Amway organization holds a Reunion Conference for top distributors in his downline. Jody can recall in detail the conference in the Washington, D.C., area. Along with their business activities, attendees took tours, went to cultural events, and enjoyed themselves with a program of what meeting planners always call "fun things."

But for many who attended, one event stood out above all others. It was an event that gave them pure joy and reminded them of the deep pride they felt in their organization and its values. It occurred when Miranda Robinson walked onstage in front of three thousand people and was interviewed by Jody. Miranda demonstrated for all that she was "a delightful, very precocious, extremely bright child." The interview focused on her scrapbook and had the theme "A Day in the Life of Miranda."

Jody revealed that he'd never felt happier, nor more humble. He put it all in perspective when he said, "Here we were trying to help this little girl, but it was really God putting her in our path to help us in the most difficult hours of our life."

Plug in to the Power Source

LIKE ALL GREAT teachers, Joe Victor could express his wisdom in short memorable phrases. He'd say things like:

If you can raise a family, you can raise a business.

If you want recognition, the best way you can get it is by being the best person you know how to be.

People will remember things if you teach them with stories.

It's a law of the universe: The more you give, the more you will receive.

If money is in the hands of good people then good things will be done.

Dream bigger dreams.

Put more passion in your dreams.

All Joe's phrases and stories and ideas together add up to a dynamic, living philosophy. It addresses the six areas of activity in a person's life—Physical, Mental, Social, Spiritual, Family, and Financial. It describes the values underlying a successful life—Faith, Family, Freedom, and Fortune. It shows how to balance your needs and attain happiness.

Joe just might have shaped his philosophy into one of the most powerful self-help books of all time. But Joe didn't put his ideas down in a book—and perhaps with good reason.

Joe was a truly humble person whose "whole goal was to be of service to other people," noted Ron. He was also an incredible teacher. And the best, most gifted teachers have always known they have a special, selfless mission. For Joe Victor that mission meant he "always had time for everyone," as Jody told a writer after Joe's death. He thought of himself as an average guy who cared about people.

He didn't want to be a guru. He didn't want to place himself between the student and the knowledge that student was learning. He didn't want to create disciples following a doctrine or obediently mouthing his unchanging words. He wanted to be a catalyst who helped the student learn and grow on his own.

> "We've grown up with the outlook that the decisions we make today are going to affect generations not yet born."
>
> —Steve Victor

"He would research everything about positive thinking. He was always looking, seeking to do better," recalls Ron. One thing he told his sons was, "You've got to read a positive book at least ten minutes every day. You gotta stay plugged into your power source."

A Plan to Stay Plugged In

BEFORE HIS DEATH, Joe Victor worked with his son Ron on a plan to help members of their organization stay "plugged into the power source." Together they carefully laid the plans for a unique facility, a center where people would be able to "find all the resources they need to build their businesses."

The center would serve as the hub of the family business as well as a corporate retreat—and much more. It would be a place where guests can go "to reap the benefits of Joe Victor's vision." Ron and Joe knew it had to be a beautiful area where you could instantly gain a feeling of peace, comfort, and serenity.

In March 1999, Ron found the ideal piece of real estate in downtown Naples, Florida—a place that will embody Joe's admonition to "dream bigger dreams." To be designed by a leading architect, the atmosphere will be that of a classic Palm Beach and Mediterranean-style mansion. Below the surface the center will hum with the efficiency of modern technology. But the visible part will studiously avoid the feel or flavor of anything officelike. "In this high-touch and high-tech environment," says Ron, guests will be able to relax and soothe their nerves from the outside world as they drink in the power of being in a place where big dreams are nurtured.

> "Success comes about through five things: humility, reverence, inspiration, deep purpose, and joy. Until one learns to lose one's self, he cannot find himself."
>
> —Ron Victor

You can imagine being a visitor, flying to the area from, say, Dallas, or Warsaw, or Tokyo and then driving onto the idyllic grounds of this global center. After checking into an executive suite you might get in the mood to learn by reclining in a quiet den in a cushy leather chair before a huge fireplace. You'd chat with other guests, because part of Joe's philosophy is that "you enhance your success through your associations." You might then stop by a library of books on self-help and positive thinking—books containing the very wisdom that inspired the Amway founders and Joe Victor and his family. At your disposal would be a media room where you could watch high-quality presentations containing the latest success stories, marketing information, and ideas to build your business.

Heart-to-Heart Counseling

The center will provide "all the videos, books, tapes, seminars, and other forms of organized knowledge" pertinent to succeeding in network marketing, says Ron. But above all, guests will get personal, one-on-one, heart-to-heart advice from family members and other people who are deeply imbued with Joe Victor's philosophy. The counseling will be "directed solely toward them." Guests will be helped to identify their wants, enrich their families, strengthen their relationships, gain confidence, and develop dreams. "We will give them resources in the areas where they are needed," says Ron. "My wife Debra and I and the staff will be like a research and development department. We'll be there to help people."

Ron envisions a showcase retreat with exquisite marble, hand-carved mantles, and a garden and courtyard on the roof—to better encourage creative thinking. The site is near the marina and city docks where the Victors will keep a yacht for entertaining guests. Visitors will be able to stroll by the shops on famed Fifth Avenue in Naples while "getting in the mood for doing some dream building," says Ron.

People will find it the perfect place to "plug into their power source."

Dream Bigger Dreams

AT THE HEART of Joe Victor's philosophy is the knowledge you can control your own destiny.

"We all can choose one of two worlds to live in," says son Jody. One is the Plan A world. That's the world most people choose. The second is the Plan B world. That's the world the Victors have embraced for three generations.

In Plan A, says Jody, everybody's day begins when a noisemaker goes off that startles them out of their horizontal positions. They dash around the house performing morning rituals. Then they plop themselves into a car and are hurtled off to a building owned by someone else where they stay until they are allowed to return home and resume their horizontal positions. The next day is the same—with their lives continuing that way week in and week out, for years. Plan A is based on having a job.

But in the Plan B world, the Victors have taught their children, you have an opportunity to enhance your life. You can also become a better person by helping others. "Our Plan B world is a dynamic and ever-changing world where we build income and security at the same time," says Jody Victor. Plan B is based on owning an asset. "And if you can create an asset that takes care of a need, you can derive an income even when you are not there," he notes. Jody also points out that, "our asset grows fastest when we have a dream. The only time it gets stale is when we are not dreaming big enough. That means the real challenge is to dream bigger dreams," says Jody.

Jody believes that if you asked hugely successful people late in life what they would have done differently, all would say, "I'd dream bigger dreams." It was a lesson his own father instilled in him, and one he has always tried to put into the hearts and minds of his own children. "I was taught that you need to get passionate about your dreams," he says. "My father would always say: 'Dream bigger. God wants you to live life abundantly.'"

How MLM Solves the Family Business Dilemma

For showering abundance on future generations, Joe Victor's choice of network marketing beats just about every other game in town. Like the proverbial loaves and fishes, opportunities for Victor family members have continued to multiply.

Joe Victor believed in the American Dream of owning an independent business. That dream involves giving your children a boost up the ladder of achievement by passing on to them what you've built. But the owner of a conventional business faces painful choices. If no one in the second generation has the drive and passion of the founder, the business will deteriorate from lack of leadership. On the other hand, if the founders produce two or more highly motivated offspring who want to run the business, they will have set themselves up for a battle over who will succeed them. Many family businesses still resolve the issue by simply appointing the eldest male, regardless of merit. If the other children don't want to become subordinates, they may leave the business altogether, or insist that it be sold. As for grandchildren, the more there are the less likely it is they will all play

"This business is even more precious to us because of our son, 'R.J.' He was born with a rare metabolic disorder caused by a strange fluke. Ron and I would stay weeks at the hospital after he was born. One day Ron said to me, 'Debra, do you realize I am the only dad in the intensive care unit?' Only because of our business was Ron able to be there for me and R.J. During that time our business continued to grow, and we received enormous love, support, and positive energy from the people in our groups. We've been able to show parents how their lives can be changed because of it. We've sponsored people with family members with disabilities, and we've shown parents a way to stay home with their children by owning and operating their own business."

—Debra Victor

important roles in the business. And, ironically, for the descendants of the founder in general, to choose to be part of the family business is to forfeit being an independent business owner.

Network marketing goes a long way toward solving all these dilemmas. It can create an unlimited number of positions for future generations. It also permits offspring to benefit from their parents' efforts while still choosing an independent or entrepreneurial path. The Victor family story itself illustrates these advantages of network marketing.

Both Ron and Jody have been Crown distributors for about two decades, and each has been able to follow in his father's footsteps in his own way. As Helyne notes, it worked out happily for all. Jody's entrepreneurial streak meant he was frequently "off chasing rainbows." By contrast, as Helyne recalls, Joe observed that Ron "very seldom does anything without considering how it is going to affect everyone

"Dream bigger dreams." Joe Victor with Jody, left, and Ron. The two sons have pursued different routes to the top. Jody built his own organization and Ron oversaw the growth and expansion of the family business. But both adhered to their father's philosophy, both reached the pinnacle of success as Crown distributors, and both have offspring in the business.

else"—a vital trait for assuming management of a family business. Fortunately, with Jody determined to build his own business, Ron was available to take charge. Ron had, after all, broken all records by becoming a Direct Distributor at the age of nineteen. As Helyne recounts: "Joe said to Ron, 'You must be the one responsible.' He gave a huge responsibility to Ron, and Ron is doing very well with it."

Finding His Own Path

Jody Victor says admiration for his father spurred him on to build his own Amway business after signing up under Joe. Perhaps it's been a mix of both admiration and competitive spirit that's driven him to achieve at the extraordinary levels he has. Clearly, he relishes his record of independent accomplishment dating from his earliest days as a distributor. "I watched my father and then I bought my own kit separate and apart," he says.

That independent path includes finding his own way and getting, in addition to his father, his own mentors—most notably, Dr.

Theodore Weisman, known as Teddy. Their friendship provides an amusing tale not only of Jody's personal growth, but of how the business brings people of differing backgrounds and cultures together. Jody met Teddy in Aruba in 1975 while on his first all-expenses-paid Amway trip. He was still struggling to master the business, but managed to show Teddy the plan on the beach by drawing circles in the sand. Weisman, an orthodontist from Long Island, invited Jody to New York to meet a group at his house.

"I had never been to New York in my life," says Jody. "There were more people stopped to pay the toll on the George Washington bridge than lived in my whole town." At Weisman's house, Jody became aware of a level of opulence he had never experienced. "I never saw anything like this in my life," not in his own house or even Amway founder Richard DeVos's. "The foyer had a foyer," he observed. "It was a three-couch living room and none of them was against the wall."

The small-town boy from Ohio immediately took charge. He reached in a bag and pulled out a gift. In a loud voice he announced, "Merry Christmas."

Teddy Weisman responded, "We're Jewish."

"Oy vay," responded the embarrassed and quick-witted distributor.

When young Victor finished showing the plan, Teddy Weisman said to his guests, "Aileen and I are 100 percent supportive of what you just heard from Jody Victor."

"He could have eaten my lunch and made a fool out of me," says Jody. "Instead, Ted and Aileen Weisman put their arms around me and mentored me." Teddy became the first of many professionals in Jody's group. "It was a relationship where I felt celebrated," says Jody. "I cherished his advice." The Weismans showed Jody the town, took him to a Broadway show, and encouraged his ambitions. They also taught him a big lesson he never forgot—that professionals need network marketing to maintain their cash flow. No one sends checks to a vacationing orthodontist.

Jody's connection with Weisman marked the beginning of tremendous growth in his business. Jody notes that he was "only a

Pearl Direct" when he met Weisman, but that six years later in 1981 he had become a Crown Direct Distributor. (His own parents had become Crowns before him in 1979.)

Emeralds, Diamonds, Crowns . . .

During the early years of Amway a distributor would pick up his product from the person who sponsored him, often driving many miles to the house of his sponsor. The sponsor also paid the distributor his compensation checks.

Then as now, the first major milestone for a distributor was to become what's known as a Direct Distributor or DD. The term was based on the DD's reaching the level where he could buy products and receive checks directly from the company. In today's era of overnight delivery and high-speed computers, most distributors of network marketing companies order directly from the company and receive their checks without intermediaries. The term *direct* is still used, but is now more a leadership title. In the early days of Amway, DD carried with it compensation roughly equivalent to what the average American family earned. After various adjustments of the Amway compensation plan over the years, the average Direct Distributor today makes even more than the average American family.

Other important Amway milestones are achieved when a DD helps others in his group become Direct Distributors. These are called *breakaways*—i.e., they break away from their sponsors and develop productive organizations of their own. The breakaway is a concept common to many MLM marketing plans.

Another major milestone in Amway is Emerald, which has three Direct Distributor or breakaway legs. A Diamond has six. Next are Executive Diamond, Double Diamond, Triple Diamond, and Crown Diamond—that is, nine, twelve, fifteen, and eighteen DD legs, respectively. The highest level of achievement is Crown Ambassador, with twenty direct distributor legs.

Bonuses are tied to each of the levels of achievement and to specific requirements. Though the ultimate dream is to become a Crown

Ambassador, a good stepping-stone is a Diamond, with its average annual income of a quarter of a million dollars.

Success Stories

Among the many success stories in his organization that Jody traces back to his close friend Weisman is the growth of Amway in New York's Chinatown, where twelve thousand families are now in the business—including two Diamonds and eight Emeralds. The area now has its own distribution centers and Web site, and "we treat it like an international market," comparable, say, to Buenos Aires, says Jody. He was led to the Chinatown opportunity by Bill and Diane Ming, whom he met in New York on a trip to visit Teddy.

"Service work is the pathway to Freedom. To give of yourself is to be happy, joyous, and free."

—*Debra Victor*

Teddy died more than a decade ago, but his wife Aileen still says the Amway years were the best of their lives. When Teddy retired he sold his orthodontist practice and his office building, but not his Amway business. Today Jody helps work the business for the benefit of Ted's family.

When Jody built a baseball field for his hometown, he dedicated it to Teddy Weisman. He'd intended to be an anonymous donor. But people figured out he was the backer and honored him with a bronze bust at the opening of the field—ultimately named Crown Field, after the highest level of achievement in Amway. It's the home of the Manchester A's—for Amway, of course.

On the Global Stage

Some of Jody's activities and influence would be a surprise even to the Amway corporation itself. In 1992, when Amway opened Poland, Jody was among the distributors who went to Warsaw and met the throngs of Polish citizens. Jody also had a long-time personal connection with none other than the vice minister of privatization, whose job it was to bring foreign business into Poland. The official's name was Andrzej Sadkowski, though Jody had known him as Andy since meeting him years earlier when Sadkowski was a college freshman in New York and Jody was in the area building his Amway business with Teddy Weisman's help. Sadkowski had returned to his native Poland, following Lech Walesa's peaceful overthrow of the communist government. When he learned that Amway was looking at Eastern Europe, he tracked down Jody and called him on the phone in March 1992. Sadkowski told Jody that Amway's registration would have to cross his desk, then said, "I can help make it happen." When Poland opened to Amway that November, Sadkowski and his wife were there to greet Jody, complete with photos from their salad days in New York. The first office Jody was to rent in Poland was none other than that of Vice Minister Sadkowski's. It was a good example of being on the inside.

Then in 1994, Jody orchestrated an astounding spectacle in the city of Warsaw. He rented a huge rotunda built by Stalin. In the very room where the central Communist government had held sway, Jody stood center stage and hailed the burgeoning free enterprise revolution underway behind the former Iron Curtain.

Jody ignited the meeting when he stepped onto a vast stage. Behind him, seated in the plush red and white velvet chairs once reserved for the Communist elite, were several thousand citizens who had embraced the Amway manifesto of unlimited opportunity for all. Some had signed up when Amway entered the country two years earlier, a day when tens of thousands of citizens had jammed hotel lobbies and meeting places between dawn and midnight and convoys of trucks bearing the Amway logo had rolled through the streets in a scene of tumultuous celebration. Fifty thousand Poles became distributors during Amway's first month in the country.

Facing him on this occasion in the giant cavern were thousands more Polish citizens happily embarking on a new opportunity and a new way of life. "When I walked out and said the word *freedom,* the place went ballistic," says Jody.

It was heady, but Joe Victor had reminded his children that doing good "is not just about being on a stage." Don't ever get so carried away by your ability to affect the lives of thousands that you forget about helping one person at a time, Joe had said. That's the real secret of being not only a successful network marketer, he'd remind his sons, but a worthy human being.

Jody's civic accomplishments, from building a ball field to helping a little girl battle cerebral palsy, led to the Polish government and the Catholic Church giving him and Kathy the renowned Heart to Heart award in 1998, the year after it was given to former President Carter. It signaled recognition of Jody's role as a significant player on the global stage. The prestigious award "had nothing to do with money," said a spokesman. Still, it might have called to mind for some people one of Joe Victor's sayings, that "a poor man can't feed another poor man." The award also "had nothing to do with Amway," noted the spokesman. But one factor was Jody's role at home and abroad on behalf of free enterprise education, a crusade that has been integral to Amway since the company was founded in 1959 in the shadow of Fidel Castro's revolution. Jody's own contribution to that crusade has gone beyond Amway rallies and has included a demanding schedule of speaking at universities and teaching courses on the principles of free enterprise.

The Third Generation

MANY HAVE POINTED out that considering his father's success, Jody need not have worked so hard. Why did he? "I wanted to be like my dad," he says, adding that he hopes at least one of his three children "will want to be like me."

Those children had the benefit of a household where grandparents and parents taught them how to set goals and visualize attaining them. "They grew up thinking that the refrigerator door was magical," says Jody—and in a way it was. Hanging your goals there where everyone could see them did indeed help make them come true. The children absorbed the fundamentals with their daily bread. "Our business is about building relationships, overcoming fears, and building self-esteem," says Jody.

Jody's son Stephen, age twenty-nine, has an organization with two breakaway legs, and is a founder's Direct Distributor. He works full-time for Jody, as does daughter Terri Sue. She is married to Greg Fraumann, the son of an Amway Diamond out of Atlanta, and they are now building their own Amway business. The two met at a youth conference sponsored by renowned Amway Diamond Dexter Yager. Jody's younger son, Joseph (Joe) Edward Victor III, is completing his senior year at Bowling Green State University and will become a distributor upon graduation.

Ron Victor, age forty-nine, also has a child in the business, his twenty-five-year-old daughter Jennifer-Helyne, or Jenah. She is on the way to becoming a Direct Distributor, "the first level of management." When six-year-old Ronald "R. J." Paul Victor II is finally ready to enter the family business, odds are there will still be plenty of opportunities available.

4

Statesmen

THEIR DREAMS ARE not merely self-serving schemes, but visions that involve us all. Their ideas are beacons that light our path. We look to these individuals. We listen to them. We draw upon their proven endurance. Because of their victories, they have credibility. They have been through the fire and come out whole. When they assure us we can outlive misfortune, we believe them because they have done so themselves while holding on to what is valuable. Through it all, they've had the courage to be themselves.

Ken Pontious

THE LATEST, GREATEST products do little to excite Ken Pontious.

Hot technology leaves him cold.

Revolutionary research?

He'd rather talk about going fishing.

People, Not Products

What is this man saying? At first Ken Pontious's blatant elevation of people over products may strike the listener as heresy, or treason, coming as it does from a distributor whose company, Enrich International, prides itself on its products. Enrich is an innovator and leader in the field of herbal supplements and personal-care products.

What could he possibly be getting at? After all, more than twenty-five years ago, his company's founder pioneered the field of putting herbal remedies into capsules, and today Enrich refers to itself as the "Father of Encapsulation." Its manufacturing facility, Pharma-tech Laboratories, Inc., is one of the largest in the industry. For the last four years in a row Enrich has been in the coveted Utah 100 list of top companies in sales and in revenue growth.

The Pontious Philosophy

Well, what he means, says Ken, is that network marketing "has always been built on relationships." Not only is Ken slow to get infatuated with products, he takes his philosophy one step further and says: "Since companies come and go, it's important to stay in touch with people."

You can bet that if any prominent employee of a big prestigious company spoke as if his organization were anything less than the immortal be all and end all, executives would be spluttering in apoplexy, and the offender would, at best, be hauled off to the company woodshed. But Ken Pontious is not a corporate employee. He's an Enrich distributor; in fact, he's the company's leading distributor. As such, he says whatever he thinks needs to be said.

Mr. Solid Citizen

Ken delivers his comments in the plainspoken style that's given him a reputation as Mr. Solid Citizen of network marketing. But—you may be asking—given his disinclination for blind corporate loyalty, just what does "solid" imply? Well, some of the synonyms you'll find are *reputable, trustworthy, dependable, respected, accountable, reliable, upstanding, honored,* and *honorable.*

Enjoying yourself with friends is part of the Enrich lifestyle. Here the Pontiouses, Littles, and Kosserts during a two-week stay at their condos on Maui. Back row, from right to left: Ken and Shirley Pontious; Karen and Tyler Little with son Kole on shoulders; Anne and Jimmy Kossert; Shirley's son Tarl Robinson. Front row, from left to right: Gina and Jill Kossert; Taylor Little, and nanny Jessica Harr.

Trustworthy? Honorable? Dependable? How can we be certain someone possesses those qualities? Well, it's true no one knows for sure what's in another person's heart or mind. It's also true that human beings are famous for talking one way and acting another. But business experts seem to agree that to succeed in any field where relationships are long-term, a person must be trusted by his associates. You could have no doubt figured that out yourself, without the help of economic theorists. But the theories do exist, and they say that if you're a card shark, pool hall hustler, or promoter of worthless penny stocks, you can be a "success" in the financial sense despite your low character, because you're moving from one victim to another as fast as you can. But in a field like network marketing, you become successful as a result of having many strong, stable relationships.

Practical and Principled

Ken says his success—and the experts estimate his annual income at about $3 million—is based entirely on a foundation of relationships. Happily, anyone can emulate the way Ken nurtures these relationships. You could even consider his life to be a model of being both practical and principled. In the first century A.D., Plutarch wrote a work aimed at "delighting and edifying" the reader with biographies of Greek and Roman heroes and statesmen. For centuries it's been studied as a guide to character and achievement in a world of strife and competition. As in ancient times, the choices for leaders aren't always easy. Were someone today to write a Plutarch's *Lives of Network Marketers* to guide people in their choices, the story of Ken Pontious would take up a prominent chapter.

Ken entered network marketing in 1977. He'd spent thirteen years in the real estate business and built up one of the largest firms in Springfield, Missouri. He decided to look for a new opportunity when the real estate business was whacked by soaring interest rates during the recession of the late 1970s. Ken had learned about MLM from an orthopedic surgeon, who explained that he became a distributor because he needed another income source in case his hands were ever injured. The comment got Ken thinking for the first time about the phenomenon of residual income.

"Put Other People First"

Ken dove in, but found he had a lot to learn. Since entering the field, he has seen a number of tattered, battered companies breathe their last. He even belonged to some of those now-forgotten entities. But during all that time, he says, he made keeping his own reputation for integrity a top priority. "Ultimately, in this business, that's the only reason people sign up with you," he says. One of his favorite sayings about becoming successful in network marketing is, "It's not about finding the right people—it's about being the right person." He also says the emphasis on self-development that pervades MLM had an immediate effect on him, and from the day he first signed up, it helped "make me a better person." His guidelines today are, "Put other people first, be humble, and control your ego."

If you're a skeptic, you might be thinking: "Couldn't Pontious's words be simply a nice-sounding commercial for himself?" It's certainly possible—especially in a business that spawns its fair share of self-promoters. But the evidence in favor of his sincerity is strong: To begin with, distributors from other companies repeatedly cite him as a positive example of the industry and seek him out for advice about their own decisions. Second, Ken has benefited on more than one occasion when groups of thousands of individuals have left failing organizations to sign up under him. You wouldn't be likely to cast your fate with someone unless you believed he was trustworthy.

Speaking Bluntly About Those Failed Companies

Ken has been a distributor in nine MLM organizations. Yes, that's a lot. But before assuming that he is guilty of hopping around, it's worth noting he has been with Enrich for the past eight and a half years. And of the other companies, six went out of business. As he puts it, "The companies left us, we did not leave them."

He has seen companies go up like Roman candles and flare out as quickly. He's observed organizations that disintegrated overnight, or that died deaths of slow agony, or that merely faded away. The conclusion he draws from it all is striking, if obviously true: "Companies don't fail because of distributors," he says. "It is always because of management." Some defenders of the industry might want to soften that judgment by arguing that every failed company wasn't all bad. What about the impact of unfair laws and regulations, of hostile enforcement by prosecutors and regulators, and of misinformed, negative publicity? All those factors may exist, but in the end Ken is right: Whatever problems face a company, management has the responsibility of dealing with them. As for distributors, while they have immense freedom, they are still playing on a field and in a game where the rule book was written by others.

Speaking bluntly about management is part of Ken's role as a solid citizen of MLM. He prides himself on telling the truth about the industry. Sometimes that means encouraging distributors to be realistic and realize that every day won't be great; on the other hand, reality often turns out to be better than anyone's wildest fantasies.

Succeeding Despite the Drawbacks

In any case, says Ken, the benefits of MLM far outweigh the negatives. Virtually anyone can succeed handsomely despite all the drawbacks. Like Ken, you can learn to turn bad news to your advantage—which is precisely what the sharpest entrepreneurs cultivate a knack for doing. They look for change and they capitalize upon it. Ken has done that on several occasions that have become legendary in the business. But his brilliant moves would not have been possible had he not laid the foundation for his own continuing success. And he did that by working steadily at developing relationships with leaders in the industry. "I wanted to know them, to learn from them," he says, emphasizing that he continues to be a learner. "When I travel around the country I find out who the big network marketing leaders are in that city. I go see them and take them out to lunch or dinner—not to sponsor them, because someone making $50,000 a month is not going to leave their company. But I stay in contact and we share information and ideas. That way, if anything ever happens to their company I've got a decent shot at recruiting them."

Crumbling Cookies

Exactly that happened in 1990 when a Nevada company with a diet product called the Phoenix Cookie started to crumble. Ken had just joined Enrich and was looking for a way to build his downline. "When I became involved with Enrich, a lot of my friends were in Phoenix Cookie," says Ken. "One of them had even made $125,000 in one month. But I honestly felt the product was a fad, and I was sure the company could not continue." As it turned out, Ken was right. The U.S. Food and Drug Administration cited the company for making "inappropriate health claims," and several states, including Mississippi, Louisiana, and Texas, went after it in court. Despite his skepticism about cookie products, says Ken, "It was an opportunity, because at Enrich we had just introduced a product called the Ultimate Cookie, and I knew there would be a lot of distributors out there looking for cookies." Within ninety days, five thousand Phoenix distributors were reborn in Ken's Enrich downline. Cookies were a hot item for a period of time, but Enrich ultimately dropped its Ultimate Cookie—proving Ken's point that diet cookies were fads. Then, to his dismay at the time, the recruits from Phoenix started dropping out. He didn't like it, but it did help prove his point that fads were not the way to build a lasting business. "Today in my genealogy I don't have one person from that group," says Ken.

Riding Out the Ups and Downs

One big lesson Ken points to from such an experience is that a resourceful distributor can ride out the ups and downs of the business, regardless of the failures, mistakes, or changes in strategy of the companies. As if telling a story with a carefully thought out moral, Ken sums up with the words, "You should never give up. Even though you suffer major hits and lose a lot of people, you can continue, and you can succeed." Okay. But what about the obvious question: How do you engineer a switch of five thousand people from one company to another? Ken's answer gets to the heart of the way MLM is done: "I only had to sponsor three or four friends who were key players— and they brought all the rest with them," he says.

The Enduring Bond with Jimmy Kossert

The following year, 1991, Ken reaped a bonanza. Again, it was the result of a company that was failing. But this time the payoff proved to be a lasting one. It also helped Ken forge a long-standing bond with MLMer Jimmy Kossert. A close companionship evolved between the two—with Ken and Jimmy surrounded by numerous other business friends and associates. It's the sort of enduring camaraderie that is natural in network marketing, but hard to imagine in any other field.

The association began when Kossert, a former real estate broker from Washington state, realized the company he'd joined, Lite 'n Rite, was in trouble, and associates recommended he speak with Ken. As Ken recalls the story: "When Jimmy was finding another home for those in Lite 'n Rite there were four different times when my name came up. He had never heard of me; I had never heard of him. Other people had referred us to each other. I flew up and met him, and we hit it off. When he made a decision to join Enrich, he brought eight thousand people with him. The impact on my income was tremendous."

A Special Distributor Named Shirley

The impact was enormous in another way also. One of Jimmy Kossert's Enrich distributors was a woman from Seattle named Shirley Robinson, who was in Ken's fifth generation. The story of how she and Ken got to know one another offers some revealing glimpses into the culture of network marketing. In 1992, Shirley was among four hundred distributors whose performance won her a place on a STAR (Super Top Achiever Award) Cruise. The cruises are sponsored by the company, with distributors earning points over a period of months.

By the time of this cruise Ken was at last feeling enormous satisfaction from seeing his Enrich business take off in a major way. Year after year, members of his own family had criticized him harshly for abandoning a successful real estate career to become a network marketer. At one point or another his mother, father, and sisters had all told him in caustic terms to get out of the field. Such disapproval from his own family was at times "very, very traumatic." His anguish had been compounded by the breakup of his marriage, a tragedy hastened by his determination to stick with network marketing. Now with Enrich he was at last beginning to see the signs of his coming megasuccess. His huge triumph, after having persevered so long, set the stage nicely for his meeting with Shirley. She was not only a fellow MLMer who'd built an organization of nearly two thousand people in less than a year, but one whose parents were still in the business after starting in Amway nearly two decades earlier.

Friends Envisioned the "Perfect Match"

Shirley had flown into Miami for the cruise on the same plane with Jimmy Kossert, who by now had gotten to know Ken Pontious well. Jimmy and his direct sponsor, Tyler Little, were playing matchmakers, cooking up a plan to get Shirley and Ken together. That night Shirley dined in a Japanese restaurant with a group of distributors from Seattle and was introduced to Ken. By the time the ship set sail, friends of the two had begun saying they would make a perfect match.

Looking back, Ken and Shirley now say that events on the cruise pointed the way to romance. They started when one Enrich distributor, Don Thompson, boarded the ship carrying a dazzling diamond ring. In front of a rapt group of colleagues, he proposed to a fellow distributor he'd met at an Enrich function in California. When his intended, Victoria Carey, accepted, both Ken and Shirley were among the well-wishers.

In a Culture of Caring Friends

Ken and Shirley dined together the last two nights of the cruise, then had their first "date" at an Enrich regional event in Vancouver. "We sat together for a whole day," he says, recalling the first symptoms of their becoming inseparable. Ken now learned more of Shirley's remarkable story and found her achievements highly impressive. He also learned more of how she had suffered the brutal setbacks that so often accompany being a single mother. Not that many months earlier she and her first-grade son had been living in a friend's garage. In her struggle to keep her child fed and clothed, she often went hungry herself. She was working two jobs and trying to hold on when she decided to enter network marketing, a field her parents had never left. Ken and Shirley reflected how in just over a year she'd gone from living on the fringes of society to being part of a supportive culture with friends who were both mindful and caring enough to steer the two of them together. After dating for eight months, they were married.

Heart to Heart Wisdom

"Those who understand the kind of lifestyle this business has to offer—and that it's definitely achievable—work with a whole different attitude. Once you see the potential, you never quit. When you start thinking of the time you can spend at home with the kids, plus the travel and all that money can do, you get inspired to give it your all."

—Jimmy Kossert, Enrich International

They recently celebrated their fifth anniversary by returning to the same hotel in Vancouver, and then leaving on an Alaskan cruise for eleven days.

Lots of Love Stories

"There are a lot of love stories in our group," says Ken. "Quite a few people have fallen in love through Enrich, and every year it seems some distributors are getting married." The most recent wedding took place in Key West during a stopover for a November Caribbean cruise. But the most unusual romance involves Hugh Leonard, an energetic and enthusiastic seventy-four-year-old whose three ex-wives all became frontline distributors—sponsored directly by Hugh—in his organization. On a STAR cruise Hugh remarried one of them—his ex-wife Terry.

Today Ken's best friends are people in network marketing. "You travel with them and have fun with them," he says. "They are not just business associates but people you share your life with." He especially shares recreation with them. As a golfer, fisherman, and all-around sports fan, Ken is never lacking for things to do or companions to do them with. Taking such excursions as this past summer's Alaskan fishing trip for king salmon—with ten of his distributors and two En-rich employees—has become a regular part of life.

Ken also uses recreation as a way of staying in touch with those in other companies, both in the U.S. and abroad. "I have a lot of friends I'm really close with in other companies. I golf with them, and I've gone on trips with them." He's laying the plans for a regular forum where top leaders from different companies can share ideas. It's a visionary concept in an industry where isolation from other companies is more often the norm. He also sees it as helping him stick to his commitment to stay in touch with his key contacts. His rule of thumb is to call or visit each of them every ninety days.

The Number One Secret

All such activities help forge friendships, and for Ken making friends is the number one business secret. To help train his distributors, Ken developed his VIP system—for Values, Integrity, and People. He calls it "a complete system for recognition and edification, using events, books, and tapes." He adds, "People will do more for recognition than they will for money."

A Special Empathy

Ken's own values include having a special empathy for those who are lacking in confidence. He himself was wounded by negative criticism all during his youth, which may help explain why today he gets ex-cited about seeing shy or apprehensive distributors come out of their shells. "When these people are told that they can do it, and are shown how to, they really grow." Perhaps he's thinking of his own emer-gence as a superachiever when he speaks proudly about "people who couldn't stand up in front of a group. Now they can lead seminars."

One wonders if his enormous success, represented by his 250,000-plus distributors, will ever make Ken feel he's gotten too lofty to care about the "little guy." Yes, that question is one of those slow, easy soft-balls that any slick talker will smack out of the ballpark. But then, Ken isn't a slick talker, and the words of his thoughtfully delivered response are saturated with conviction: "I am where I am because of a lot of wonderful people. That's why I will always be around to help those who want to succeed." That's not exactly exalted rhetoric. But it is a very solid statement.

Integrity—A Concrete Example

So much for Values, and People. As for the "I" in VIP, Ken defines integrity as "doing the right thing." He uses a practical example of the kinds of issues that confront network marketers: "Someone recently told me he would sign up if I would personally sponsor him. But this person had first learned about the company from another distributor. I told him I would never, ever agree to sponsor anyone in such a situation." No ducking and parrying here. It's simply a question of right and wrong. Period.

For the Record: What Went Wrong?

Speaking of the type of questions that many network marketers tend to dodge, there's still the nagging one of what went wrong with all those companies in Ken's past that didn't make it—vanished enterprises such as Gold Plates International, Nu/Trend, and Meadow Fresh?

One example should suffice: Meadow Fresh Farms, Inc., was a Utah company where Ken, naturally, progressed right to the top level. Meadow Fresh produced a weight-loss drink made out of whey and other ingredients. In the early 1980s, Mormon families were standing in long lines to buy the product for their home food storage programs. From there it had explosive growth across the country. But the company grew too fast, and management became overwhelmed. A modern network marketing company is unable to function without intact computer systems to calculate bonuses and commissions, and Meadow Fresh's original systems were sadly outdated. Then a slew of states stretching from New Hampshire to Arizona went after the company on a variety of charges, forcing it to fight legal battles on every front. For example, Wisconsin, a big dairy state, was among those that moved to bar Meadow Fresh for being an imitation milk product. News stories accompanied each legal action, and the sour publicity helped speed Meadow Fresh down the road to confusion, then paralysis, and finally oblivion.

Looking Carefully at Enrich

Examples like that were burned into Ken's mind in 1990 as he debated whether to sign up for Enrich. He wanted every assurance that the company would be both competent and ethical. At the time the company had a mere $3 million in sales, though its origins were impressive. They went back to 1972 when founder Ken Brailsford and his family devised a way to encapsulate the herb cayenne, to treat the bleeding ulcer of one of Brailsford's uncles. Prior to that time, he'd had to take cayenne by spoon.

By 1990, the company had built a manufacturing facility and positioned itself for major growth. To make sure it stayed on track, Pontious moved for a time to Utah, to be near company headquarters. With a new marketing plan and Ken's leadership among distributors, the company was growing dramatically by 1994. It has appeared several times on the *INC.* list of the top 500 fastest-growing companies in North America. As it turned out, Ken's vigilance over the company's ethics was unnecessary, he says. The management—which includes CEO Richard Bizzaro—was outstanding. With his concerns set to rest, he left Utah and now has homes in the Seattle area and in Scottsdale, Arizona.

The Pontious Lifestyle

Ken and Shirley spend summers in Burien, Washington, overlooking Puget Sound. After three years of construction and $3.3 million, their newly renovated house became ready in the summer of 1998. It's a place where they can look out the window "and watch the whales, the seals, the freighters, the beautiful boats." A thoroughly high-tech home, "it's got everything"—from heated floors in the bathroom, to push-button draperies and blinds, to walls wired with fiber optics so Ken and Shirley can stay abreast of the ongoing communications revolution for years to come. It's also about forty minutes from the house of Enrich buddies Jimmy Kossert and Tyler Little.

"Every Day Like Paradise"

Shirley finds it easy to rhapsodize about their winter house in Scottsdale, also completely remodeled. Its spacious, sunny warmth seems light years removed from that bleak period when Shirley was literally out in the cold. "Imagine," she says, in a voice that ripples with delight, "our beautiful Santa Barbara-style home on a lovely lake, with the sun shining and the sky blue, and every day like paradise."

She describes the pleasures of "looking up at the mountains while basking in the sun beside the pool, or stepping onto our backyard deck and catching a largemouth bass out of the wonderful 43-acre lake that comes up to the house." The sunsets are breathtaking and the nights are enchanting, perfect for a cruise in their boat while looking at a moon that seems so big you feel you're in a fairy tale. When Shirley speaks of her feelings about her life, it is with a sense of wonderment: "I can't believe it," she says. "When I was small I always dreamed I would be somewhere like this. As I grew up I lost that dream. Now I have come full circle and I'm here." Though Ken's father has since died, Shirley and Ken both brought their parents to the area, away from the cold North, so all could live in comfortable visiting distance of one another.

Fathers, Sons, and "Action Motivators"

Whether he is talking about his parents' influence on his life, or his gratitude to people in his downline, Ken's trademark seems to be giving credit to others. The debt he owes his late father, though, is a bit complex. In fact, his father raised him the way he himself had been raised—in an atmosphere with no knowledge of the kind of positive thinking that's infused Ken's life in his adult years. His method of motivating Ken was the verbal equivalent of a cat-o'-nine-tails. The ceaseless lashings "finally made me say to myself, 'You are going to be the absolute best. You're going to show your father.'" From that moment onward, Ken was determined to excel at everything, which helps explain how he rose to the number one spot in so many undertakings.

After many heartfelt and tearful father-son discussions, Ken's father repudiated his childrearing methods as being more likely to produce a son with an inferiority complex than, as things fortunately turned out, a first-class fortune. But here's the irony: In those moments when things aren't working out, Ken refers to his Action Motivator. That's a device he recommends that absolutely everyone in network marketing have. An AM is nothing more than a word or phrase with a very personal meaning that will "snap you back into reality"—something written on an index card you can pull out when there's a cloud of gloom on the horizon, or when your best-laid plans have gone awry. So what is Ken's Action Motivator? You guessed it. It's "Father."

Giving Back

While it sounds a bit like a cliché, Ken feels that, all things considered, his life has worked out enormously well, and he's full of a sense of gratitude. "We are very fortunate and we need to give back," he says. Ken and Shirley give generously to causes that they believe in. They've funded all sorts of projects for schools and gave $10,000 a month for a year to subsidize the incomes of teachers. They are supporters of Mercy Corps International, and give a dime from the sale of every VIP tape to a program to feed the hungry.

Ken says such good works benefit him also by making him feel good. However, such feelings, while warm, are anything but fuzzy on one critical point: He knows his happiness, prosperity, and lifestyle are the result of his dedication to network marketing, and he simply can't imagine how you could achieve comparable success in any other field. Shirley adds her own strong belief on this subject: "Network marketing is the last type of free enterprise for ordinary people to do extraordinary things with their lives," she says.

The Future

As his own company soars toward the $130 million mark in sales, Ken has some concerns about the industry as a whole. He views the emphasis on using technology to sell products and recruit distributors as something that "is going to hurt the network marketing industry." He sees overreliance on the Internet, on mass mailings, and on voice-mail as inhibiting genuine heart-to-heart contact among people. "It bothers me," he says, "because this is a relationship business." You can't base it on "people you don't have contact with, whom you don't train, whom you don't talk to. That's not network marketing." Technological gimmickry will indeed produce "limited success on a short-term basis," he says. But like those diet cookies of yesteryear, you won't be able to build a business on them.

What Will Make People Stay?

As for new products, they of course can have an impact, and he notes that over the eight and a half years he's been in Enrich there have been new products that have caused sales to spike upward. Just remember, he says: "People may come into a business because of the product, but whatever the hot product of today may be, somebody will try to knock it off tomorrow. People won't stay in simply for a product. For that you've gotta have something else, and that is the relationship. You need to be bonded." He quotes another network marketing leader in saying the business can be boiled down to three elements: "Getting them in, keeping them in, and moving them along."

That quote indicates an idea at the heart of the Ken Pontious philosophy: It tells you that while he doesn't get too excited about new technology and new products, there is one new thing upon which he puts tremendous value: New friends.

One of those friends is Mark Victor Hansen.

Mark Victor Hansen

PREVENT WARS? That's right. You heard Mark Victor Hansen correctly. As usual, he's speaking at such a rapid clip that his words and ideas come at you like a hurricane. In fact, his wife, Patty, has said she wishes at times he had a "stop" button she could push.

Big, Big Ideas

What Hansen just said is that network marketing has the power to end war—and that was just one thought in a stream of eye-popping ideas issuing from Mark's mind, as well as from his heart and soul. He also said that support for network marketing can be found throughout the Bible, and that everyone in the country ought to belong to a network marketing company. "We can all have unlimited wealth," he's now saying. "If you really believe you have the opportunity," he notes, "then stuff will happen for you that is miraculous." Does his enthusiasm never end? Well to tell the truth, he confesses, it doesn't.

Mark Victor Hansen for years has shared with network marketers his insights, often subtle and profound, about creating wealth.

A Special Breed of Individualists

Now it's true you're apt to hear some innovative, stimulating, leading-edge concepts anytime you talk to a trainer in the MLM field. Attend a major rally or function and you'll find huge crowds abuzz with the special crackle of electricity that comes from experiencing mind-expanding new ideas. One reason for that is the willingness, indeed the eagerness, of MLM companies to spend whatever it costs to get the top speakers in the country at their events: Former Presidents Bush, Ford, and Carter. National leaders like retired General Colin Powell. Bestselling authors and television celebrities. Super motivators like Zig Ziglar. Top athletes. Brilliant scientists. Even egghead economists. You'll hear them all regularly at MLM meetings and conventions. Perhaps another reason for the intellectual and emotional excitement that is part of MLM is that people in the field—distributors and company leaders alike—make up a special breed of individualists who are open to visionary thinking.

Because of his appeal to this special breed, the revved-up Hansen may over the years have reached more MLMers than almost anyone in the country. Does Hansen have any fleeting doubts that you'll think the ideas pouring forth in an uninhibited torrent of words from his mind and mouth should be labeled outlandish, preposterous, or maybe even a bit nutty? After all, he's talking about MLM being "a giant mastermind." He's saying that the field is marked by "esprit d'-corps, love, belongingness, and surrogate spiritual experiences."

Go ahead and call his ideas far-out. That won't bother Mark Victor Hansen a bit. That's just what was said about his mentor, the renowned Buckminster Fuller, and at one time about his mentor's mentor, Albert Einstein. Some of those who went on record rejecting Hansen's ideas include the thirty-three publishers who turned down a chance to publish one of his books. Many of them disliked one certain book manuscript so much, in fact, that they made a point of saying belittling things about it. They said the title was dumb. They said the content would hold no interest for today's readers. They even threw Mark out of their offices, expressing their contempt for his being so out of touch with the marketplace. So not long ago, Mark, his coauthor Jack Canfield, and the thirty-fourth publisher—the one who said "Yes" and published the book—took out an advertisement thanking those thirty-three nonbelievers. Those rejections, they said with gratitude, had ultimately made possible the scenario that resulted in *Chicken Soup for the Soul* and its dozens of spinoff titles selling 40 million copies and becoming one of the most astounding publishing success stories of the decade. Creating a megasuccess out of warmhearted inspirational stories seems to be a natural for someone who puts love notes from Daddy in his daughters' peanut butter and jelly sandwiches while also teaching them to visualize winning at sports.

Clicking with MLMers

As the co-mastermind behind the multimillion-dollar triumph, Mark considers the *Chicken Soup* series to be just one relatively small manifestation of his fertile mind. If you don't like his other ideas, this salesman-philosopher may enjoy trying to persuade you to his way of thinking. But, if the truth be known, Hansen could go his entire life without coming up with another commercially viable idea and he, his wife Patty, and their daughters Melanie and Elizabeth would continue for a long time to enjoy the riches of his past marketplace victories.

Speaking of the marketplace, one of the reasons Hansen clicks so well with so many MLMers is the way he combines useful business training with both visionary global concepts and bighearted, open-minded, soul-bearing, self-help advice. For him, harvesting millions is just one step along the way to making yourself a better person, saving the world, and having a great time in the process.

He Saw the Future

Years ago Mark stood in front of his first cheering Amway crowd and saw the future flash through his mind. As a self-professed super-intuitive macro thinker, he did not need to hire researchers or crunch numbers to know that he was witnessing a leading indicator of a trend that was going to be stupendous. In his mind's eye, he could see "massive coliseums around the world filled with hundreds of thousands of people." While that future was coming to pass, he did training for dozens of MLM companies and today has no hesitation in telling everyone, from Fortune 500 CEOs to national leaders of every stripe, "You need to be part of an MLM." One reason for signing up is simply "to go to the greatest cheerleading session in the world." Another reason is that, "MLM meetings are the only place the layperson can come to hear the greatest minds and finest thinking on the planet."

Implicit in Mark's comments lurk some subtle but profound insights about creating wealth. The insights are not always explicitly articulated, but you can find them woven into his beliefs. Indeed, they are perhaps his hidden secret to building fortunes—and they are easily overlooked by all those serious-minded, so-called practical people who promise you they aren't going to waste your time with frivolous stuff like ideas, emotions, theories, or philosophies. Just focus on my 1-2-3-A-B-C system, they tell you, and forget about all the stargazing. Squelch your curiosity, stamp out your feelings, smother your soft-hearted impulses and get down to the hard, cold, selfish, dog-eat-dog

Heart to Heart Wisdom

"This business changes you. It makes you a better person. It helps you get in touch with what you value. It gives you choices. It makes it possible for you to have what you *really* want—not just what you wanted because that was what you could or could not afford."

—*Tyler Little, Enrich International*

business of making money. Compare that to Hansen's description of speaking to 38,000 Amway distributors at the Georgia Dome: "I stood there praying that I might take them to the next level. You could feel the wind of emotion and spirit. It brought me to tears."

Resonating with Customers

This is not to say that Hansen's secret to wealth-building amounts to crying in public. The secret—at least the first part of the secret—lies in his openness of mind, emotions, and spirit, an openness that the dog-eat-dog school always calls "unrealistic." It's the kind of openness that enables you to resonate sympathetically with the marketplace and understand intuitively what your customers will want despite the preaching of experts, the numbers, or conventional wisdom. It's also the kind of openness that enables a Hansen, or a Bucky Fuller, or an Albert Einstein to hook together two seemingly unrelated things, be they objects or ideas, and come up with a third entirely new brilliant thing that nobody else could see before. It's the kind of entrepreneurial receptiveness that helps you see first what is good in an idea, rather than only seeing what is wrong with it, which is the way we are generally conditioned by the corporate and professional world.

Great, Inspired, "Ridiculous" Goals

In place of realism with the blinders on, Mark advises: "You've got to set great, inspired goals. I believe you ought to write ridiculous goals." It's certainly a lesson that he himself follows, if you define ridiculous in terms of a "sensible" person's judgment. For example, before ever finding a publisher, he and his coauthor had mapped out a plan to publish dozens of spinoff titles from *Chicken Soup,* titles that would go on for years selling in the millions. It was a ridiculous idea, though that is exactly what has happened. And just so no one will miss the point, Mark adds: "I teach, believe, and practice that you've gotta have way too many goals, and you gotta have goals that are outrageous." Can you give us another example, please, Mark? "Goals that are way out of the book—like feed unfed humanity." Mark talks fervently on the subject of how reading heartwarming stories such as those in *Chicken Soup for the Soul* enlarges your mind and spirit and opens your eyes, helping you see possibilities you didn't see before. He even has anecdotes to show how the positive emotions evoked by the book strengthen your immune system, and how the intense involvement with the stories helps dyslexics master reading.

Tune in to the Abundance Mindset

The second part of Hansen's wealth-building secret is that simply being part of an MLM culture will stimulate, excite, and embolden you in ways you never imagined. Nobody in a conventional corporation or typical business seminar is going to say things like, "We can all have unlimited wealth." But Hansen says it, as did his genius mentor Bucky Fuller. And as you get tuned into Mark's "abundance mindset," you gain an optimism and belief in the future that enable you to see the world and yourself in entirely new ways.

A third part of Hansen's unspoken wealth-building secret involves having a genuine, enthusiastic curiosity about many things that lie outside your immediate self-interest. Far from wasting your time and diverting you from the straight and narrow path of getting rich, as the dog-eat-doggers are constantly saying, these wider interests serve to expand and enrich your vision.

Not So Far-Out After All

Hansen's big-picture thinking, for example, leads him to focus on MLM's political impact. He believes that "network marketing can end war." While skeptics may roll their eyeballs at such grand claims, a closer look at the idea suggests it may not be as far-out a possibility as you'd first think. Unlike the legions of stereotypical pacifists who over the years have pegged their hopes on utopian dreams and schemes, Mark sees his new era of peace stemming from self-interested free enterprise. Going back to 1776, none other than the patron saint of capitalism himself, Scotsman Adam Smith, believed that people united by common commercial bonds would place their economic well-being ahead of national agendas. "World trade and world war don't mix," as Mark puts it. The bottom line, simply, is that "no one wants his country to go to war against people in his own success line," says Hansen. He might have added that grassroots efforts to encourage peace, such as the American Field Service, affect a minuscule number of individuals compared to the hundreds of thousands or millions that can be part of a distributor's downline in another country. As for the likelihood of this happening, it's already well underway. "There are enough people who are globally minded to build tremendous worldwide organizations," he notes.

Nonstop Self-Improvement

Back home in the realm of improving yourself, Mark can speak with the sincerity of one who has been there. His first business venture went bankrupt twenty-five years ago, leaving him rudderless and living in the hallway of a friend's apartment. It was his exposure to self-development books and tapes that "saved my life." Today he tries to make sure his audiences hear and absorb a message learned in those days—a message essential to network marketing: "Whether you succeed or fail is not due to the economy, or the Republicans, or the Democrats, or circumstances. It is ultimately up to you."

At the heart of Mark's prescription for succeeding in MLM is ongoing, nonstop, uninhibited self-improvement. Uninhibited? In other words, don't be embarrassed about having big goals or "learning to love yourself," says Mark, showering his own arms and shoulders with rapid-fire kisses. A good way to get started on your quest is "listening to tapes every day." In other words, "start working on yourself." For a novice, hitting the tapes means that "in just a few days you will know the protocols and techniques for your business." He advises distributors to sponsor people more capable than they are as a way of automatically helping themselves become better. "Sponsor someone with better connections than you, someone who's worked on his Rolodex more," he urges. And while you are at it, tend to your own Rolodex. Mark clearly loves his connectedness to countless people. He loves talking with others and sharing ideas, and so it's easy to understand his enthusiasm for a way of life he terms "the ultimate conversational business."

Networking and the Bible?

Mark converses as easily and fluently on topics involving spirituality and religion as he does on any other subject, and in this realm he has notions that are no more conventional than are any of his other ideas. Take the Bible. Mark says, "If you look at the Bible right, you'll see that it is a whole book on how to do network marketing." After hearing him cite one reference after another from Scripture in support of this hypothesis, you're inclined to say, "Hmm, you may have a point there, Mark." In one account, Mark tells how "Moses and God had an opportunity meeting with a burning bush. God tells Moses, 'Take off your shoes and sit down, we're about to have a meeting.' What does Moses do? He starts giving God a long list of objections—just like people often do when they are first told about MLM. Moses says, 'I'm too old. I stutter.'" Mark laughs as he pulls out other examples from the Bible, all of which might indeed be seen as reinforcing the validity of the networking approach. Good theology or not, it is certainly good conversation.

The Nitty-Gritty

Getting down to the nitty-gritty, Mark believes there are three things you need to do to succeed in MLM:

1. Go to events. "Leaders are born at events," he says, quoting Doug Wead, an Amway Diamond and personal friend. Events are where "you catch the fire. You catch the flame. . . . By the time you walk out of an event you're going to have the wind beneath your wings."

2. Listen to tapes. It's a point worth repeating, as it changed his life. To make sure you get beyond mere good intentions, set a minimum of a half-hour of listening a day, he says. "There are great tapes in every MLM and on MLM as a business," he notes. By getting to know thoroughly the lessons of the leaders in your own company, "you can own it."

3. Support your upline, and use their influence to strengthen your own efforts. It's a powerful process some call "edifying your upline." While the term may be strange, the benefits can be astounding. "If you're my upline and I praise you to my group, I raise me," he notes.

Edify, Edify, Edify

"Edifying the upline" involves putting your upline directly in touch with your downline and facilitating the communication. Like a skilled introducer, a good networker will get his downline in a receptive frame of mind by letting them in on the fact that the upline person they're about to hear from can veritably "walk on water," Mark notes. With such a buildup, folks are bound to listen.

Hansen marvels at what a galvanizing force edification can be. "The upline has the precious information that will make the whole thing move at a very high clip," but they can be maximally effective only if their downline has "created the mystique through edification." He stresses giving "a million dollars worth of praise" to your upline.

Such praise works wonders. In addition to the respect and attention it will evoke from the downline, it serves another important psychological purpose: Because everyone's upline is actually made up of human beings (who often have a tough time walking on water), the recognition your praise gives them will motivate and mobilize them to ever higher levels of performance. Don't think they are above wanting and needing praise, says Mark. "Everybody needs recognition," whether they admit it or not. Yet another payoff from the multifaceted edification process is the way you, the networker, gain from doing the praising and facilitating of communication. Your prestige, leverage, and effectiveness are all enhanced.

What happens in a highly motivated MLM where people are sharing information and working together is, "you get a vehicle where everybody's greatest talent starts to show up. Then the thing grows like a prairie fire on a windy day."

What an outrageous, ridiculous, unrealistic idea.

5

Believers

THERE'S MAGIC IN believing. When you have the will to try, and the faith that what you are attempting is possible, nothing can stop you. Over and over people discover that when they overcome the doubts that hold them back, they prosper. Belief has a tangible power that makes things happen. It's likely to involve a belief in yourself, a belief in life as worth living, and a belief in the future.

For the achievers in this chapter, belief also involved their personal faith. It sustained them and turned life around for them. For network marketers, the words of the Roman writer Livy are on the mark: "When you are under the firm persuasion that you can command resources, you virtually have them."

Neta Irwin

NETA IRWIN WAS jogging one day when she stumbled and fell. Then it happened again. The first few times she thought her coordination was out of kilter. After all, she knew she was in great shape. She was a highly motivated, radiantly attractive, hardworking, professional salesperson—and she loved to run.

Her Darkest Hours, Her Brightest Triumphs

Neta had spent ten years getting to what she then considered the top of her field, a $50,000 annual income. Since her divorce she had grown self-reliant and independent. Then suddenly that independence was threatened. Not only was she stumbling, her life was falling apart. Neta learned she had multiple sclerosis.

Neta had grown up in rural Oklahoma and attended two years of college on a singing scholarship. After her father died and the scholarship ran out, she left school. She went to work for a dentist for five years and then became the first female sales rep for a large dental supply business. She got the job "because I was a woman and they could pay me less," she recalls.

Neta was resourceful. She knew how to get things done.

"They threw me a phone book and said, 'Go develop a sales territory,'" she says. It was simple for her. She prided herself on her excellent service. She even delivered product in her car so her clients wouldn't have to pay freight. She was the top salesperson—until she started to stumble.

Her Worst Fears Were Happening

As her coordination worsened her fears grew. She lost the fine motor skills needed to write, and the speed, strength, and reflexes needed to drive. "In corporate America, being a woman, divorced, and with a medical problem was frightening," she says. Her desperate attempts to keep the illness a secret—for fear of losing her insurance—eventually failed. So did her efforts to hold onto her job after a period of rest.

Her request to work part-time was denied, and she was forced to resign. Then she lost her insurance, and then she lost her home. "Sometimes it is tough to go back and relive this story," she says with emotion in her voice. Finally Neta found herself starting all over with nothing—and thinking about the very worst-case scenario: "I was certain that I would be living in a wheelchair, disabled," she says. "I thought things were over for me. To say that I was devastated—that's putting it mildly."

The Customer Who Changed Her Life

Neta had to start looking for something else, something that she could handle physically. She found a part-time job at an upscale boutique that sold gowns. It was 1990, and she was making just over $4 an hour. She was delighted to wear the evening gowns—by then the five-foot six-inch blond had dropped twenty pounds and was down to a size 4—but she had a terrible time with the high heels on the marble floors. She couldn't hold a pen to write up a bill, but she could type orders into the computer. One day, a customer walked into the bou-

"I jumped in," says Neta Irwin.
When the chips were down she seized
an opportunity with Arbonne and
achieved remarkable success.

tique and changed her life. The woman was on her way to a training for Arbonne, a Swiss producer of health-oriented beauty and fitness products. The two "sales types" chatted. Neta was excited by Arbonne's sophisticated European slant and the idea of selling its high-quality products.

The snag was that Arbonne was a network marketing company, and Neta came from a different world, that of the professional salesperson. Though being an Arbonne independent consultant would allow her to set her own goals, she had a deep fear and reluctance because "it wasn't a company job with an expense account. I didn't really believe in working my own business," she recalls.

But she was intrigued that her new friend had come shopping in the middle of the day. That sort of freedom was enticing. Trying the products all but convinced her. But when she looked at the compensation plan, it was unlike anything she'd seen in her whole selling career. In fact, it appeared to be "completely foreign." (And what newcomer to MLM wouldn't sympathize with that objection?) She took the plan to the man who would become her fiancé, who had an accounting background. He assured her the numbers made total sense. "So, I jumped in," she says. Within two years she replaced her old $50,000 a year income and kept on going.

An Amazing Group of Women

Neta and the people she recruited did what many newcomers to MLM do to become successful. They adapted their old skills and knowledge to their new situation. Because of her sales background, Neta knew the importance of training and self-improvement. She started off by organizing a regular training meeting.

The very first meeting in her living room was attended by a group of women who would soon amaze everyone with their remarkable accomplishments. They began by sharing their stories and drawing on each other's strengths. Neta's sister, Sonja Peach, was there. A teacher, Sonja took charge of teaching the women how to present. Joyce Owens, a nurse, took the job of understanding and explaining the products. Neta taught sales. Cecilia Stoll didn't know it, but she was a naturally gifted trainer. Martha McIntyre was a mother who understood the needs of women who wanted to earn money from home while taking care of their families.

An Explosion of Growth

Each of the women from that first meeting in Oklahoma City went on to became national VPs. "These were five powerful people who developed a phenomenal group," says Neta. "It grew with an explosive surge when they got together," she remembers. "We didn't know enough to be greedy. I didn't know about the Mercedes-Benz awards. I never thought about any trips. I just came in to take care of myself and it grew into something greater than that."

What was greater than helping herself, Neta found, was helping others reach their goals. She wanted to see Martha get that $200 a month. She wanted to see the others get what they wanted. She was thrilled to see them work hard and have their incomes grow each month to levels they had never imagined possible—to $12,000, then $15,000, then $16,000—with no end in sight. As they progressed from one level to another, Neta was deeply moved by their accomplishments.

"Seeing what happens to other people can motivate you when you are down," Neta says, admitting there were times when she found it hard to stay motivated. "How did I hang on? How did I stay in? Every time I would decide to quit, something positive would happen," she recalls. Neta was also driven by the desire "to prove to my sister Sonja that it would work," she says laughing. Most of all, she worried, "If I quit, all these other people will quit. So I didn't," she says. "When my focus was on other people, the cars and the trips came naturally."

> With her dark days far behind her, Neta is extremely grateful. She knows she need never again be scared of being poor or alone.

With her disease in remission, Neta resumed driving—and one day was told to go to the Mercedes dealership and pick up her VP award car. When people saw the "Benz" their rejections softened. They became more receptive. Now they actually wanted to talk to her about Arbonne. A doctor who had laughed at her for "selling lipsticks" saw her drive up in the new Mercedes. "Nice wheels," he said. "Yeah, I got it selling lipsticks," she responded. He looked at her car and then back at his. She had the better car. Right then, Neta's confidence grew a bit.

A Stunning Example of Residual Income

As Neta's business expanded she turned more of the responsibilities over to her downline leaders. She visited the Phoenix area, fell in love with it, and bought a dream house in the Foothills. Her fiancé, Rick LaGuardia, who originally encouraged Neta to join Arbonne, bought a business in the area. When Neta left Oklahoma after four years of diligent work, her checks continued to increase—a stunning example of "walk-away residual income." It happened because her leaders were established and ready to run their own shows. In fact, says Neta, she is proud that when she moved, the group blossomed.

Their performance was a shining example of what happens when you have genuine teamwork and cooperation. Today Neta spends little time on day-to-day concerns and instead tends to the important long-range issues, especially the development of leaders and their organizations. Of the fourteen current National Vice Presidents in Arbonne, five are in Neta's organization, which means her group moves a lot of volume.

Giving Thanks

The frightened, vulnerable woman who was shoved out the door by a corporation in the darkest hours of her life has shown herself to be a capable, caring individual who puts the needs of others before her own. Rather than brood over the past, she gives thanks for those who surround her today. "My gratitude is extreme," she says. "And I am most grateful for the fact that I didn't do it alone." She could have added: Nor will she ever need to be alone, now that she is a network marketer.

Of the way it all turned out, Neta says simply this: "I believe with every ounce of my being, that this was one of those 'God Deals,' as we used to say back in Oklahoma."

She adds: "It was like God was saying, 'Neta, this is what I want you to do!'"

Rich Ruffalo

YOU NEED TO know certain amazing mental, emotional, and physical facts about Rich Ruffalo in order to understand his impact on MLM audiences around the world. These crowds know he has a special message for them, and so they pack the halls. They give him standing ovations before he even starts talking. During his speeches they weep, laugh, and burst into wild applause while furiously scribbling notes and straining to catch every thought. After his talk, they flock around him and his wife and daughter, clamoring for yet more insights and motivation. Rich does all he can to help them.

A Compelling Story

One reason audiences find Rich's story so compelling is that in his early twenties he went blind from a rare disease. Thinking he would be incapacitated, he tried to resign from his position as a schoolteacher. But his understanding principal wouldn't hear of it. Rich later won top awards for being an outstanding teacher. His students at Belleville High School in New Jersey talk about him with awe. "Ruff is tough," and "You don't mess with Mr. Ruff," they say. Disney found his story so inspiring that they decided to turn it into a film.

Amazing. Inspiring. Richard Ruffalo's triumphs thrill audiences. He often brings wife, Dianne, and daughter, Sara, to his talks.

How He Reached New Heights

All of which is nice—but we haven't gotten to the amazing stuff yet. You get a hint of this when you notice Rich's mighty six-foot–three-inch, 225-pound frame. You wonder: Could that physique be part of the story? Then you learn about the slew of national and international gold medals he began winning for track and field events in javelin, shot put, discus, and powerlifting—including four world titles. When you learn that he had not even taken up the shot or discus until he had reached age thirty—and then add to that the fact he won his medals against both blind and sighted competitors—you start appreciating the triumphs of this world-class athlete. You realize that he is one of those extraordinary individuals who not only overcame his difficulties, but reached new heights because of them.

But there's more. And don't jump to conclusions that his is a story about someone who has always been the ultimate role model, because that's not at all the way he tells it. When he first learned he was going blind, he reacted with a rage, despair, and bitterness that nearly destroyed him. Only later did he realize that you can turn your weaknesses into strengths, your setbacks into triumphs.

When he was a toddler, Rich's family knew he had problems and tried to find out the cause. He was given an EEG to see if a brain defect was making him constantly move his head from side to side. He was actually trying to take in more visual stimuli and compensate for his narrow field of vision. By the time he was three years old he was already wearing glasses. Despite the handicap he was a good athlete, competing in football, baseball, and track. "But right out of high school my night vision started to go. I kept driving a lot longer than I should have," he admits. "I couldn't accept it at first. I was like Mr. Magoo's brother." He chuckles when he talks about it now. The problem didn't prevent him from becoming a javelin thrower and co-captain of the track and field team at Montclair State College in New Jersey. Then he fulfilled a dream by becoming a high school science teacher. From the time he could read, Rich had wanted to teach. Starting in elementary school, he'd kept mental notes on teachers, "culling, categorizing, and filing away" their techniques.

> "Though MLM is a microcosm of life, there is a difference: Here, if you work really hard, someday you'll hardly work."
>
> —Richard Ruffalo

A Devastating Diagnosis

He was in his early twenties when he started to miss balls and looked like he was getting clumsy. In 1975, a few years after starting to teach, he was diagnosed with retinitis pigmentosa, an inherited, incurable eye disease that gradually destroys the retina and optic nerve.

Rich was crushed. He now couldn't drive and didn't know how he could go on. One of his first reactions was to walk into the principal's office and resign. But the principal refused to accept his resignation. "I don't want to lose a good teacher," he said, and gave him a teaching assistant. Looking back, he now says with brutal self-honesty, he realizes his response to going blind was to have a "pity party" that lasted for years. Life got even worse when his first wife left him. He could barely care for himself. He felt worthless.

Look What Happens When You Try

After sinking to the depths and spending years "blaming God" for his plight, "I started competing as a way of getting some self-esteem back. I started lifting weights and punching a heavy bag." At first he would flail in rage at his fate. "I was so angry I even punched a concrete wall," he remembers.

But gradually he grew more focused. "I would hit that thing for an hour straight," he says. Now that Rich was at last taking action, God seemed to answer his efforts by saying, "Look what happens when you try." What happened was Rich Ruffalo's astonishing rise to world-class athlete. You could fill a book with his accomplishments, but briefly: He won four different world titles in shot put, discus, javelin, and powerlifting. He earned fourteen international gold medals, won twenty-four national titles, set nine world and fifteen national records, and has won eleven USA Track and Field Master's State titles against sighted competitors. He received the cherished Victor Award as the nation's most inspirational athlete. His bushel of awards for teaching and coaching include Outstanding Coach of the Year and Outstanding Teacher of the Year. And then there's that movie on his life, to be aired on the *Wonderful World of Disney*.

Obstacles Help Us Grow

What can a network marketer learn from this tale of tragedy and redemption? In Rich's words, "People with faith realize that their finite and mortal nature must be tested in the great race of life."

The obstacles and setbacks one meets in the business world are there for a reason, says Rich. "Everyone needs humbling blocks. If you lack vision, you call them stumbling blocks. But people with faith know they are placed in our way to help us grow," he says.

"In regular business there are actually not enough built-in humbling blocks to help you reach your full potential as a person," he says. "In network marketing there are humbling blocks that test your strength, your resolution, and your resolve. People in network marketing share their humbling blocks. They share the pitfalls and potholes. That's a neat thing because it is in a sense a support team. You see, not only do you build income and wealth, you build character through a sense of support."

MLM Versus the "Square Business World"

When it comes to helping others, the upbeat "Mr. Ruff," as his students call him, sees a profound distinction between MLM and the "square business world." In a phrase, the difference is that "people are truly happy when someone else succeeds," he says. "They clap for the person who has achieved the next level of success because next time it could be them. The applause is an affirmation that the method really works."

Ruffalo feels a closeness with network marketers because, like him, they are willing to learn and grow. They want to take a little piece of the speaker—the "sage on the stage"—with them. They want to uplift themselves and strengthen their minds and their spirits with motivating words. "They are more inclined to feed their vision of the future by using books and tapes. They are trying to pull threads of excellence from the speakers and authors to weave a quilt of inspiration to warm and protect their families."

Crowds Hungry for Information

Corporate audiences respond to Ruffalo with much the same enthusiasm as MLM crowds, though they are rarely as passionate. Like MLMers, they roar with approval at his signature motivational line: "When the world says, 'You can't,' champions say 'Watch me!'" But he's keenly aware that in a corporation a superior scheduled the event and told the employees to attend. At MLM events, "You have people who may have missed a meal or will do without to buy your tapes."

They're people who are hungry for information and inspiration, who take copious notes and listen intently. Another distinction is that MLMers "are not afraid to say, 'Maybe there is something this speaker has that I can take with me to create freedom for my family.'" Ruffalo sees people from corporate America as having more of the pieces of their life's puzzle locked in place, while the MLMer is still discovering new pieces. He feels an enormous responsibility when he speaks to these groups because he knows that every presentation he gives may hold a crucial piece of that puzzle for someone.

"Everyone Can Be Successful"

Ruffalo knows that not every person makes it to the top, but everyone who wants to be successful badly enough can and eventually will. As he puts it: "MLM is a microcosm of life. But there is a difference: If you work really hard, some day you'll hardly work." Some other favorite phrases that this skilled and eloquent motivator uses in his talks to network marketers:

- "These people are lifelong learners who become lifelong earners."

- "In this business the more you learn, the more you earn."

- "You build a monument through your efforts that generates a cash flow and lasts the test of time."

- "You are your own boss, make your own hours, and have the freedom to choose to do things when you want."

Work That Suits Your Lifestyle

He also notes that as the job description for parents constantly changes, an MLM lifestyle can be adapted to meet those needs. "You can mold your business around your family's needs"—even when you're in a nontraditional "split" or "blended" family. Rich loves bringing his wife Dianne and his daughter Sara whenever he speaks to MLM groups and notes that "it is more appropriate to bring your family to these functions than to events in the corporate world." He adds, "I feel like I felt at my wedding reception as the people come up and greet us."

As Rich has poured his athletic energy into speaking, he's found that the experience of changing people's lives has stimulated his desire to write. He recently wrote *Invisible Gold Medals,* a full-length poem for children that he dictated while on a cruise. "I like to write poetry because I can describe things in visual terms—so that even the blind can see what I am saying."

As for those "invisible gold medals," he believes you win them by helping other people.

For MLMers looking for the secret of success, no message could do more to open their eyes.

Bobbie Soetaert

HOW COULD GOING through two network marketing disasters strengthen anyone's commitment to the business? Here is the story of someone who walked away from two failed companies—then went on to become super-successful in a third business.

Disaster Left Her More Committed

"Dear God, please get me out of the ghetto," pleaded little Bobbie Reardon in one of her frequent prayers. She was sitting in an old galvanized metal bathtub looking at the teapot heating on the stove, waiting for her mom to pour the water into her bath. One powerful, ever-present motive for her prayers was the not-so-fragrant smell of the nearby Armour meat-packing plant.

At nine years old, Barbara—or "Bobbie," as her family called her—realized that the Armourdale area of Kansas City where she lived was the wrong side of the tracks. She already understood the word *ghetto.* "I used to hear the neighbors say, 'I can't get out of the ghetto.' I knew I could and would." To make sure she got out, the young girl from the strict Irish Catholic family kept on praying.

"Please God, Get Me Out of the Ghetto"

Bobbie became excited about drama after watching the school play, so "I changed my prayer a bit," she says. She changed it to, "Get me out of the ghetto and get me on stage," she recalls with a laugh. "You have to be really specific. I thought God understood I meant show business," she says. "I forgot to tell God what stage, so he put me on the MLM stage," says the girl who grew up to become a super-successful distributor for a company dealing in health-oriented products.

"Under my picture in the high school yearbook were the words, 'Joan of Arc, the girl most likely to succeed in the people business.'" The words suggested both her religious and her worldly sides. The religious side seemed to have won out when after high school she decided to enter a convent. But once she encountered the

The magic of network marketing. When Bobbie Soetaert investigated her check, she began to understand the nature of the business.

discipline of the nuns of Mount St. Scholastica, Barbara realized she had made a grievous error. "They were stricter than my father!" she says. She lasted six weeks, then fled to the home of her grandmother, who helped Barbara convince her parents that she would never adapt to convent life.

Researching Cancer and Nutrition

Barbara did office work, attended night school, and began a career in real estate. But her life came to a turning point when her sister-in-law, who had breast cancer, died in her arms. She became convinced there was a relationship between nutrition and cancer—specifically breast and ovarian cancer—and so threw herself into a mission of researching women's health. "I wanted to find out what caused women's cancers," she says. She talked to health food specialists and read nutrition books. In time she became something of a self-taught nutrition expert—all the while achieving ever greater success in real estate.

She had met and married Jerry Soetaert and had become a mother, while working in real estate, when in 1981 she mentioned to a physician friend that she wanted to spend more time with her children. The doctor enthusiastically told her about MLM and introduced her to the Cambridge Diet. She decided to give it a chance, but to do so without leaving her real estate career.

Checks That Kept Growing

Her first check was for $63.05. She was making more than a hundred times that each month selling property. "He wants me to change careers for sixty-three dollars and a nickel. I don't think so!" she remembers saying to Jerry. But the amount kept growing, and soon she was surprised and puzzled to receive a check for $8,000. Jerry, an accountant, looked it over and solved the apparent problem. "The decimal point's in the wrong place. Send it back," he said.

Barbara phoned the company. The woman assured her she had the right check. She then sent Barbara her group genealogy, listing the names and addresses of people in her downline who had purchased product that month. When the printout arrived in the mail, Barbara examined it, leafing through page after page of names. "I don't know these people," she remarked to herself. That's when the magic of network marketing hit her. "I tell a few. They tell a few, and then they tell a few." The check that arrives reflects the cumulative effort of all. "It was so easy," she recalls. "People were ready for that product. I could have strapped a can of products on my cocker spaniel's back and sent him out to sell and he would have been very successful." Her checks continued to grow, and over three exciting years she made a lot of money and met a lot of friends, some of whom are still close to her seventeen years later.

A Wildly Controversial Company

But the Cambridge Diet came to be one of the most wildly controversial episodes in the annals of network marketing. The company rose like a Roman Candle and almost as quickly burnt itself out, leaving thousands of distributors in the lurch.

The product, a very-low-calorie milkshake-type drink enhanced with vitamins and minerals, was based on a formula devised by Dr. Alan Howard, a chemist from Cambridge University in Britain. In February 1980, entrepreneurs Jack and Eileen Feather introduced the liquid Cambridge Diet through their small mail-order operation. One year later they began selling the Cambridge Diet via the multi-level method. By the end of 1982, revenues had soared to nearly $400 million, thanks to 150,000 distributors or "counselors" who had sold the diet to more than five million people.

Several factors were involved in the company's implosion, which resulted in it filing for bankruptcy in September 1983. The owners spent money with undue optimism, determined to do everything "first class." Competitors like the "Oxford" and "University" diets came on the scene. The medical community and the FDA criticized the product. Though the company was resurrected and continues to this day, it suffered a severe setback.

> Despite the catastrophe, Barbara now knew she was committed. She couldn't go back.

Barbara's Second Adventure

For her part, Barbara vowed never to be a quitter and headed straight into her next network marketing adventure. It was with Cernitin America, a company founded in July 1983 and based in Yellow Springs, Ohio. It was the exclusive North American distributor of natural food supplements made with pure flower pollen from A. B. Cernelle in Sweden. It also handled a broad line of other nutritional and personal care products as well as the Dick Gregory Slim-Safe Bahamian Diet.

After the Cambridge experience, Barbara was attracted to the Bahamian Diet because it had been developed with safety concerns in mind. Jimmy Carter, M.D., from Tulane University had worked with Gregory to ensure the safety and efficacy of the diet. Once Barbara flew into action, her group rapidly grew to an enormous size. The

Cernitin America period marked a time Barbara calls "magical." She found "such warmth and love among distributors that I can't even put it into words." Where the Cambridge distributors had rapidly fallen into disarray, the Cernitin distributors seemed to be functioning effectively, and the products were perceived as excellent.

Barbara's response to what happened next explains the essence of network marketing for many who are in it. In 1986, the company appeared to be riding high. Projected annual revenues were at $146 million. Its employee base had grown to more than a hundred workers. It had warehouses throughout the United States, with top-notch buildings, equipment, and office furnishings. Then disaster struck with the force of a tornado when revenues failed to materialize as planned. The over-optimistic forecasting had shattered expectations and started a downward spiral that ended in ruination. Sales plummeted to between $3 million and $4 million. All warehouses but one had to be shut down. Ninety percent of the staff was cut.

Heartache and Commitment

Once again Barbara and the friends she had made through MLM had their income suddenly stopped. Yet—and here's the amazing part—despite the almost unmitigated business catastrophe and all the heartache it caused, Barbara was more committed than ever to MLM. As she put it, the bug had bitten her and she knew, "I could never go back and do something else after that."

To anyone outside the field her reaction must seem extraordinary, and it raises one question: Why? Why put yourself through that again? Why endure the chaos, uncertainty, and embarrassment of committing yourself heart and soul to the same kind of venture that twice left you shipwrecked? Half of the answer, says Barbara, is that she had tasted the excitement, the thrill, the satisfaction, of making an income in the high–six figures. She knew MLM was the best way to recreate those earnings. The other half of the answer is that she had loved "standing on stage motivating people to believe in themselves."

Searching for the Right Company

She looked carefully for her next company. She was cautious this time and gathered more facts before making her decision. She sought out a company that was everything she needed. She wanted a product mix that suited her personally, one she could take pride in selling. She also looked for solid management, and she asked questions to make certain she was getting it. When she found a growing company in the neutraceutical field she decided she had looked long enough.

How does Barbara go about building her business? "I approach each new person that I meet as someone I will know for a long time. This is a family-friendly, heart-propelled industry. If you put your heart and soul into it you will make a lot of friends." Barbara emphasizes the profound difference between working together in MLM and in a job, where "no one really wants to help you." In regular jobs people are deceived because coworkers will "smile and be friendly," but in the end they often don't see helping you as benefiting themselves. In MLM, precisely the opposite is the case.

Helping People's Dreams Come True

Barbara is barely able to contain her enthusiasm when she says, "You help people's dreams come true." She remembers working with a woman in her downline to help her achieve the dream of her lifetime, a trip to Italy. When the distributor expressed her gratitude by saying she wished Barbara could accompany her, Barbara, who lives in Kansas City, Missouri, dropped everything and went with the woman. "Going to Rome was priceless. There is no way to explain it to someone with a job," she says.

At rallies and seminars it often takes an hour for Barbara to reach the front of the room because everyone wants to say something to her personally. "It's so exciting because these are the people you are trying to help," she says. On stage, Barbara is known to be a wild and crazy lady. At a weekend seminar she entered the center isle with a gigantic gold sombrero covered with one hundred dollar bills. The music started playing the song, "She Works Hard for the Money," and Barbara started dancing. "I love this industry. I wouldn't do any other business. It allows me to be myself."

It allows Barbara Soetaert to be free, enthusiastic, zany, and accepted for who she is. It allows her to get on stage and tell everyone, "The income is very nice, but the friends are wonderful." She encourages the audience to think about all the wonderful people they are going to meet as they build their fortunes. "Think about what it would take to get someone you like in the business. Focus on them, on what it would take to get them to see it. You have to get emotional about the products and emotional about touching someone's life. Make a purpose for your life. Decide that you are going to enrich the lives of others."

Barbara says she always held a secret belief that business could be emotionally fulfilling. She also knew she would get out of the ghetto.

She just didn't know that MLM would be the answer to her prayers.

6

Partners

W HO WOULD BELIEVE the fun we have, the lives we lead?" asked one husband. "We could not have had this lifestyle with any other business," added his wife. Out of shared effort comes deepened respect and affection, and a stronger, happier family. The struggles bring you closer and make the big rewards all the more exciting.

"Buddies Forever"

YOU HAVE TO hand it to Sheri. "I believed in Gregory," she says of her husband. "I always believed in him." She says it a lot.

So, when Gregory Lagana got down on one knee and proposed in the Windows on the World restaurant in 1986, Sheri accepted, having no doubt that life together would be an adventure.

When Sheri looked at Gregory, she saw a smart, soon-to-be successful guy. They would make a great team, and together they would conquer any obstacles that stood in their way.

As befits two soulmates, when they married the following year they exchanged wedding rings inscribed with the words, "Buddies forever."

And today, in their residence in exurban New Jersey, where the big houses are separated by wide fields and winding roads, the two buddies sit at side-by-side desks in their luxurious home office. Now, "luxurious" may not be the ideal word for this office. You could also say elegant, or exquisite, or some other term to capture the quality displayed in the furnishings, which range from a desk of just the right style, topped with granite of just the right shade, on through the rug, wall hangings, and other tasteful appointments. You could go on all afternoon noting each aspect of rich decor, but you could sum it up by saying that more money went into that one room than many Americans earn in a year. Yet such a description completely overlooks the casual, spontaneous atmosphere of the household with its three children watched over by an attentive nanny.

In describing Gregory, master of the house and co-hero of this tale, you might say he's the model of a successful businessperson. He's confident, articulate, and a superb presenter, someone who can keep a roomful of listeners laughing, smiling, and nodding their heads in agreement and appreciation. If his presentations are not quite on the level of a paid entertainer, they are at least a few thousand times more interesting and enjoyable than the typical speech by a corporate executive.

A Tragedy of Errors

But back when he and Sheri met, in 1983, Gregory was a twenty-four-year-old aspiring entrepreneur with a ninth grade education. The fact he came from a well-off family with a highly successful father had done nothing to put him on the path of achievement. Gregory's school career had been a tragedy of errors, starting with his being ousted from kindergarten for "hitting a kid in the head with a block." It took two more schools and a year of being left behind before he finished first grade. All in all, he served time in seven institutions of lower learning before high school. After first grade, he was left back in second, kicked out in fourth. He then endured the injustice—apparent to him, but not to others—of being sent to a school for those deemed handicapped and retarded. Though the path was not smooth, he emerged from there, finished the ninth grade, and then said good-bye forever to an education system that for years had failed to diagnose the source of his problems—and of his intense frustration: It was nothing more and nothing less than dyslexia. Not lack of intelligence or emotional problems, but dyslexia. Looking back, he says, "Frustration with education led me to where I am today."

The next stop for eighteen-year-old Gregory was the U.S. Army. Though he saw Korea and other spots, the stint did little to lay the foundation for a lasting career, and his attempts to attend college "did not get anywhere."

Lacking in credentials but never in energy, in 1983, at age twenty-four, he earned a living traversing the urbanized environs of New Jersey and New York, selling merchandise out of the back of a van. He sold pots, pans, fake leather bags, clock radios, Naugahyde, cutlery, glassware, plates, cups, and even telephones, with markups of up to 300 percent.

One had to admire Gregory for his ambition. On the other hand, mature citizens of common sense and good judgment might have cautioned any young woman against giving her heart away to an uneducated peddler, however enterprising and energetic. Sheri, at the time they met, was a college senior who had wrapped meat in a butcher shop during high school and held three different jobs to put herself through college. A prudent adviser would have told her to set her sights on ascending beyond the struggling world still inhabited by her parents—a world where luxuries were rare and bills were omnipresent. Surely, the last thing she needed to do after coming so far on her own efforts was to hitch her fortunes to someone whose future was anything but assured. She could do far better, it seemed. From a purely statistical standpoint, at least, Gregory's future earning potential was considerably less attractive than that of other men

Heart to Heart Wisdom

"Most people have no clue about residual income."

—*Sheri Lagana, Melaleuca*

she might meet, including virtually all of the guys at her college as well as half the male population of the United States. Not surprisingly, she quickly decided on that first blind date that "I really wasn't interested."

Sheri Saw Larger Possibilities

At the end of the evening she would be done with him. But that very night, at a bar in Saratoga, New York, a little event opened her eyes to larger possibilities. She stood there as Gregory pulled out a brochure and proceeded to persuade a group of people he'd never seen before to buy his merchandise. The admiration still echoes in her voice when she says, "Right on the spot they bought $150 of stuff. I thought, 'This guy is cool. He has this magnetic personality. He has really honed his skills.'" Sheri had come to see something that the teachers and experts with their tests and measurements had failed to see, and so she came to believe in Gregory.

During the first several years of their marriage Gregory hustled on a variety of fronts, including holding down a job as an installation technician with a private phone company. The fact his father owned the company did nothing to ensure that his job was cushy, or, as we shall see, secure.

At the same time, Sheri's career was off to a good start. Leaving school with a degree in psychology and business, she took a job as a secretary at Citicorp. "I kept getting promoted and promoted. I worked for mergers and acquisitions. It was the late 1980s, a good time to be in that."

As for Gregory's career, you will find experts who say that genuine entrepreneurs not only *will not* work for others, they literally *cannot* do so. Whatever the case may be, on January 3, 1990, after working on and off at the telephone company for eleven years, Gregory was fired, leaving open a world of possibilities.

Exciting Initial Results

By April, he had been introduced to multilevel marketing. He signed up as a distributor for a large company, and the initial results were exciting to both him and Sheri. "We always wanted to have our own business," says Sheri. "At the time, I had seven people reporting to me and at least five had been working in Citicorp longer than I had been alive. But I didn't like it. I was not happy there at all. I wanted so badly to work with Gregory and leave my job and build the American Dream. That's what I wanted."

Shortly after he became a distributor, Gregory's efforts produced a monthly check for $2,400. The reaction of both was to say, "Can you imagine if both of us did that?" Encouraged by their upline, Sheri quit her job, losing all benefits. "We were young, naive, and ambitious," she explains. "We wouldn't listen to Gregory's father. He told us we were crazy." They had an outstanding loan and a mortgage and had just taken out an $11,000 car loan.

Dangerous Advice

The Laganas now acknowledge that they should have been exercising thrift. Instead, they were taken in by the statement of one of their upline sponsors to "Live life like a Blue Diamond." Among the frequently misleading and even dangerous pieces of advice disseminated to young achievers is the notion that one should "imitate the successful." Having role models and heroes to look up to can clearly have its benefits, but for every instance where imitating the successful is a good idea, you can probably find a case where it is a potential recipe for disaster. This is especially true when the advice is aimed at getting people to spend money they do not have. In the corporate world, sales managers with commissioned salespeople once made a practice of urging their charges to think big, to raise their sights, to have the courage to commit to that hefty mortgage or that more expensive car. "Make the commitment you're going to raise your income, and then go for it" was the advice. In the best situations, these managers served as mentors and coaches, spurring their younger salespeople along the path to greater achievement and encouraging them to take moderate, attainable risks while accepting new responsibilities. The salesperson produced higher sales, and everyone benefited.

Heart to Heart Wisdom

"The company convention in 1992 changed our lives. We met so many people who were plain old folks, regular people making $5,000 to $10,000 per month. After that convention we said, 'We can do this.' It changed everything.'"

—*Gregory Lagana, Melaleuca*

In network marketing an upline sponsor can also play a valuable role in helping a distributor he's signed up expand his vision. But the advice to live beyond your means can represent the worst sort of selfishness on the part of a sponsor, especially when it involves encouraging inexperienced young people to take on debt. As far as emulating the successful, the best tactic is often to imitate what the successful people did when they were still trying to achieve success.

Encouraged by others, the Laganas retained a housekeeper and took on more debt, living briefly with the illusion that their financial status was improving. Then, as if to amplify the warnings of Greg's father, Sheri soon got pregnant. Within months their initial optimism had turned to concern and then desperation, and before long the two had entered a terrifying downward financial spiral that was to exhaust them both over the next year and a half.

Heartache and Stress

Adding to their heartache and stress during that period was the unexpected death of Sheri's father. What pained Sheri most about the loss was that "he never had the chance to live the kind of life he dreamed of. He worked so hard, but he never got anywhere. Finally, one day he did all he could to get a boat, so we could all spend time together and have some memories." Her father and mother sailed from Long Island to Mystic, Connecticut. Sheri and Gregory drove up. "We spent a couple of days up there and had to rush home." It was the last time Sheri saw her dad alive. "He got home and saw the bills from that trip," she says. "We know that's what did it."

"It was Sunday night, the time when people have heart attacks because they have to go to work the next day," adds Gregory. "He had gotten home from vacation. There were piles of bills."

Meanwhile, the financial screws kept turning tighter on Sheri and Gregory. That initial $2,400 check, the one that had inspired their optimism and led Sheri to resign, turned out to be the biggest check they would ever receive from the company.

In order to qualify for their commissions, the Laganas were buying $500 to $1,000 worth of product a month. In addition, they were encouraged to purchase thousands of dollars in videotapes, sales aids, sample packs, and training materials, many of which were sold to them as a side business by their upline. Soon they were running meetings simply to collect the $5 at the door. As their situation worsened, the company was hit with a wave of negative publicity. They especially remember a July 19, 1991 *Nightline* episode with Barbara Walters on the company and network marketing that "devastated our business," says Sheri.

Before long, "creditors were calling our house night and day," says Sheri. "There were messages stacked up on the answering machine from people demanding what we owed them. Sears wanted its vacuum cleaner and dishwasher back," says Sheri, adding, "We were demolished. We got in so far over our heads. The phone was turned off, and then the electricity."

Maxed Out

They used their ingenuity to survive. "I remember going down into the basement (of their apartment building) and tapping into other units," says Gregory. At the same time, says Sheri, "Gregory's mother was giving us groceries. She'd open the trunk of her car and there'd be cereal and pasta."

Their credit cards were maxed out, their bills were mounting, they were falling further and further behind on their mortgage payments, and their monthly income was less than $1,000.

In place of her promising job in management, Sheri now did typing as a temp. "I was out-to-here pregnant," she says, holding her hands over her stomach. "I was wearing borrowed maternity clothes and $10 overalls, working as a typist and secretary, driving around in a Chevy with a taped-up back window because a tree had fallen on it and knocked out the glass. The brakes squealed so loud you had to shut the windows and turn up the radio to block out the sound."

Their 540-square-foot condo, a fourth-floor walkup in Hoboken, New Jersey, had begun to seem like a trap. "We called it 'the cage.' Everything we owned was in that apartment," says Gregory. As they maneuvered to survive, they seemed to add to their problems, including Gregory's getting $1,300 worth of parking tickets.

As Sheri's pregnancy advanced, they started using a milk crate hung out the window to haul up groceries or laundry or lower packages. Walking up and down the stairs was agony for her.

With the world closing in on them, Sheri recalls, the sheriff "came to the door to serve us a notice to vacate the premises" because of the overdue payments on the condo. He returned in thirty days, and then again after thirty more. Their sense of desperation kept increasing.

Gregory found a new job as a cable installation technician. Though he refrains from complaining, Sheri recalls the work as being "sweaty and dirty and terrible. He would come home exhausted after twelve- to sixteen-hour days." She herself had borrowed a car in order to supplement her temp work by selling ad space for a local publication. "It was a tough time," she says. "We needed money." Adds Gregory, "Sheri was pregnant and we were broke."

In November 1991, they decided to give up on the multilevel marketing company. Says Gregory: "We had enrolled fifty-three people on our first level and only four people placed an order—after all that blood, sweat, and tears. We said, 'That's it. It's not worth it.'"

After agonizing over the decision for months, they felt they had no alternative to filing for bankruptcy protection. "We tried hard to pay our bills up until the day before bankruptcy," says Sheri. "We didn't want to go that route. We aren't that kind of people."

He Refused to Give Up

After such a searing experience, you might have thought the Laganas would flee from all so-called "business opportunities" and settle for a more secure but less exciting life as wage earners. Lots of people would have advised them to do just that—lower your horizons, retreat from the struggle, put your hopes in a job. Why didn't they? Maybe one result of Gregory's difficult childhood was the creation of a fighter willing to withstand criticism and make his own judgments. After all, people had been wrong about him all his life. Despite all he and Sheri had been through, Gregory's spirit was far from broken. "I never give up," he says.

The following month, December 1991, Gregory learned about a company called Melaleuca, which had a wide range of household, nutritional, and personal care products—many of which were made with the oil of the melaleuca tree. Melaleuca stressed that it was not an MLM, but a "consumer direct marketing" company. They learned about Melaleuca from someone who had been signed up for only two weeks. The person's name was Russ Paley, and he started calling the Laganas.

"Not another one of those!" said Sheri, horrified.

"Let Me Sit with You"

Russ kept on calling, and Sheri got more and more irritated.

Gregory himself was reluctant to listen at first. "I kept on telling Russ, 'No,'" he says. "But Russ kept saying, 'Let me sit with you.'"

Right before Christmas, when Sheri was out, Gregory told Russ to come up. "He came up and he sat down with me. Within an hour I said, 'Okay, I can do this.' I gave him $19 at the time to sign me up in Melaleuca."

Again, the question arises: Why would Gregory even consider signing up with Russ Paley and a company he'd never heard of after such a horrendous prior experience?

Gregory says it was partly "the fact I had nothing to lose" by exploring the opportunity. In addition, he saw it as a way of partly salvaging his past experience. "I really was feeling, 'If I don't do this I'll have gotten nothing.' The $19 fee to sign up was not a lot,'" he says, adding: "I was also thinking at the time, 'If I say no to Russ and he succeeds, I will really have screwed up.'"

Gregory adds, "I had never given up on our desire to succeed in a home-based business." After signing up, he says, "I took the portfolio kit and put it in the kitchen next to the cookbooks. I didn't want Sheri to know what I had done," he says. Few spouses will be surprised to hear that Sheri "found it an hour after she got home." Then nine months pregnant, she had a predictable reaction. "She went ballistic. She went ape," says Gregory

"That's an understatement," says Sheri.

Sheri Was Determined to Say "No"

"We fought for three months," says Gregory, "because of her determination not to have our family suckered into one of those deals again."

"I don't believe we ever had such fighting," says Gregory. "I almost quit. I would have, but I never sent the fax to Melaleuca."

The situation did not improve when Gregory realized a little later that "Russ signed us up to be preferred customers with a backup order" of seventy-five base points—amounting to about $89 per month. That meant that even if they failed to place a monthly order, they would receive that much worth of product and would automatically be charged for it. "I tried to get my money back. Thank God I didn't have a fax machine or I would have succeeded," says Gregory. "I almost quit."

"A Miracle We Survived"

Adding to the stress was the birth of their first child, Matthew, who was born by c-section. "It cost us $11,000 to have the baby. We had no insurance," says Gregory. The transition of going from their first company to Melaleuca took its toll on Sheri. "It is a miracle we survived it. I was so negative. I didn't want to do it. We had a tiny little apartment with everything in one room. Gregory would come home from work and would go into the bedroom and would call from 6 to 10 P.M. For the first three months he worked Tuesday and Thursday nights for a four-hour period."

One crucial fact Gregory had to face was that, "We couldn't go back to people we knew."

"When you build a business, like we had tried to do, your heart is in it," says Sheri. "When it fell apart we lost friends. People still don't talk to us. We lost credibility with everybody we knew."

But they began to realize that Melaleuca was what they wanted. There was no pressure to buy loads of product they did not need, and they were now doing the business right. During the first year in Melaleuca the Laganas worked part-time and earned about $18,000. They also attended the convention in August 1992, where they saw hundreds of successful individuals. After their first year of full-time work, they had earned $101,000. They doubled their income in each of the following two years and by November 1996, when they were written up as the cover story in the monthly corporate magazine, *Melaleuca Country,* they had earned $546,000 in commissions and bonuses over the previous twelve months.

"If we knew we were going to make the money we have, we would have taken it more seriously a lot sooner," Gregory has often said.

The Laganas joined Melaleuca when the company was more than seven years old—it was founded in 1985—and climbed to the highest level. In discussing all that their residual income has made possible, the Laganas focus on their second child, Alex. Now a smiling, laughing three-year-old, his life began in an agonizing, terrifying crisis. The Laganas have no doubt that their present happiness and the health of their second child are results of the income and lifestyle made possible by their business.

The year before Alex was born, when Matthew was two, Sheri had a baby that died shortly after birth. The Laganas then took six months off from the business, but their residual income checks from Melaleuca continued to arrive every thirty days. Then, when Alex was born, "he was monitored like you can't believe," says Gregory.

Soon after his birth, the nurse noted he was having seizures—what turned out to be a major stroke. "It was so massive that half his brain was black on the CAT scan," recalls Sheri. "On the whole right side, there was nothing there. It would have killed an adult," she adds. The parents were told that "he may never walk, he may never sit up, may never feed himself." The Laganas refused to accept the gloomy prognoses. Instead, they flew into action and committed themselves to playing an active role in his recovery.

"We fought really hard, thank God. A lot of people would have wanted to crawl under a blanket. There were incredible obstacles, but we fought to do everything for this baby," says Gregory.

Sheri began reading everything she could find about the development of young babies. "I learned about the brains of kids and that they are very resilient. I learned that in the first three years babies are constantly building connections in their brains, and the more connections the better off he would be." Nothing was going to stop her from learning and from helping her child. She strove constantly to lovingly stimulate Alex in every way—from encouraging him physically, to singing songs, to providing toys to engage and excite him. She sought out every book on how to raise a smarter, healthier baby.

Nonstop Treatment, Thanks to Melaleuca

Without Melaleuca, the Laganas see no way they would have been able to give Alex the combination of personal attention and nonstop therapy he required. Had they been working regular jobs, they would have had neither the income to pay for his sessions nor the free time available to care for him. Sheri went to therapy with Alex every day. For the first three years of Alex's life, the Laganas were spending $600 a week in therapy, involving three different kinds of sessions each week. No insurance programs available through employers would have covered the amount and quality of care he was getting. In addition, "there was a waiting list for therapists," says Gregory. Had the Laganas not had the funds, "there would have been someone else who would have paid cash," says Gregory. "There's no way he would have gotten the kind of help and therapy he did without our having the cash to pay for it," he adds.

Under constant care, Alex got better and better—and ultimately thrived and flourished. When you know their background of heartache and hope, it's easy to understand why Sheri has tears of joy in her eyes when she grabs the laughing boy in her arms and calls him, "the biggest miracle in our life." All the while Alex was rallying, the Melaleuca business was growing.

A Picture in Their Hearts and Minds

In November 1997, Amanda was born. As Kim, the nanny, readies Matthew, Alex, and Amanda for an afternoon out, Sheri says, "This is how we work. This is our lifestyle." It's a lifestyle that was painted vividly in their hearts and minds before it ever took shape in reality. For years the Laganas had on their refrigerator a picture of a house taken from a magazine. It was a picture of what their dream house would be like. "It has moved with us into four different homes," says Sheri. The house is strikingly similar to the one where they now live—except that the real house is notably larger than the dream version. Not present in the magazine picture are such details as the Mercedes that sits in their driveway with the license plate "$7 Bucks." Explains Gregory, their Melaleuca car allowance is $800 per month, and the car payments are $807. "So we're basically getting that car for seven bucks a month."

Sheri and Gregory work together like partners in just about every aspect of the business. Often, when faced with a decision, Gregory will remark that he wants first to get Sheri's input or opinion. One reason he values the togetherness is the ability it gives him to consult with a highly knowledgeable individual who has the best interests of the business in mind—that is, Sheri.

Companionship and Kids

For her part, Sheri values the companionship, the presence of Gregory in the house, and the ability to flow smoothly back and forth between the business and tasks of household management. "It's a good mix of being with the kids and being together. Working from the house is the best thing you could imagine. Having Gregory here is wonderful," she says. "Can you imagine what an impact this is going to have on our kids when they get older? He spends more time in one day with the kids than some fathers do in weeks."

Matthew, seven, is now aware of having a lot more access to his father than his friends do to their dads. Recently he said to Gregory in astonishment, "You mean you once had a job?"

With the security of their residual income, the Laganas are able to keep life in perspective. For example, says Gregory, when things get too busy or hectic, "We can just forget all this and go jump in the pool."

They Recognized Their Mistakes

Gregory says an important part of their success was being able to acknowledge that they had made mistakes. He notes that "everything we did wrong eventually caught up with us." Even their old credit record sometimes comes back to haunt them. On the other hand, getting a mortgage was not a problem for the simple reason that "money talks."

"Any one of the things that hit us—losing a child, having a child born with problems, going through bankruptcy—would be enough to break up a lot of marriages," says Sheri. But, she adds, "We always had each other. We pulled together. Things that would have ripped other marriages apart made us closer. I remember the lowest of the low times. We were so in the dregs. But we survived and succeeded because we had each other."

Putting his arm around his wife, Gregory agrees: "Buddies forever. That's us," he says.

Bella's Recipe for Nonstop Happiness

"GORGEOUS!" EXCLAIMS BELLA Werzberger. "Beautiful!"

Bella, whose richly flavored Brooklynesque speech overflows with enthusiasm, is talking about all the great, terrific, wonderful things network marketing has done for her and her husband, Nick. Is there anyone who can listen to Bella's excitement and not feel joyful? As they might say in Brooklyn: Maybe if you're dead, or have a similar problem.

"We now have time to play," enthuses Bella. "What a thrilling way to live with your spouse," she rhapsodizes. And just so you don't forget, Bella adds, "This business has had an absolutely beautiful effect on our relationship."

She Got It All Started

Nick would no doubt agree, but Bella does the talking because, "I am the mouth. He is the brains." To tell the truth, that neat division of labor may not do justice to Bella, as she was the entrepreneur who got it all going. But no one's complaining, because life is too good.

She dreamed of their working together in a family business. Bella Werzberger seized an opportunity, then got husband Nick to join her.

What has network marketing meant to them? "We are both excited at the same time. We go to training together. We fly together. We vacation together and we work together," says Bella.

Don't think Nick and Bella didn't appreciate the wonderful attractions in Brooklyn. But now they go to the most exotic places in the world. They stay in the nicest rooms in the best hotels. They go whenever they want, and they go without any guilt, because those fat residual checks keep coming.

And forget about that old two-room apartment they were once crammed into. Now they have a beautiful five-room condo in Brooklyn's Borough Park. Large? Like you can't imagine. More like "a villa or small mansion." It's a brownstone, the kind people in Brooklyn say they'd kill for. Their business is downstairs and their home is upstairs, which makes for more of that togetherness Bella loves. And here's the inside info: With the cost of the renovations alone you could buy another house.

"A Total Whammy"

Yes, people are talking and gossiping. But as everyone knows, that's good for business. "Our being in Herbalife has affected a lot of people in our Jewish community," says Bella. "It has been a total whammy, seeing an Hasidic couple doing well in network marketing."

To understand how such an untraditional thing could occur, you have to go back to the beginning. Back to when Bella was a psychologist. Well, actually, she was a beautician. But it's close, because, "It's just like being a psychologist. You have no idea. I took all these skills into the Herbalife marketplace."

Bella had worked at a hair salon since she was a teenager. It was a perfect job for her because she was gifted with her hands and also because, "I love talking to people." A good friend of hers who knew Nick played matchmaker. Here was the thinking: Bella was a people person and Nick was a computer technician, so the friend figured it should work out. Were they compatible? "Perfectly," says Bella. It just shows you can't beat logic like that. At age twenty Bella opened her own salon and for the next ten years was very successful. "I had more customers than I could ever handle. I had secretaries. Everything." But it wasn't paradise. "You have to show up at the salon every day. There is no residual income. I was ready and looking for something," says Bella. She ran into a cousin of hers who was wearing a button that read, "Lose weight now. Ask me how." Bella did ask, of course.

That was eight years ago. Now, everything is changed. Everything? Not her deep faith. Not her wonderful family. But her life? Yes. Completely. Now it's paradise.

"A Way to Unleash My Power"

It all happened so quickly, says Bella, because with Herbalife, "I found a way to unleash my power." To be specific, "I was a maniac. I started talking like crazy. We did $26,000 the first month. We became celebrities." If you're wavering about taking that first step in network marketing, here's how Bella handled things: "At first, I didn't even know what the hell I was doing." It all worked out, though, because, "People had trust in me and faith in me. I love people. I love helping people. I was using my true talents."

Someone who recognized her abilities was Mark Hughes, CEO and founder of Herbalife, a public company with weight management and nutritional products. When the Werzbergers visited Hughes at company headquarters, they shared their vision for Herbalife developing a kosher line. Bella had asked her rabbi about taking the Herbalife products. "The rabbi said, 'Okay, take the vitamins, but not the shake, because that you enjoy,'" recounts Bella. When they explained the situation to Hughes, "he knew we weren't just talking. We were producers. He said, 'If you help us, we will come out with it.'" Now the company has a complete line of *glatt* (meaning "strictly") kosher products that are selling like hotcakes.

Finding customers for these products comes naturally to Bella. When she decided to close her salon, her clients and staff all cried. They remembered her skills as a "counselor" who listened to what her clients cared about. Those are the skills she's now using to develop new business at Herbalife—with the help of Nick's brains, of course.

In the beginning, Nick helped Bella with the paperwork. "Then just one year after starting," she says glowing with pride, "I retired my husband." What happened was that "my business went completely out of control. It got so big so quickly that I needed serious help." She recalls the day she confronted Nick with the words: "You're not going back to work tomorrow. You're staying home and working with me. We're going to get rich together." She laughs and says, "Isn't that amazing. I forced my husband to retire!"

She Dreamed of a Family Business

Bella had always dreamed of working with her husband. Hasidic Jews grow up with family business as a model, believing it is not only good business but that it encourages closeness and commitment.

Heart to Heart Wisdom

"Have faith. Have patience. Never lose your dreams and goals. You're gonna get there."

—Bella Werzberger

Believe it. Bella knows that she's now a walking advertisement for just that. Her message to other women is "Wouldn't it be nice to have your best friend around to play with?"

Play for Nick and Bella has meant four luxury cruises at the company's expense. They included trips to Bermuda and Hawaii—both to Maui and to Kona—and to the Bahamas, aboard the *Ecstasy* (appropriately named, in Bella's estimation). "I would never have gone on such exotic vacations before Herbalife. I would have been thinking the whole time: How many heads am I going to have to do to pay off this bill? Now it's no problem." Now when she reserves a hotel room she simply says, "Give me the nicest place you have." Among the countless great memories is the stay on Paradise Island, in a suite with stunning rooms, their own verandah, and a Jacuzzi. "It was right out of *Lifestyles of the Rich and Famous.*" As for the whole lifestyle the Werzbergers now lead: "It has such a beautiful effect on us. We hired an assistant to help us manage so we can play more. We want more time off with each other. It is beautiful to work with your spouse when you have a common direction and common goals. It was much harder when I was going in one direction and he was going in the other."

A common direction includes worship on Shabbat, which means you won't see the Werzbergers at any Saturday rallies. To stay abreast, they simply pop a tape of the event in their VCR. The company often helps out by sending footage of corporate events. Their many friends in the business sometimes send tapes, too. How do they deal with the impact their absences have on people in their downline? The Werzbergers say they work harder to turn people into leaders who can take care of themselves. As one person who knows them said, "In the beginning, Bella could have used many things as an excuse. But she was motivated enough to find her way past the obstacles. Her determination really does put excuse-making into perspective." As this book went to press, the Werzbergers had just achieved their biggest triumph—qualifying as members of Herbalife's elite International President's Team.

Staying Motivated Every Day

To stay motivated, Bella starts each day listening to tapes. "I mentor myself every day. I listen to tapes every morning and I don't step into my office until I'm flooded with amazing positive thoughts. That gives me the power to inspire other people." Bella places a high premium on being a good communicator, and says, "If you don't have the skills, start mentoring yourself. Read books. Listen to tapes. This is an added perk in building an MLM." She also recommends that her downline read *Working at Home* magazine for inspiration in creating the lifestyle of their dreams. Since Bella had no direct upline leaders, she had to find the path of self-development herself. One of her favorite MLM motivators is the well-known speaker Jim Rohn.

Rohn is now also a personal friend who visits the Werzbergers when he's in New York, and that gets Bella on a topic where her enthusiasm truly knows no bounds—namely, all the wonderful, fantastic, magnificent, marvelous, precious, priceless, absolutely thrilling friendships she and Nick have formed. She wants everyone to know about the people who helped them build their business, people who weren't even in the same organization. Bella would adore having these people mentioned in any story about her. Sorry Bella, but space does not permit. Suffice to say, it's a long list.

Bella now does all she can to help others build and dream. To all she says, "Have faith. Have patience. Never give up. Never lose your dreams and goals. You're gonna get there."

"Fun Is Essential"

THE PINNOCK FAMILY will never forget the day Tommy walloped a homer over the centerfield fence with a power hitherto unseen in

Heart to Heart Wisdom

"The more people's lives we touch, the more money we make. But while making money is great, what we have become in the process of making money is far greater!"

—*Bella Werzberger, Herbalife*

The network marketing lifestyle is ideal for sharing experiences and continuing to grow together, say Karen and Tom Pinnock.

any Little Leaguer in those parts. His dad, Tom Pinnock, had tears in his eyes as Tommy rounded third base and headed for home, delirious with joy as he followed two teammates across the plate to score the winning run of the game.

Every nuance of the scene was sweet to savor. To say the ballpark triumph created a memory of a lifetime would be a vast understatement. Not only had Tommy made the winning run, he'd done it in the final inning, with his team trailing by two runs, and with two outs and two strikes against him.

Statistics, however, only hint at the reasons behind Tom's emotion. They had to do with his knowing that "if I had a regular job, I probably never would have shared that moment." Beyond that, Tommy's victory smash represented much more than a single event with a proud father in the role of observer. It was the culmination of hours spent together working on Tommy's hitting, including daily visits together in the winter to the indoor batting cages, and countless pitches thrown by Tom.

A Rich Family Life

And baseball was just a part of Tom's story, though an undeniably glorious part for a former semipro ballplayer like himself. The time he spent with Tommy was woven into the fabric of a rich family life involving his wife Karen and daughters Lindsay and Ashley. It included time for camping and hiking and going on field trips and cruises and having more adventures and more fun in perhaps a month or two than the average family might manage in all their years together.

Heart to Heart **Moments**

When Joe and Carol Felger joined Reliv International they held a vision of
traveling the world together with their friends. It was their dream to have free
time and the friends to enjoy it with. It wasn't long before they took their first
trip to Maui. "It was one of those typical Hawaiian days under a blue sky on
a catamaran," Joe recalls. "Carol was sitting next to Pat Rodgers, who had
sponsored us into Reliv. It was in that moment on the blue waters of Hawaii
that it dawned on us: We were traveling the world together with people we
deeply cared about. We had already begun living our dreams."

One powerful emotion that seems abundant in the Pinnocks' lives
is a sense of constant gratitude. Tom and Karen say their household
overflows with thankfulness. They are grateful for one another, and
for their family, and for the fact their lives are such an exciting, enticing mix of fun and new challenges. They are full of eager, youthful
curiosity, and are forever doing new things and experiencing new
pleasures together. They are a striking contrast to the many parents
who, "caught up in the toil of day-to-day survival, take the fun out of
the home," in Tom's words.

A Bit Like a Fairy Tale

Traveling whenever they please to places like Maui, Cancun, the Bahamas, Australia, and New Zealand, and surprising one another with
gifts like sports cars gives the Pinnocks' lives a bit of a fairy-tale quality.
But unlike those born with silver spoons in their mouths, Tom and
Karen have the deep inner satisfaction of knowing they themselves
earned everything they have—and that they did it by working together.

When Tom first joined Reliv, he and his family were living in a small house in Central Florida that backed up to a mosquito-filled swamp. "The mosquitoes were so big that the kids couldn't play in the backyard," Tom recalls. Pinnock worked as a journalist and Karen was a full-time nurse at a hospital.

To put their former financial situation in perspective, Tom recalls a pivotal event at a time when "I only lived nine miles away from Disney World, but I couldn't afford to take the kids there." After some effort the Pinnocks managed to save $500 for a short Disney vacation.

"We had packed the suitcases for the weekend. My three little kids were so excited. We were going to stay at a hotel and visit Disney. Then late Friday night, on my way home from the newspaper, I fell asleep at the wheel. The car careened off the road and crashed into the side of a bridge. I had to be towed to the garage and pay for a new tire and repairs." He ended up spending all his Disney savings.

The next morning, the children were standing at the bedroom door with their suitcases waiting for him, bubbling with excitement. "I had to tell them that we weren't going. I couldn't afford both the new tire and the trip. I didn't have the money," he said.

"I Decided to Do Better"

"Seeing them cry, their not understanding why we couldn't go, left me feeling like such a failure." Tom went out in his yard, put his head against a tree, and felt hot tears burning in his eyes. As a former firefighter, U.S. Army tank commander, and now, tough-minded reporter, Tom was no crybaby. But the thought he was an inadequate father who couldn't show his wife and kids a good time gouged his insides. "That night I decided that I was going to do something to take better care of my family. I was going to build an income that was as big as I wanted it to be," he says.

Tom's journalistic training and his job at *The Orlando Sentinel* had taught him how to gather facts. Using his investigative skills, and with Karen's help, he set out to find a worthwhile business opportunity—a search that would eventually lead them to Reliv. He was realistic enough to know that launching his own entrepreneurial business would take skills, experience, and capital that he did not possess. After looking at franchising, he also ruled that out, considering that the up-front investment was often in the hundreds of thousands of dollars or more.

Tom was beginning to wonder if there were any viable business opportunities for someone like himself, who had no capital and no real business experience. At about that time, someone stuck a card on the windshield of their parked car while Tom and Karen were in a mall. It was an advertisement for a business opportunity meeting. Tom had to work, so Karen was the one to attend. It turned out to be a meeting for an MLM. Karen heard the testimonials of individuals who were making $25,000 and $30,000 per month and more, and relayed them to Tom. At the time, Tom would have been happy to find a work-at-home opportunity that paid that much per year.

Handicapped by Skepticism

Seeing the gap between his own limited aspirations and what some individuals were earning led him to realize one of the drawbacks of his professional background: He simply could not imagine himself becoming wealthy because "I was handicapped by the skepticism ingrained in me as a reporter." But the examples of real people who had succeeded inspired them, and Tom and Karen began consciously learning about the field. They might have signed up with someone at that very first meeting Karen attended, but no one from the meeting ever followed up with them—a lesson Tom did not forget.

The testimonials they would hear made Tom and Karen realize the power of heart-to-heart storytelling. Hearing people tell their stories in their own words was more convincing than all the arguments, statistics, and compensation plans they would hear about. As Tom puts it, "Networking is a story business, and the more stories you have to share, the stronger you are, and the stronger you are, the bigger your business will be."

Tom explains, "Networkers sell from their hearts. As a rule, most aren't professional salespeople. They are homemakers, truck drivers, teachers, lawyers, firefighters, and just about any other thing you can think of. They sell their products to friends and family . . . because they use it themselves and believe in it. That's our foundation and power. It works because it is honest. People are not stupid. They can tell if you use and believe in what you are marketing."

Bill Collectors and Alligators

Eventually Tom met Mike Williams of Reliv International—a public company with nutritional supplements for optimal health—heard his story, and signed up under him. On the way to getting established the Pinnocks had to maneuver through some tight financial squeezes. That meant staving off the bill collectors until their income grew. Tom employed some zany survival skills, born of necessity. At one point, he recalls, "I caught a six-foot alligator and tied him to the mailbox. I was glad when we didn't get any bills for a while."

But Tom's eagerness came back to bite him at least once. In one case, he accepted a bad check for $2,000, for product he had sold a distributor. "It was all the money we had," he recalls. It was a painful incident at the time, but it ultimately served to bring Tom and Karen closer together.

"All I could think of was to sell Karen's car. It was a big old Fleetwood Cadillac that she inherited from her grandfather. It was the only thing he had left her in his will," says Tom. Karen used the big car to get around town, her petite form almost hidden from view as she sat behind the wheel.

"Karen really cherished that car," says Tom, recalling the incident. "She was standing at the kitchen sink shucking corn and crying. She turned to me with big tears in her eyes and said, 'You just sell that stupid ole car, 'cause I know you can do it.'"

Karen's Faith in Tom

Knowing his wife believed he could do it and was counting on him was all Tom needed to start conquering the world. Tom sold the car and bought more product. Then he sold the product and made money.

He repeated the process and taught others. Whenever he felt himself slowing down, he'd see Karen standing by the sink, her eyes full of tears. "And whenever I was afraid to talk to someone about Reliv, I would just think about the day I couldn't take the kids to Disney." That was enough to keep him motivated. In less than a year, Tom was able to quit his job on the newspaper—a career he had pursued since high school and while in the military. "I'm just an average guy who spent two of the best years of my life in eleventh grade," he quips. Whatever his past shortcomings might have been, at Reliv this average guy came to understand the immense power that focused effort could bring to an endeavor. "I made $100,000 my first year. In a few short years, we became millionaires," he says. Eventually he became the company's top distributor.

Along the way the Pinnocks also took that long-awaited trip to Disney World, where they stayed a full week in a huge suite that was bigger than their original house. Mickey and Goofy came to breakfast with them. The three children still talk about it.

Every Day a Holiday

Today Tom considers himself "at a point where every day is a holiday. Success is measured in what makes us happy. For me, it is my family and my freedom." Tom adds: "The only reason we are here is to bring up healthy children and help them become well-adjusted citizens. As a stay-at-home father, I'm there to help them and keep them in line. I spend more time with my kids in a week than most dads spend in a year," Tom says. "I was the only dad on the field trip to the St. Louis Zoo," he says, recalling how the boys on the outing flocked around him, eager to be in the presence of a male figure. He was amused when one of the children asked, "What's wrong, mister? Don't you have a job?"

Heart to Heart Wisdom

"People who understand the relationship part of this business will succeed. People who do MLM just for the money may bounce from company to company and miss the biggest blessing in this business."

—Joe Felger, Reliv

One of the small daily pleasures he enjoys telling about is the way the family gets started in the morning. Because Tom and Karen don't go to an office, "We don't have to wake up to an alarm," he notes. "From the day the children were very small, the Pinnocks relied on "a snuggle alarm—my kids come in and snuggle with us to wake us up." Contrast that with most all-too-common family wake-up scenarios, which tend to be hurried episodes marked by tired bodies and jangled nerves as parents prepare to meet the pressures of the day. Time with the kids is cut short. It's a contrast that hits home with Tom. "The most important task of a person's lifetime is to raise good children," he says. "Nothing else comes close." Above all that means having time for your children. Tom believes his drive to succeed was fueled by what he knew would be the emotional fulfillment of being a full-time dad to his daughters Lindsay and Ashley and his son Tommy.

At times, it seems hard to say whether it's the parent or the child who gains the most from time spent in children's activities, especially judging from Tom's enthusiasm for everything from coaching Little League to hunting for arrowheads near their house in the fields where Lewis and Clark once camped. While time is the most important gift Tom gives his family, he enjoys being generous in other ways too. For example, he had no hesitation in getting his son a new special edition Mark McGwire baseball bat. Though it cost $250, Tom confesses, "I didn't even think twice when I got it." An avid fan, Pinnock was once drafted by the St. Louis Cardinals, but says he lacked the skill to become a professional ballplayer.

Tom also makes sure his daughters get their fair share of his attention. "There won't be many dads at Lindsay's field hockey game today," he says, "but Tommy and I will be there." Such in-

Heart to Heart Wisdom

"Friendships help people develop their potential. Everybody has gifts of genius that God has given them. Often you can't recognize your own gifts. Our job is helping people find and believe in the gifts they already have."

—*Joe Felger, Reliv*

volvement "is really important for me," he says, hastening to add, "I know my kids love it, too."

Helping Friends and Family

The Pinnocks have also gained enormous satisfaction out of helping friends and other family members succeed. Tom's very first Reliv customer was his father. Tom's sponsor, Mike Williams, went along with him on the call to make sure all went smoothly. The second person to buy products from him was Karen's dad, Davie Sims. Both parents became retail customers and later signed up as distributors under Tom's sister Nancy Pinnock, who lives in Altamonte Springs, Florida.

Tom's parents have developed a thriving Reliv distributorship and today the senior Pinnocks' large residual income means they finally have what they never dreamed possible—financial independence. "My dad was a fireman. Now at eighty years old he's making more money than he ever did," says Tom. For Tom's parents, being a part of Reliv has turned their golden years into an entrepreneurial adventure that the family can excitedly share with one another, especially when they all get together at conventions. "Who do I meet at the corporate events but my mom and dad? Imagine having the freedom that we all have of traveling and working with people we really care about."

Almost from the time they joined Reliv, Tom and Karen made building upon close relationships a part of their successful business strategy. Eleven months into the Reliv business, Tom received a call from his best friend, Larry Garner, who was living in Atlanta. They had been childhood buddies and played on the same Little League and high school baseball teams. Larry's company had downsized, leaving him out of work and ready for a new opportunity. "Karen had a sister in Atlanta, too," says Tom. "So we decided that it would be nice to move to Atlanta and work a new market."

For about two years, the Pinnocks worked the Atlanta area while Larry became financially independent. Network marketing is always about "helping other people realize their goals," notes Tom, "but it becomes even better when you do it with your mom and dad, older sister, and best friends. These are the people who mean the most to you."

A Spectacular Home and Lifestyle

Their strategy has enabled them to travel in a few steps from living in a cramped house on the edge of a swamp to a spectacular home atop a hill that looks down on two of the most magnificent golf courses in all of Missouri. From his home office Tom looks out across a green valley nestled between rolling hills and etched with sparkling creeks.

The route to success has also taken Tom on excursions around the world to sign up other people and teach them the business. He even wrote a book about it called *You Can Be Rich by Thursday,* in which he points out opportunities and warns of misrepresentations in network marketing. His basic advice underscores the self-development ethos that you find everywhere in MLM—namely, to become the best person you can be, and to learn to care about others. Next, you must get customers, and teach others to do the same. Says Tom, "You will work like a son of a gun in the beginning. You have to find other people who are willing to work hard too. But in the end you wind up with a distribution network just like the big corporations." The difference is that once your network is in place, you can go home and play with the kids.

Having a Blast and Living Longer

Playing and having fun is something the Pinnocks believe in strongly—both for its own sake and as a business strategy. Another of Tom's books, *The Male Homemaker's Handbook,* humorously extols the virtues of having a blast while being a stay-at-home dad and helpmate—roles in which male network marketers often thrive.

Now that the children are older and he and Karen are millionaires, some of the housekeeping chores he describes in the book have little relevance for them. But one benefit of the work-at-home lifestyle he extols in the book is having fun—and lots of it. For example, he is sure there is a boon to one's health and well-being that comes from enjoying yourself with your kids and their friends. In the chapter, "Can

Your Husband Come Out and Play?," Tom reveals how he became convinced that "the guy who sheds his shoes and socks and jumps into the sandbox with his children has a better chance of living longer."

The book also recounts Tom's laugh-provoking adventures as the leader of fourteen rambunctious kids on his block. With his knack for organizing and making up games, Tom led the neighborhood young-sters in such all-consuming activities as an ongoing water-balloon war. That particular rivalry culminated in a massive showdown one day that saw some 2,500 water-filled missiles hurled in a historic con-test in which dozens of men, women, cats, dogs, and children all saw action in the streets, driveways, yards, and garages of their neighbor-hood. It all sounds like more fun than a lot of people have in their en-tire lives as parents.

Have Fun, and People Will Follow You

Tom also thinks it is essential to use fun to build your business. In his words, "if you're having fun, people will follow you, because people like to do fun things." He describes meetings with fellow distributors where guests were invited simply to be shown "how much fun we had together." Fun is part of the Reliv culture, and is actively pro-moted by the company in such activities as cruises to exotic places.

Above all, he urges, remember that working hard at something you passionately believe in is not really work, especially when you are sharing it all with someone you love. Tom and Karen Pinnock say their network marketing lifestyle is ideal for keeping the flame of ro-mance burning. Sharing experiences and continuing to grow together is certainly easier in MLM than in corporate America, where hus-bands and wives often get pulled apart and end up strangers.

Many outside of network marketing will be surprised to learn what the Pinnocks consider "one of the most romantic things this business has to offer"—the conventions and activities put on by their company, Reliv International. That may sound odd to the typical businessperson, for whom conventions have limited romantic ap-peal—despite time set aside for entertainment, dinners, and dancing;

but then dining and dancing with your loved one alongside a feared boss or hated rival is more likely to make you mutter hostile fantasies than whisper sweet nothings.

Awakening Warm Feelings

For network marketers, however, conventions and other get-togethers highlight and celebrate what a husband and wife have accomplished together. As such, couples say, these events have the power to awaken in them warm feelings of mutual happiness. One network marketer said the following about why big MLM events seem alive with a special expectation and electricity: "Unlike employees, for whom corporate gatherings may simply be a reminder that they are puppets on someone else's strings, a network marketing meeting is a council of independent men and women who don't kowtow to anyone. These people feel they are achieving great things. They are full of pride and self-respect, and they are among friends who are happy for their success and who celebrate them as individuals. The whole atmosphere sets the right scene and enhances the sense of mutual attraction."

Magic, Excitement, Romance

For Tom, forty-six, and Karen, forty-one, Reliv conferences are one more thing that keeps alive both the friendship and the romance in their marriage. Tom says such events offer "an opportunity for all couples to recharge their lover's batteries." Tom adds, "There is a lot of magic in the air at an event. The excitement is intoxicating. You dress up, and see your wife looking beautiful in a lovely gown. You stay in beautiful suites. You have time away from the kids to be alone with the woman you love. You romance your wife. It makes for a wonderful time because you are with your lover and best friend." Corporate events, he adds, "help us hold on to the passion that we have in our marriage."

Perhaps Tom is just a very romantic fellow. Perhaps he and Karen are simply lucky they have an affectionate marriage. But the evidence suggests that the lifestyle that goes along with network marketing gives you a better than average shot at health, wealth, and romance.

The Pinnocks' lifestyle does set them apart, of course—even from many of their well-to-do neighbors—in that Tom need not rush off to work each day. After seeing the kids off to school, Tom and Karen often enjoy a leisurely breakfast together, then play a few rounds of golf. Another benefit of their way of life is the health and vigor they feel as a result of the Reliv products.

They also do the flamboyant and exotic at times. Karen surprised Tom with a '98 Corvette convertible for his birthday. She and the kids dragged him out to the garage first thing in the morning to help him discover his gift.

The Pinnocks also follow a tradition they started a few years ago. On every vacation or trip, they buy a piece of jewelry to help them recall their time together. Now, when Karen dons one of these beautiful jewels, the hours sparkle not only with the fire of the gems themselves but with the recaptured radiance of their days and nights in the West Indies, or in Patmos or Mikonos in the Greek Isles.

> ## Heart to Heart Wisdom
>
> "Who says the American dream is dead? We're proof that it's alive—and it's called multilevel marketing."
>
> —Tom Pinnock, Reliv

Recently the Pinnocks went to the Vatican with a group of Reliv distributors who were leaders in contributing to humanitarian causes. The party was received by the Pope, and the distributors' efforts were recognized by a special plaque hung on the walls of the Vatican. The affair included formal dinners, dancing, and shopping in Rome on the Via Condotti.

As one attendee put it with a smile, "It was heavenly—in more ways than one."

Working Together

IF A POPULAR documentary were made on the lives of Jerry and Debbie Campisi, the previews might include a glimpse of them happily cruising the sparkling waters of the Caribbean in their large

European-built motor yacht, laughing at the dolphins leaping along-side their boat. You might also spy them flying by small plane then hiking through the uplands of New Zealand to witness a colorful aboriginal ceremony. "They lead interesting lives," you'd say to yourself. "I wonder what their story is."

What is refreshingly different about the story of Jerry and Debbie Campisi of Nu Skin is also what makes their experience in network marketing such a practical guide for anyone entering the business.

To sum up the plot, during the past decade they've earned more than $10 million by sticking with one company, applying sound business skills, and continually learning as they went along.

They especially illustrate how a couple working side by side can support and bolster one another by bringing different but complementary skills and perspectives to the table. Here the filmmaker would have ample opportunity to show Jerry at home working late into the night, poring over numbers and scrutinizing the results of his past month's performance. On those occasions when an expression of discouragement or depression seems about to overwhelm him, you'd see Debbie entering the room with fresh information, new ideas, and commonsense counseling, all of which fills Jerry with renewed clarity and determination. It may not be high drama, but many a married couple who aspire to a better life can sure relate to it.

A Lesson for Others

The Campisis' success also raises the question of whether other couples might have avoided some of their great difficulties had they pursued a strategy similar to the one chosen by Jerry and Debbie. Above all, that means having a mutual understanding right from the start and working together rather than at odds with each other.

Neither Jerry nor Debbie were experienced in network marketing. But Jerry had been in business since leaving Boston College, and had a decidedly entrepreneurial outlook. For Jerry, though, entrepreneurship never consisted of that popular yet misguided romantic notion of taking wild gambles or getting rich overnight. Rather, for him entrepreneurship was a more sophisticated concept— the art and discipline of intelligently pursuing opportunities while systematically working to minimize your risk. Debbie's outlook was more operational and managerial, making her the perfect companion for an entrepreneur. Both had analytical minds, though Jerry's acumen was aimed at identifying and evaluating opportunities, while Debbie used her skills to make sure they were pursuing those opportunities in the most

Lessons for other couples: Jerry and Debbie Campisi have earned over $10 million in Nu Skin by applying sound business principles.

effective way. He had big dreams, and she was a constant but supportive "reality check." Most important, says Jerry, "it was always *our* business, not my business." One important point from which others can learn: Experienced businesspeople don't expect to banish all disagreements and live in a state of perfect, unceasing harmony. That's a formula for a tea ceremony, not a business partnership. Seasoned businesspeople like the Campisis feel free to challenge one another, and then work things out.

In building their business they worked extremely hard to meet their goals, but they stayed in control of their lives. While other couples tell tales of being lost in a dark and scary wilderness without guideposts of any sort, Jerry and Debbie, by contrast, seem to have been engaged in a tough, challenging game—but one they were confident they could figure out and master. If one of them faltered, the other was there to coach and encourage.

Lest we go too far before you think the Campisi story is all business, with no flesh-and-blood human drama, let's flash back to the event when they first met and started to fall in love.

It was in Rhode Island, at a fund-raising event for children with muscular dystrophy, when Jerry sat down at a table with Debbie, and the two started talking. They were from similar backgrounds—average, middle class, Boston. Jerry was there donating his time to run the event, which gives you a little insight about him already. Interested, Debbie asked: "Do you do a lot of this?"

A Life-Changing Event

Perhaps it's a bit of New England reserve, but Jerry exhibits a certain restraint when speaking of his private life, which provides a nice change of pace in this era of instant, California-style confessionalism. He didn't tell Debbie at the time, and even now is a bit reticent about revealing an event that occurred at the age of eighteen, one that changed the course of his life and led to the opportunity for some uncommonly deep introspection for a teenager. While doing back flips on a trampoline, Jerry landed incorrectly and injured his spine. He was in bed for six months, fully conscious but immobile and uncertain as to whether he would ever be able to move again. In that state of utter helplessness, while he depended on others to feed, bathe, and care for him, he made a fervent vow—he swore that as long as his mind was functioning he would always figure out a way to be financially self-sufficient. When movement at last returned to his limbs, Jerry had become a young man with a deep resolve and an inner strength far beyond his years. For Debbie, it may have been a sense of that inner strength, plus the similarity in their backgrounds, and their shared work ethic, that provided part of the attraction. She was 31. He was 40, and had never been married—had in fact always pushed the prospect of marriage into the future, to a hoped-for point in his life when he would have managed to free himself from the unceasing demands of his business and financial consulting practice. It would be a time when he was no longer "exchanging hours for dollars." How he would get there he did not know.

Debbie, too, was inclined to think about gaining freedom from the punishing routine and grueling hours of her profession. "She was going in one direction, and I was going in another," recalls Jerry. After the two had moved to South Florida, Debbie, who was trained in neurodiagnostics, ran the seizure unit of a children's hospital. The job sounds far removed from anything related to network marketing, but in fact the skills Debbie practiced—people skills, managerial skills, analytical skills—were all ones she ultimately adapted to making their business work. Despite the complex-sounding nature of her work, the real lesson, says Jerry, is the following: "Whatever you now do for a living, you can use it as a base for your success in network marketing."

The chance to think about a new way of life arose when a colleague told Jerry about network marketing. Jerry used all his business background to critique the opportunity methodically, even doing interviews with regulatory officials to understand the legal implications. Once he was convinced the business concept was sound, he and Debbie decided that they would neither deplete their assets nor funnel their current income into the business. She kept her job until his monthly income had matched her yearly salary.

It's common when building any sort of business to cut back on your lifestyle in the early years. But you need to bear in mind, says Jerry, that "there's a big difference between money being tight and your being so strapped that you can't even pay your electric bill. Getting over your head in debt is a mistake." Jerry adds, "the biggest mistake is for people without resources to stop their income. Most people should start part time."

Heart to Heart **Wisdom**

"Getting over your head in debt is wrong. The biggest mistake is for people without resources to stop their income."

—*Jerry Campisi*

A shared outlook on such practical matters enabled Jerry and Debbie to work together during the difficult times. When things got tough, Debbie would pointedly ask if Jerry still thought the Nu Skin opportunity was sound. At one point, Jerry spent thousands of dollars buying the products of competing companies and having them evaluated alongside the Nu Skin products. Like any good operations person, Debbie questioned the expenditure. It seemed extravagant, unnecessary. But it paid off by enabling Jerry to assure himself that the company's products were indeed superior.

Debbie left up to Jerry the role of determining whether the products and market represented good opportunities. When obstacles arose—as they always do—she would ask: Are the products good? Is the company honest? Is there a market? Once assured on these points, her response was: "Then let's not talk about that anymore because that's not the problem. Let's see what the real problem is."

Understanding That It Takes Time

In the early days Debbie would often find that the problem lay in Jerry's expectations having gotten out of whack. She'd remind him what he already knew about launching a business—that sustained effort is always required to get it moving. She'd look Jerry in the eye and play back to him the very convictions he had spoken earlier:

- "You don't get something for nothing."

- "You know success does not come overnight."

- "You are expecting things too fast."

- "This is a legitimate industry. Results take time."

- "We're committed to a long-term strategy. To make it work, we may need to change our tactics."

At one point early in the process of working the business, she said, "Jerry, you are acting as if you've already graduated and have ten years experience and you haven't even gone through the first semester yet." In other words, she said, "You don't get the money until you've put in the effort."

Today, Jerry says gratefully, "If it were not for Debbie, we would not be in this business today. She was always absolutely consistent about the importance of putting in the effort." He adds, "Many times I wanted to quit when things were not going right. That emotional support was extremely important."

But Debbie's contribution went far beyond simply keeping Jerry focused and motivated. When his efforts were not producing results, Debbie would say, "Let's find out why. Let's do research." Using the skills of a medical investigator, she interviewed customers to learn the reasons people were dropping out and then helped Jerry adjust his approach. In one case, she pointed out to Jerry that, "I was not qualifying the leads. I was talking to everyone. That was a big mistake. I wasted a lot of time persuading people to join the business instead of finding out whether they were self starters."

Debbie interviewed the top-performing people in their burgeoning group. She put all her brainpower to work trying to understand the keys to developing successful leaders. Once Debbie had outlined the traits of success, Jerry intensified his efforts to find people that fit her criteria.

As their organization grew, they began a division of labor that more or less continues to this day: "I do the building of the business and getting people involved. Debbie supports and trains," says Jerry.

The Turning Point

A turning point in their lives and psyches came "the day we had no mortgage payment, no car payment, no boat payment." Not only was there "a big relief," but the entire way they did business underwent a transformation. As Jerry puts it, "You should always care about others in this business, but knowing you don't have to work allows you to concentrate on other people's goals even more than your own."

It took the Campisis four and a half years to reach Nu Skin's top level of Hawaiian Blue Diamond. Says Jerry: "Most of our leaders did it faster. We plodded away and stuck to our strategy." Working steadily, they developed an organization that now has fourteen huge legs and spans the globe in a network that encompasses twenty-five countries. The amount they have earned from their business to date is represented by their membership in a very exclusive organization— the $10 Million Circle. Success has meant time to travel, to spend with friends, and to devote toward altruistic activities, such as helping people with muscular dystrophy and spinal cord injuries.

If the documentary on the success of the Campisis followed the desires of a filmmaker, he might end it here. He'd splice in some mountains and sunsets in faraway places, choosing scenes from some of the thirty countries the couple has visited with Nu Skin over the past five years. He'd show Jerry and Debbie touring China, or Austria, or traveling to Lake Rotorua on New Zealand's North Island to watch the aborigines dance, or eating breakfast aboard their fifty-eight foot, Italian-made Azimut after spending the night anchored in a serenely beautiful cove in the Abaco islands.

That would be a pretty ending. But unfortunately for the film-maker, the Campisis' lives aren't going to follow such a pleasantly predictable arc.

A New Cause for Excitement

After arriving at the brink of retirement, fifty-one-year-old Jerry has suddenly come flying back into action with renewed vigor. The cause of his excitement: The opportunity to join Big Planet, the Nu Skin-funded company aimed at capturing a piece of the Internet. "I couldn't sit still," he says. "I realized this will be the biggest shift of wealth in our lifetime—much bigger, in fact, than the $400 billion computer revolution of Microsoft and Intel." This giant opportunity means "we will be able to help a lot more people," says Jerry.

Big Planet is a good indicator that Jerry's entrepreneurial drive and instincts have not diminished, meaning Debbie will have plenty of work keeping him on track in the coming years. "We believe this division will be ten times the size of the Nu Skin personal care and nutrition business because of the tremendous potential of the Internet," he says.

They'll still be taking the boat trips to the islands and flying to exotic locales around the globe, but in place of the placidity of retirement the Campisis will be filled with the electricity of a couple setting out to write a whole new chapter in their partnership. "We're going to be helping many more people achieve their goals and dreams," he says.

And as before, the basic guidelines will be the same. As Jerry puts it: "If we don't both agree, we don't do it."

7

Givers

BEING ABLE TO give generously to others is what some network marketers value most about their way of life. The bighearted people profiled in this chapter all feel strongly that it is more
blessed to give than to receive. And throughout the culture of network marketing it's commonplace to hear that you must give to get,
that you must sow the seed before you reap the harvest.

Tears of Joy

BECOMING THE NUMBER one contributor to research into cystic fibrosis is the goal that's driven Collette Van Reusen to become her
company's leading distributor.

How did Collette Van Reusen do it? What special talents does she
possess?

A deeply inspiring story: Collette Van Reusen helped her family overcome their tragic loss and find new purpose and prosperity.

What skills or knowledge enabled this warm, outgoing, forty-six-year-old woman to begin earning nearly $1 million a year so soon after starting in network marketing?

She cites just one advantage: "I know all about motherhood," says Collette. "That's my area of expertise. A lot of what I do in building my business," she adds, "is just Parenthood 101. I use lots of motherhood analogies in training."

With ten children between her and her second husband Gerry, no one should be surprised at Collette's characterizing herself as above all a mother.

And as a mother, the immense journey she and her family have traveled together is one that is filled with intense, often excruciating emotion. At times it is almost unbearably sad and wrenching—the story of a single mother with almost no income and five children, two of whom needed her almost constant attention.

But it is also a deeply inspiring story—one of a family saddened by the deepest tragedy who found a new life with rewards beyond their wildest dreams.

It's a story that thousands of people know. Yet whenever audiences are reminded of it they are likely to weep again. And because, for Colette, so much grief was followed by so much happiness, perhaps the most poignant moments are when the audiences find themselves laughing and crying simultaneously.

For Collette, motherhood has meant lots of tears—and even more of those tears flowed freely as she told her story. The tears were in remembrance of the pain she had endured. But they were also tears of joy, hope, and gratitude.

As a mother, Collette knew how to love unstintingly. She knew how to nurture the offspring in her large, energetic family. She also knew how to help them learn, and how to stand back and let them grow up on their own.

Surprised by Her Fighting Spirit

And much to her own surprise, she found she also knew how to fight for survival when the chips were down. That fighting spirit helped her seize an opportunity as a distributor with USANA, now a $120 million public company, founded in 1992, that develops and manufactures antioxidants and other nutritional products. At the time, she and her family were swamped with medical bills and overdue mortgage payments and were facing certain bankruptcy. That spirit helped her—once she had set her sights on the goal—to become the number one distributor in the company year after year. It's no wonder that her presence onstage will spur thousands of fellow distributors to cheer their hearts out.

They are cheering for someone who has come a long way. As Collette puts it, "I had no background and no education, and very, very limited business experience."

The story as she tells it is remarkable indeed. "I was the oldest of ten children from a family in Idaho. I married out of high school against my parents' wishes. I had my first baby at age twenty. I was married for twenty-one years. We had five beautiful children. But it was a very difficult relationship and a very difficult divorce. I ended up getting $202 per month in child support, and I didn't always get that. There was lots of pain. There was the hardship of the divorce. It was emotionally and financially difficult."

A Reason to Succeed

In network marketing it is said that to succeed you need a "why."

Collette says it needs to be "a big bright burning 'why.'" Collette's first why, upon being introduced to USANA, was to use the products to improve the lives of those she loved. She swiftly saw results in that area.

Beyond that her why was to save her family from bankruptcy. That goal was accomplished as well.

And then there was the why of prosperity for herself and her family, plus travel, pleasure, and security. All that also has become a foregone conclusion.

In fact, Collette has been so successful in her few years in network marketing that she could retire now, never make another phone call, and her lifelong wealth would be assured.

Her Biggest "Why"

So today she has a new why, one that drives her to keep attaining levels of affluence unimaginable to the girl in Idaho. Such accomplishments put her in the company of some of the country's most prominent speakers, entrepreneurs, and businesspeople.

Today, her new, deeper, and much more profound why is the direct result of having given birth to two daughters—Lexi and Sharlie—with cystic fibrosis. Her why is to become the country's number one contributor to research into cystic fibrosis.

Collette's two girls shared all the dreams of normal children, including a desire for sports and physical activities that were often too rigorous for them. Then, in August 1993, at the age of thirteen, Lexi underwent a double lung transplant.

Over the next eighteen months Lexi struggled valiantly. "She got to where she could walk again," recalls Collette. "Her hair grew back in. Her legs regenerated. After the wheelchair she used a walker and then a three-pronged cane. She had braces on both legs."

As the family prayed and hoped, Lexi gained strength. "We took her to see *Forrest Gump*. Do you remember when he starts running and breaks off his braces? After that movie, she made me take off her braces. She did get so she could walk."

Precious Memories

The memories of Lexi are precious to Collette and the family, and a vital motivation in their lives today. "I remember Lexi's first boy-girl dance in junior high," says her mother. "She was so nervous. She was just barely walking. She went in her wheelchair. Her friends took her.

She was absolutely beautiful, but with these tiny, wobbly legs. I carried her in, but she wouldn't let us stay and watch. At the end of the evening, one of her friends carried her out. I grabbed her and hugged her. She was so, so happy."

She said, "Mom, I danced every dance."

"How?" Collette wanted to know. How could she have danced?

"They bearhugged me," Lexi laughed.

"It was such a wonderful experience," says Collette. "We have hundreds of stories like that."

Sharlie and Lexi "were absolutely inseparable," says Collette. The two spent months of every year in the hospital together. Even though Sharlie was not ill enough to require hospitalization, the doctors put them in together for mutual support. Sharlie dropped out of school to be with Lexi in the final months of her life, when her body rejected the transplant. Sharlie and Collette were holding Lexi in their arms when she died.

Two days before she died Lexi was so weak she could hardly talk. "I slept with her," recalls Collette. "Lexi would squeeze my hands three times to say she loved me."

She whispered, "Mom, I'll never give up."

"I know you won't," said Collette.

"But, Mom."

"Yes, Lexi."

"I may have to let go."

A Group Offering Love and Support

Lexi died on March 5, 1995, at the age of fourteen. Her funeral four days later drew a thousand people who knew the brave young girl.

At the funeral, Collette realized something new.

"It was one of those insightful 'ahas,'" she says.

Many of the people there knew Lexi from Collette's activities in USANA. "She had been there at the meetings in her wheelchair," says Collette. "All these people had become, truthfully, like a family to me. At that point I was still a novice. I was thinking this was my part-time business. My realization that I was part of a group offering love and support opened up a whole new path."

It was also a turning point where Collette found increased motivation. Lexi's medical expenses were $1 million. Insurance covered much of it but not everything. It didn't cover physical therapy or many of the drugs. "We still had tens of thousands of dollars in expenses," she said.

Collette had started the business a year earlier because "we literally had reached the point where we knew we had to declare bankruptcy. We began months of survival mode." Eventually it got to the point where "we were so deeply in debt we had maxed out four credit cards. We had borrowed from family members. It took me my first two and a half years to climb out of debt." She and Gerry had married in 1993, hopeful that their faith combined with his impressive financial skills would steer them out of the deepening crisis. But the situation did not improve. "After getting married we had no income because Gerry was refinancing homes and interest rates were on the rise," she explains.

From the Products, New Energy

Along with the rest of the family, Gerry had tried the USANA products and was convinced of their efficacy. In fact, they had given him relief from his own allergies and asthma. "We loved the products," said Collette, who had felt her own energy increase. However, Gerry was skeptical of the business opportunity. But Collette saw little opportunity to do anything else. Unable to afford nursing care for Lexi, she needed to be at home much of the time. Collette had been introduced to the USANA products by her brother Dallin Larsen, who had gone to work in the corporate offices of the company after meeting founder Dr. Myron Wentz. Dallin had sent Collette products, and she eventually signed up as a distributor in April 1994.

Today Collette hastens to point out that her success at USANA was earned on the same terms as all other distributors. She did not benefit from her brother's corporate position, other than by having someone she trusted introduce her to the products, assure her she was making the right decision in signing up, and encourage her along the way. On the other hand, as a distributor, Collette has not hesitated to help her family share the benefits of USANA. "I brought in all the rest of my family," she says proudly. "All my brothers, sisters, parents, our numerous cousins, and their children who are eighteen and older."

In addition, children Dax, Zak, Chelsea, and Sharlie are thoroughly involved in the business. Their confidence and sophistication in all aspects of network marketing are in marked contrast to Collette's early start. She recalls her first meeting, to which she invited forty-four people. Four came, and two went home early. Two people were left. "They signed up more out of pity, I think," says Collette.

Hopeful in those early days but deeply conscious of her own lack of business experience, Collette attended her first national convention in Las Vegas the summer after signing up. She did it on a shoestring, sharing the travel costs with three women and even taking food with her. To make certain she understood the compensation plan, she went to four identical sessions on the subject, which provoked some teasing from her brother about the scrutiny she was putting into a $39 investment.

> "I realize now that there are very few people, including corporate presidents, who make my income. Today, I wouldn't trade what I do for anything. We've gone from financial devastation to incredible prosperity. I'm living such a dream life that I literally wake up every morning so excited I almost can't stand it."
>
> —*Collette Van Reusen, USANA*

A New Rush of Confidence

Like so many other people in network marketing, it was in watching that year's achievers—seeing people in many ways similar to herself—that Colette felt her first deep rush of inspiration and confidence. "I said to myself, 'Next year that's me.'"

Once fully committed, Collette became unstoppable. With ever-increasing focus and discipline, her life became a purposeful regimen of meetings and three-way phone calls.

"I was a Gold Director within a year," she says. "At that level you are making at least $1,000 per week plus leadership bonuses. I went Ruby and Emerald without realizing it. I got clued in when I was about to go Diamond. I was a Diamond within two and a half years. At that level you have four business centers, with at least $1,000 a week in each center plus other income. Now I'm becoming a Four-star. (A Diamond averages $5,000 to $6,000 per week. A Four-star Diamond earns about $1 million per year.) This will be my first Four-star year. God bless America. To go from the edge of bankruptcy to living the life I live."

That life includes travel wherever and whenever she wants. Aware that USANA would be opening up Australia, Collette's oldest son Dax had suggested, "Hey Mom, maybe we ought to go there." Collette's reaction was, "Why not? We have the time, we have the energy, we have the finances."

Leaving Gerry and the others behind, Collette, Dax, Zak, and Sharlie arrived in Australia on New Year's Day 1998 for a five-month stay. "We traveled the entire country. We stayed in the great hotels. We rented a van and drove through the outback."

Mixing business with pleasure in typical network marketing style, Collette began her Australian downline on February 16, 1998. By January 1999 it had grown to more than twenty thousand.

Collette recalls vividly the family's arrival in Australia. "As we flew in, I saw the Sidney Opera House. Twenty-five years earlier I had written out my goals for my life, and had put down a trip where I would see the opera house.

"When I saw it out the window of the plane, I started crying. I said, 'My dreams are coming true.'"

A Cheerful Giver

FINDING A NETWORK marketing diamond mine in her own backyard has helped Dr. Kathy Bliese do what she loves best—be "a cheerful giver."

Anyone who learns about this soft-spoken physician from Omaha is likely to wonder just how many lives have been saved and how many hearts have been touched because of her. She is someone whose life and career seem to carry a special message for anyone who's ever found themselves searching for a purpose.

Dr. Kathy Bliese, left, a physician and minister, found a company and leaders she trusted with WIN and founders Cathy and Ralph Oats.

You, for example, may be among those who are inclined to think that "nothing I have done to date has prepared me for network marketing." On closer examination, you may come to find that virtually all your experiences have paved the way for you.

The Perfect Solution

Take the story of Dr. Bliese. Only after many years did she realize that network marketing provided the perfect solution for fulfilling her dreams. Dr. Bliese is a healer who's treated starving war victims in Nigeria and lived in a mud hut among the impoverished citizens of Bangladesh. She's a builder who's overcome massive obstacles to create hospitals and health care systems in the midst of poverty. She's a dynamic leader who's directed relief efforts with the commanding authority of a general amid the blood, sweat, and turmoil of war and its aftermath. And she's an entrepreneur who's rustled up money and equipment to carry out her dreams.

In addition to her medical work, Kathy Bliese sends weekly messages of hope and inspiration to millions of people outside the United States. Her broadcasts reach three-quarters of the area of the world.

In short, the scope of her work has been immense. She always had big dreams, but she was also stymied at times, wondering how she would ever get the funds to carry them out.

For Doctors and Professionals

Today, her wide-ranging efforts are supported by the growing wealth she receives from a network marketing company that has won the confidence of many physicians.

The company, Wellness International Network, Ltd., or WIN, has a wide range of health-related supplements, a compensation plan, a training program, and many other distinctive characteristics that appeal to M.D.s and other professionals.

The path that brought this dedicated doctor to WIN goes back almost half a century, to the childhood of young Kathy Bliese in Elk Horn, Iowa, a Danish community. Her father was born in Denmark, and her mother's family was from there.

Some will see an almost uncanny chain of events in Kathy Bliese's life, a series of experiences that left her uniquely prepared for her current role.

Long before she built a downline in MLM, Kathy knew what it was like to care about the destiny of thousands of people under her sponsorship. She knew also how effective a good network could be, and what a powerful function it could perform in passing along information. She knew too that no matter how successful or important she became, she would never want to sacrifice the kind of heart-to-heart communications and relationships that inspired people to be their best.

A Sense of Higher Purpose

Perhaps the first time she recalls feeling a sense of higher purpose was at the age of seven, when she heard a nurse at church tell about caring for the sick in Africa. Young Kathy listened with rapt attention as the nurse described performing medical procedures while living in primitive conditions with few doctors available.

She especially remembers the nurse's description of operating on a woman to remove a huge cyst. After the talk, "I said to my mom I was going to do that. So that was one of the sparks that lit a fire in me." Years later the dedication to serving others coupled with the belief in a dream would still mark Kathy Bliese's life and be a powerful force in her achievements in network marketing.

A Dynamic Role Model

As a girl Kathy read a book by a dynamic Scotswoman, Mary Mitchell Slessor, an enormously energetic Victorian missionary who was also known as the White Queen of Calabar and the White Queen of the Cannibals. In 1876, the twenty-eight-year-old former mill-worker became inspired by the work of another Scot in Africa, the famed Dr. David Livingstone. She boarded a steamer and went to an area called Calabar, now part of Nigeria, to bring education and to raise the living conditions of the people there.

Mary Slessor encountered such local practices as "putting new-born twins into the forest to die, thinking they were evil," says Dr. Bliese. The young Scotswoman "began rescuing twins and showing how nothing bad happened to her." She ultimately rescued hundreds of twins and put an end to the practice of infanticide as part of her energetic, years-long campaign to combat poverty and superstition. Among her many accomplishments was building the first hospital in the area in 1897.

Young Kathy Bliese noted the impact Mary Slessor had on those she helped. "She turned their lives around, and I was intrigued by that," says Dr. Bliese. Mary Mitchell Slessor provided an example for Kathy Bliese of strength, energy, and inspiration—a practice some call "modeling." Years later, Kathy would participate in the ultimate application of modeling—the transmission of positive traits and behaviors through an MLM network of many individuals.

During high school, a teacher who was also a minister helped fuel Kathy's ambitions. He told her not to think of being a nurse, but to set her sights on becoming a doctor. "That sparked that sense of call in me," Kathy says.

She later entered Dana College on a Lutheran scholarship, but started out in sociology because "I was not convinced I could become a doctor."

A Desire She Couldn't Ignore

She soon realized her desire to become a physician was too strong to be ignored, so she switched to pre-med and did a year of research on hypertension to qualify for getting into medical school. She attended the University of Nebraska Medical School and then did her internship in Omaha.

An opportunity to do volunteer work abroad came when the Lutheran World Relief Organization, under the auspices of the Red Cross, asked her to go to Nigeria. It was a journey that would take her to Port Harcourt in Southeastern Nigeria in the vicinity of the city of Calabar, where her heroine Mary Slessor had arrived nearly a century earlier.

War—and a Better Way

Kathy Bliese was named medical director of the relief team during the catastrophic civil war that was then attracting world attention because of the misery it was inflicting on the tribespeople of Biafra. As the two-year war ravaged the country—fighting and starvation ultimately killed a million people—the Nigerian government was too busy fighting to attend to the needs of the population. "They let us handle all relief," says Dr. Bliese.

She visited local mission hospitals and realized that if she limited her approach to the conventional practice of medicine she would be failing to address some of the country's most serious problems. "They needed a better way," she concluded. Out of necessity she got involved in the total picture, which included helping improve nutrition and sanitation. "It didn't take me long to figure out that one of the things they needed least was Western medicine," she says. For example, indiscriminate use of antibiotics could actually "make the situation worse."

She set out to make sure the population was getting enough to eat. Taking charge of four camps with some sixteen thousand refugees, she oversaw the distribution of supplies that were arriving at Port Harcourt on relief ships from abroad.

Then, when the fighting ended, her team began helping everyone who was a victim of war, which meant "a lot of starving people."

Leadership During Crises

She oversaw clinics and makeshift hospitals in seventeen places. Keeping them functioning while dealing with ongoing crises meant staying constantly on the move, often traveling 200 to 250 miles in a day. "That was a pretty scary deal right after the war because of the possibility of land mines. I was fortunate not to find any. Others were not so fortunate," she notes. She drove with three nurses from village to village in a hatchback Land Rover provided by the International Red Cross. She and her team visited several hospitals a day, at times being chased down by barefoot runners with word of an emergency she had to confront or a decision she had to make. "One of the blessings of no electricity was that you could only work from sunup to sundown—6 A.M. to 6 P.M.," she recalls.

The devastation was enormous, and in fact can still be seen nearly three decades later in the large number of maimed and disabled citizens who hobble on crutches or struggle along in rusting wheelchairs.

At the time, and in the face of such overwhelming challenges, says Dr. Bliese, "I started training and sending people out because the task was too large for me to do myself."

It provided a potent learning experience for her about the need to have others who can do what you yourself do—a lesson that would later serve her well in network marketing.

Lessons in Bangladesh

After two years in Nigeria, Dr. Bliese began a ten-year mission in Bangladesh, arriving amid the upheaval of its independence struggle with Pakistan. Her work there would be even more striking in the way it foreshadowed her entry into network marketing.

Called to Bangladesh because a medical director was needed to start a hospital, she soon realized that the task awaiting her was far greater than that. She redefined the challenge not as building a hospital, but as in Nigeria bringing health to the local population. Because she knew that hospitals often deteriorate when the expatriates running them have to depart, she was determined to create a health program that could "leave some of our expertise and education behind if we had to depart." "Most people just want to build a great big hospital even though there's no hope that such an approach will function effectively over time," she says.

She wanted to build on the culture, beliefs, and practices that already existed. Like an MLM network, her program would be self-sustaining.

Residuals Worth More Than Money

The benefits that the system would deliver would be comparable to the residual income that a network marketer continues to receive long after he or she stops working. The difference was that in this case the "residuals" Dr. Bliese would get were much more valuable to her than money—they were the ongoing improvements in the health of the citizens of Bangladesh.

In her quest for knowledge and insights that would make her philosophy effective, she devoured knowledge about Bangladesh.

Like Mary Slessor, she learned the languages of the people she sought to help—in this case Bengali as well as Santali, the language of Bangladesh's aboriginal people, the Santals, who had long been victims of neglect and humiliation.

In setting up a system, her approach paralleled the one she would use years later in network marketing.

"I realized I had to duplicate myself," she says.

Rather than assuming that the way to build a successful system was by hoarding all knowledge in the hands of Western professionals, Dr. Bliese's program aimed at teaching the local people sound health practices.

I designed it almost like a pyramid system," she says, ignoring the extreme skittishness with which network marketers generally use the "P" word.

Passing On Vital Knowledge

In her health care system, a doctor trained his or her assistants and each of those assistants trained others. In so doing, knowledge was quickly spread from assistant to assistant and village to village. For much of the valuable work done by these assistants, there was no need for a central office to regulate their activities and pile up paperwork on their every action.

In any kind of large organization, increasingly large amounts of money and effort go into building up the inside of the company—the inner workings that don't have any contact with the customer. With any such traditional organization, the bigger it gets, the smaller the proportion of its total mass that is in touch with the outside world. It's for this reason that centralized, "top-heavy" organizations are slow to react and lose touch with their customers.

In network marketing companies, by contrast, a much smaller part of the company's resources are devoted to internal processes. The important part of the company is its distributors—and they are out there in direct touch with the world at large and the people who are buying and using its products. Indeed, distributors and customers tend to be one and the same. The brains of the organization are not all up in the top of the pyramid, but spread throughout the network.

> Dr. Bliese's experience included feeding the poor, building hospitals, and raising money. She knew how to create effective organizations. The lessons she learned all proved relevant when she entered network marketing.

Her Focus Was on Improvement

Dr. Bliese's health care system was built along the same principles.

"The focus was on improving health in the local villages," she says—not on developing expensive infrastructures. The advantages of her program included keeping costs low, reaching out to many people, and putting plans into action swiftly.

"I started out training nurses. I had two, sometimes three nurses. I trained them to do routine things that a Western physician would do," she notes. She and her nurses then recruited people in the villages that could be their "front line." These included individuals already involved in treating the local population. Typically, these were village practitioners "who weren't trained but maybe had worked for a doctor in a larger city." They were accustomed to "going out in the village and hanging up a sign and offering their services," explains Dr. Bliese. Dr. Bliese made these people a vital part of her system.

The local people embraced her system. By contrast, it was "difficult to get doctors to accept anything different from what they knew."

Independence Equals Motivation

It's a challenge that is mirrored today every time a network marketer tries to show someone from corporate America how individually motivated, independent workers are a more powerful force than people under the command of a central authority.

Again and again network marketing illustrates that what makes people effective has nothing to do with possessing impressive credentials or accumulating years of experience in the ranks of a major corporation. In fact, bringing your corporate baggage into a network marketing company is almost guaranteed to thwart your success.

Dr. Bliese was out to illustrate a similar point: Developing a network of local people and teaching them what they needed to know about health care made more sense than keeping all the answers in the hands of a temporary contingent of educated white coats from abroad.

The time Dr. Bliese spent studying what already existed in the way of health care in Bangladesh helped her understand how to motivate the individuals there. It gave her a sensitivity and insight that few outsiders could match.

"We started classes for the people we were training and they would come every week for two hours. They got a graduate certificate they could hang up in their place of business. They wanted to earn that," she says. "I started working with them, giving them training, not totally taking away what they did but convincing them to take out what was harmful," she adds.

The case of one local freelance health practitioner she trained is a good illustration of Dr. Bliese's practical frame of mind. As she tells the story, "He treated burns with egg white, grass, and manure. I thought, 'Well, the egg white is okay.' So we taught him to wash the grass. As for the manure, now that could cause tetanus. So we talked him out of that, and taught him that when the burns reached a certain level they would need more care. We taught him other ways to care for the health problems he was dealing with."

Big Results from Few Resources

Like an entrepreneur driven by a vision, Dr. Bliese figured out how to get big results out of minimal resources. Entrepreneurs are known for getting things done without making the cash outlays that traditional decision makers take for granted, and here Dr. Bliese was profoundly entrepreneurial.

The rural health program Kathy Bliese launched in Bangladesh so many years ago in the face of resistance and skepticism, has not only survived, it has been recognized as the best in the world.

She learned there was a better way to motivate her village assistants than putting them on a payroll, which she could not afford in any case. The assistants continued to get paid the way they always had, by the village residents that they treated. Dr. Bliese worked with them on the basis that the more they learned effective medical practices, "the more we would reward them by allowing them to send their patients to the hospital. This gave them 'face value' in the village."

"We were training them in better medicine, and this gave them credibility," she says.

It should come as no surprise that among her Western-educated colleagues "not many were keen about" the revolutionary system she conceived and implemented.

Many were like corporate executives and bureaucrats everywhere. They overlooked the value of genuine, heart-to-heart contact and communications. They were fixated on massive, top-down solutions. They sought to impose their ideas, practices, and institutions on a culture that they had little interest in understanding. They were determined to make the people they were supposedly trying to help fit into solutions that had nothing to do with them.

The Best Program in the World

Despite the conventional opposition, Dr. Bliese forged ahead with her vision. Today this same rural health development program that she launched has been recognized as the best in the world in an award given by The Evangelical Alliance Relief Program (TEAR) in England.

Like a solid downline that keeps on producing, the program she built two decades ago is still going on today. It has been expanded to encompass a mobile teaching clinic for such needs as maternal health care, sanitation, and other aspects of public health. Today, as she planned, the teachings, screenings, and immunizations continue, and the village health workers that were part of her downline continue to work with trained doctors on issues such as sanitation and safe drinking water. They also work training the local midwives.

The project has helped the local Bengali doctors get an education, and today she is proud that the medical director is a Bengali. The fifty-bed hospital that she founded as medical director—it's known as a LAMB Hospital, which stands for Lutheran Aid to Medicine in Bangladesh—has "stuck with the basic principle" of working with a network of village health practitioners.

During her years in Bangladesh, Dr. Bliese traveled in Europe and America to raise the equivalent of millions of dollars in funds and equipment.

A New and Different Battle

With her impressive background and leadership skills, she returned to Omaha in 1980. She then spent the next sixteen years developing a group of family health clinics. It was in Omaha that Dr. Bliese would face a foe that would test her spirit more than any of the challenges she had confronted in Africa or the Indian subcontinent.

The antagonist this time was more insidious than those she had faced in the past. In place of a clear-cut daily struggle to feed starving children or immunize impoverished villagers, she now found herself stumbling through an enveloping gray shroud known as "managed care." The battle was sapping her energy and spirits, and leaving the doctors with whom she worked exhausted and demoralized. The doctors were also faced with a loss of income.

By 1995 Dr. Bliese was having to deal with those losses—not only for herself, but for the doctors with whom she worked. She also would have to face the kind of loss that only other business owners can truly appreciate—the loss of seeing something that they have painstakingly nurtured pass out of their hands and out of their control. Those who have undergone such a loss testify to the particular type of wrenching pain it causes as they contemplate the years of effort and sacrifice that suddenly seem to have gone to waste.

> Dr. Bliese was searching for a way to fund her overseas ministry and her volunteer efforts. She wanted to get back to pursuing what she had always known was her real purpose in life.

The Seeds of an Opportunity

At the time, the last thing Dr. Bliese could imagine was that the dispiriting difficulties she was enduring would be the seedbed out of which a major new opportunity would grow.

The seemingly no-win situation in which she found herself arose only months after the sale of her clinics to new corporate owners in June 1995. It soon became clear that the clinics were heading for trouble fast. The new owners were projecting a possible $2 million loss by the end of the year and she saw that "the possibility of all the clinics being closed was very real."

The new owners asked Dr. Bliese to become medical director and turn the situation around. In December 1995, she accepted the offer "because I didn't want to watch what we had put together for sixteen years disintegrate."

She initiated a successful turnaround, but the performance demands of the corporation continued to escalate. Dr. Bliese was forced to make cutbacks that placed a severe strain on the doctors in the system. "They were working at full capacity and they were stressed," she said.

Her Purpose—Hope and Healing

As she struggled with the task of running the operation, she saw with increasing clarity the way corporations can trap people, drain them of their energies, then toss them aside. She also saw how what she was doing seemed ever more distant from her real purpose in life—bringing people hope and healing. "I realized that administration in medicine was not going to be the avenue to get me into doing more volunteer work and ministry overseas," she says.

She spent 1996 wrestling with the impossible demands of the corporation, and then, in February 1997, she was suddenly removed from her job. It was one of those inexplicable corporate actions that left everyone baffled and shell-shocked. But it also released her from the purgatory in which she had been suffering and allowed her to spend the next six months exploring how she would fulfill her mission in life.

The time would give her the freedom to travel during the first half of 1997. It would give her the chance to reflect on the course of her life. And it would allow her to think about an opportunity that some friends had put right into her hands nearly two years earlier.

Dr. Bliese had first heard about the Wellness International Network in March 1995. When friends first told her about WIN she could barely take the idea seriously. She'd actually had experiences with other network marketing companies. It would take her some time to learn that the companies with which she had been involved were nothing like WIN, the creation of a remarkable husband and wife team.

The Saga of Ralph and Cathy Oats

WHETHER KATHY BLIESE was learning the language of an aboriginal tribe or building a private business staffed with doctors in the United States, the orbit of her life seemed far removed from that of a couple named Ralph and Cathy Oats. But events were drawing them closer and would soon bring Dr. Bliese directly into the pioneering path the couple was blazing with their extraordinary organization.

Before getting into network marketing, Ralph Oats had spent twenty-three years driving a truck, earning a top income of $35,000 a year. Then Cathy Oats learned about a network marketing company that sold home water filters. In just four months of working part-time, her income reached $14,000.

Ralph quickly joined forces with Cathy and after the first year they'd made $100,000. After six years and more than $7 million in earnings, they quit working and moved to Florida.

But the couple was not cut out for retirement.

Ethics and Education

Using their thorough understanding of network marketing, Ralph and Cathy decided to create their own company, one devoted to total wellness—mental, emotional, and physical. In the early 1990s, they launched the Wellness International Network. They had seen the growing number of professionals joining the ranks of network marketing companies, and they wanted WIN to be a company in which educated people with high ethical standards and a long-range perspective could feel completely comfortable.

Beth and Rance Rogers

Among the individuals who heard about WIN in its early days were Rance Rogers, a former corporate manager with Proctor & Gamble, and his wife, Beth. Thanks in part to the skills and discipline Rance acquired in his ten years at P&G, the Rogers were among WIN's top five producers by 1994 (and today are members of the Winners Circle for earnings of $145,000 achieved during a single month).

Kris and George Hase

One of Rance's golfing buddies was George Hase, an award-winning architect. George and his wife Kris started doing the business part-time in August 1994. They went full-time after eight months, and by the end of their first year had monthly earnings of more than $40,000 (now grown to $60,000).

Kim and Brian Peterson—and Brett

George and Kris conveyed their enthusiasm for the business to Kris's brother, Brian Peterson, and his wife, Kim. In April 1995, Kim signed up, and two years later Brian retired from their franchise business and joined her. Working together, the pair soon entered the company's circle of top producers (and now have a monthly income of some $45,000). Along the way a third Peterson sibling—Kris and Brian's younger brother, Brett—also caught the WIN vision.

The WIN Comet

BY NOW THE WIN comet was streaking over the horizon in the direction of Kathy Bliese. It would take just one more event to bring it into her view, and that was a call from a pair of old friends, Dallen and Glennis Peterson.

The Peterson Connection

Dallen and Glennis first joined WIN in order to stand behind their children, Kris, Brian, and Brett. When they saw the success of their offspring and the company, they became enthusiastic supporters of WIN.

The Petersons had known Dr. Bliese for years, and knew about her commitment to helping others. Dallen was also on the board of Hope International Services, of which Dr. Bliese was founder and president.

"They knew that I had a passion for doing medical work overseas and that I had a heart for the ministry," says Dr. Bliese. They also knew that though she had raised millions for projects in which she was involved, "I don't like to ask for funding for my own causes," she says.

"When Dallen and Glennis got involved in WIN they called me because they saw that WIN would allow me to fund my ministry and support projects," says Dr. Bliese.

An Influential Voice

Peterson's successful career as an entrepreneur lent considerable weight to any recommendation he made for a business opportunity. He was the founder of the highly successful Merry Maids franchise, which he sold in 1989 for $25 million. A demographic trend watcher, Peterson said he started Merry Maids—a home cleaning service—because he foresaw the impact of the two-income family. The success of that company and of his other investments made Dallen Peterson a man to whom the business community listened.

The Petersons had first introduced Dr. Bliese to WIN in March 1995, when she was negotiating the sale of her clinics. The Petersons had visited Omaha and invited her to a WIN meeting at the Marriott Hotel. Happy about seeing her old friends, she went to the meeting but had no intention of pursuing a business opportunity.

"I Felt Great"

She recalls arriving at the meeting. "I had been on call all night before and was very tired. They gave me an energy drink and then I felt great."

She also started using some of the products, and "I had a seven-pound weight loss the first week." Meantime, "Dallen sent me $3,000 worth of product" that Dr. Bliese started providing to patients as samples. She decided to sign up and work on WIN part-time, or when she had the time.

Results, Results

She was soon impressed when she saw that her patients were getting results. Equally potent was her own experience: "I lost thirty-seven pounds on the product and felt really great." She adds, "I had been getting tired and lethargic and so I was excited."

The financial results were also eye-opening. "During my first month working part-time in the business I spent probably four to six hours." Her total earnings during that period from both retail sales and commissions were $7,000. "So I was impressed by that. I thought, 'No way could I make money that easily in medicine,'" she says.

In telling Dr. Bliese about WIN, Dallen Peterson put his recommendation in the strongest terms. "He said it would be like being on the ground floor of Merry Maids twenty years ago," she says.

A Valuable Tip—But No Decision

Many smart people would have paid handsomely to get a business tip from Peterson. Dr. Bliese was getting it for free, but despite his recommendation she was still stopping short of jumping on the bandwagon and going full-time. Instead, she waited two full years.

She went through the grueling experience of trying to save her clinics. Then, after being replaced in February 1997, she decided to spend time traveling. She visited Bangladesh and stayed a month and also went to other countries. By that summer she still had not made a decision about what course of action to follow. She was not even sure where to look.

In Your Own Backyard

"Acres of Diamonds" is a speech that was delivered countless times by the minister, lawyer, and educator Russell Conwell, founder of Temple University. It reminds us that immense opportunity may lie close at hand, and is easily overlooked.

The speech includes a story that Conwell called "essentially true"—that of an ancient Persian, Al Hafed, who leaves home in search of a diamond mine. He sells his substantial property and spends his life roaming across the continents in search of his fortune. After years of disappointment, his clothes in rags, he throws himself in despair into the Bay of Barcelona and drowns.

Back at his former home in the Indus Valley, the farmer who bought Al Hafed's land comes across "a black stone with a strange

eye of light in it which seemed to reflect all the hues of the rainbow."
He picks it up and realizes there are many more such black stones on
his property. In fact, across all of Al Hafed's former land similar
stones lie in abundance just under the soil. "Thus were discovered
the wonderful mines of Golconda," Conwell would intone, adding
the clincher: "Had Al Hafed remained at home and dug in his own
cellar or garden, or under his own wheat fields, he would have found
Acres of Diamonds."

Conwell, who believed both in getting rich and in giving generously, goes on in his speech to relate a dozen factual instances of
American capitalism where enormous opportunity was indeed right
under someone's nose, or in his backyard—like the unpolished black
rocks overlooked by Al Hafed.

Diamonds in Omaha

For Dr. Bliese, there was indeed a "diamond mine" in Omaha.

The diamonds were lying all about the town, like the rocks in the
story. These diamonds were her many friends and contacts, especially
the large number of doctors who had fallen under the pall of managed care and were looking for a better way. The question was now
whether she would uncover these opportunities or turn away.

On returning from her travels in mid-1997, she recalls, "I decided
to start looking at what I was going to do." She had reached a turning
point in her life, where pursuing WIN full-time made more and
more sense.

Weighing the Pros and Cons

She considered the facts:

- She had personally experienced the WIN products.

- She had seen others benefit from them and said to herself:
  "The products do work. People get results immediately. That
  is what people buy."

- She liked "the credibility of the products—the fact they are in the *Physicians' Desk Reference.* That made me comfortable."

- She saw it "as a way to work in something related to my field of medicine."

She was excited by the compensation plan. "The pay plan was excellent. You earn and make a living and do so quickly," she says, adding, "When I saw the numbers and how they were organized I had the background to realize they were paying people very very well."

Dr. Bliese also gave great importance to the individuals who founded WIN. "I realized Ralph and Cathy Oats were very genuine and authentic, and had tremendous people skills. I was impressed by the Oats—by who they were and what they had accomplished," she says. "I also realized that though Ralph may not have had a lot of education, he was a very intelligent person with desire and skills and the ability to help others."

At some point she looked at the other people doing well in WIN and "I thought if they could, I could too."

The Big Decision

Most importantly, WIN provided a way to fund her medical and missionary work—just as her friend Dallen Peterson had pointed out two and a half years earlier. "In August 1997, I made a decision to go into WIN full-time. I started September 1. My first big earnings were in November—$55,000."

Dreams Fulfilled

THE DREAMS OF Kathy Bliese's youth, far from fading away, today burn more brightly than ever.

Using her skills as a leader and providing her own funding, she has taken medical and missionary teams to Nigeria, Bangladesh, Kazakstan, Belarus, and Russia, where she has provided medical care, "planted" churches, worked in orphanages, ministered to women in prison, and provided all manner of practical assistance such as painting, cleaning, and repairing. Her teams, made up of doctors and laypeople working together, may include several doctors plus nurses, occupational therapists, physical therapists, "and whoever else wants to go."

One of her projects was helping plan and fund a fifty-bed hospital in Nigeria—an achievement completed one century after Mary Slessor built the first hospital in the area in 1897. Using her wide network of contacts and acquaintances, Dr. Bliese was able to recruit individuals and secure contributions of funds and materials, including equipment from rural hospitals in Nebraska.

Her radio broadcasts and their translations reach 75 percent of the world, including the Near East, the Middle East, Russia, South America, and all of Africa. Listeners hear her playing the guitar and singing the theme song of her program, a piece entitled *Kindle the Flame* that she wrote years ago during a car trip. Despite the volume of mail that pours in as a result of the broadcasts, she still tends to speak of her audience as individuals, and eagerly recounts the story of a listener from Malawi who started by getting friends to listen to her broadcast on Friday nights and was soon ministering to a church of sixty people.

> She "plants" churches and works in orphanages. She heads missionary teams and provides all sorts of practical assistance, such as painting, cleaning, and repairing. She takes teams of doctors abroad. She helped plan and build a fifty-bed hospital in Nigeria. What is most impressive: She is funding her good works with her income from WIN.

Telling Others about Her Good Fortune

Today Dr. Bliese finds that telling others about the WIN opportunity is a natural thing to do. "A lot of times it comes up in general conversation when I'm out among people," she says. Or, she adds, "I may have people on my list to talk to that day. I arrange to meet a lot of them for lunch."

The fact she has changed from practicing medicine full-time to being in WIN is often what provides the opening in the conversation. Whenever people ask her about her changed circumstances, she finds their questions provide "the perfect opportunity" to talk about WIN, she says. That's especially so, she adds, "when people ask why I am so relaxed and happy." Add to that description "cheerful," she notes, recalling the Scriptural phrase, "God loves a cheerful giver."

Among the things that attracted Dr. Bliese to WIN was its method of providing free samples. In her words, "You build your business by giving things away. That is why I felt so comfortable with it." She recalls another phrase from the Bible: "Give and it shall be given unto you."

> Dr. Bliese's radio broadcasts and their translations reach 75 percent of the world.

That's part of the lesson she teaches at her Omaha training center. She has opened a second training center, called Heartland Wellness Center, "as we are growing so fast." That growth has enabled Dr. Bliese to become part of WIN's elite Presidential Leadership Council for doing $600,000 in Personal Group Volume in a six-month period.

At the training center, "we do business opportunity meetings for people who want to take a look at the business. And we do training. That includes training in the concept of MLM, the compensation plan, how to build your business, how to develop yourself and other people, and how to avoid pitfalls."

Primarily, she emphasizes, "this is a people business, so personal development and learning to work with all kinds of people are key."

Help Others, and You Will Grow

Shining like a diamond at the core of her networking philosophy are her words: "If you will help others build their business, your business will automatically grow and you will be successful. If you have a strong desire to help people, then this business was meant for you."

As she sees it, the messages all reinforce two principles that have guided and given meaning to her remarkable life: "Be a cheerful giver," and "Give it all you've got."

For Dr. Bliese that's good advice for medicine, for the ministry, and for business.

"A Very Powerful Thing"

THE LITTLE GIRL sitting next to William Todd on the airplane was one of the cutest and "most excited little chatterboxes" he had ever met. She was telling him and everyone within earshot on the plane all about her recent trip to Disneyland and what a thrill it had been to meet Mickey Mouse and all of his cohorts and to experience the entire unforgettable spectacle. She was, to put it mildly, "off her rocker with happiness." William made a remark to the girl's mother about what an exciting vacation it must have been. The mother began explaining that the trip was not exactly a vacation, that it had been made possible by an organization called the Make-a-Wish Foundation. As she was speaking, the girl's hat fell off, and William saw the bald head of a child who obviously had been undergoing chemotherapy treatments.

Arriving home that evening at their house in Redmond, Oregon, William told Jan, his wife, "I've decided what charity we are going to support." He then related what he'd learned from the girl's mother about how the Make-a-Wish Foundation has helped thousands of terminally ill children take trips, meet celebrities and sports heroes, or achieve some special dream that the child would otherwise die without realizing.

Golf Outings for Charity

One way the Todds support the charity is through a golf outing they hold each year. Dozens of players participate in the event, after which Jan and William present a large check to Make-a-Wish.

"It's a great feeling to be able to do that," says William. "I can't begin to tell you what it's like. It is a very powerful thing that has happened to our lives."

What makes their giving feasible is the income and lifestyle the Todds have created as a result of being in network marketing.

*"It was something I had been looking for all my life,"
says William Todd. Joining Nikken changed
everything for him and his wife Jan.*

Disaster Once Loomed

The richly fulfilled life the Todds now lead is in striking contrast to the path they were both on just a few years back when, as William says, "As a couple we were headed for total disaster."

A construction superintendent, William felt trapped in the twelve-hour days and backstabbing of corporate life. For relief, they'd cram their weekends full of frenzied activity, "skiing and drinking until we could find our way home at five o'clock Monday morning. It wasn't a balanced life."

To make matters worse, Jan had been suffering from—and seeking treatment for—a bad back for nearly five years. Eventually she was told that her chronic pain was incurable and that she needed to learn to live with it.

Then a friend loaned them some products from a firm called Nikken. A Japanese company that entered the United States in 1989, Nikken employs what is often called "magnet therapy," a field that has received increasingly respectful attention from researchers. While Nikken avoids making specific health claims, some believe magnet therapy works by increasing blood circulation by attracting the iron in the blood's hemoglobin molecules. Nikken's products include mattresses, pillows, shoe insoles, seat cushions, and body patches with small magnets embedded in them.

Relief at Last

Very quickly, Jan gained the relief that she had been unable to find during her years of drug treatment, chiropractic, and physical therapy.

Despite the great results, when William heard Nikken was sold via network marketing, all his defenses went up, and he refused to consider seriously any presentation on the business opportunity. He actually knew nothing about the industry, but he held a number of preconceived notions that he had learned from friends. His favorite was, "MLM means 'Many Losing Money.'" Closing his usually open mind, he refused even to investigate. "You just didn't do something like MLM," he said.

Entrepreneurship—and Debt

Nonetheless, he counted himself as a happy consumer of the products. Then in 1991, William Todd entered history as a statistic, which is to say he was downsized. During this episode of their lives, the Todds came close to filing for bankruptcy. As their finances deteriorated, the Todds moved in with William's sister and brother-in-law. "We received an instant family," he says, laughing now about an event that was surely less humorous at the time.

Entering the entrepreneurial world in 1992, William started his first venture, called Breakthrough Media, Inc., marketing books and tapes on the subject of positive thinking. Despite an optimistic start, in two years he found himself heavily in debt. Determined to find something, and under the lash of necessity, he decided to overcome his past reservations and talk to his friends in Nikken.

This time it was Jan who was the naysayer. Imprinted on her mind was her exposure to MLM at the age of twenty-one when she had been "ripped off" by a pots and pans deal. Jan pursued a career (in William's words) as "a computer knucklehead"—a systems analyst for Unisys who did contract work for other companies such as Nestlé and Carnation. MLM was not for her.

Unable to persuade Jan, " I went off on my own," says William. With or without her, he was going to do it, and his determination convinced Jan not to try to hold him back. Rather than support him, Jan says she merely tolerated his involvement. Meanwhile, she took over their Breakthrough Media business.

William quickly became enamored with Nikken and its approach to business, which contrasted sharply with the mistrustful corporate environment that had tormented him for so long. "I always seemed to get wrung out at a certain level," he says of his previous career, a dissatisfying experience even though he had supervised crews of up to seventy-five men on various projects and helped run the largest branch of his company in the country. "There weren't a lot of attempts to help me climb," he recalls, noting that he believed he was being "held back because of jealousy." Even being offered the job of the superior who was thwarting him provided little satisfaction. He did not want to win the rat race, he wanted to escape from it.

"What I'd Been Looking for All My Life"

Finally, in Nikken, "I learned a Japanese style of network marketing," he says. "It was something that I had been looking for all my life." The principles were clear: "Take my eyes off myself, focus in on other people, and add value every day."

The Nikken style of networking teaches balance in all areas of your life, says William. "It teaches mind, body, family, societal, and financial balance. To achieve balance you have to stop being so concerned with yourself and start helping other people achieve their dreams and goals."

William and his upline established a mastermind team and set about guiding their downline in how to attain a balanced life. He helped the members of his group focus on their dreams and how to fulfill them in a balanced way. In turn he found his own life becoming immensely more satisfying. Unlike corporate life, he saw that here an ambitious individual would be pulled ahead and encouraged to succeed.

Jealousy of the downline is hardly a factor because it doesn't make sense. If a distributor has a burning desire to climb the MLM ladder, he can find leaders at the top to offer a helping hand.

Rapid Success

Highly motivated, William became successful quickly. Within eleven months, he became a Diamond. Few others in the company's history had done so in a shorter time. "The best thing," recalls William, "was that as soon as my checks went over $10,000 a month my wife became my biggest supporter."

Jan had continued running the book and tape sales operation, and that would have some payoffs the two had not foreseen. It came about when they began carrying the works of John Kalench, one of the most successful authors writing for network marketers. Kalench's works had sold in the millions. By handling them, the Todds developed a customer base for their business among network marketers.

Even more important was the friendship that developed with John Kalench. When Kalench got cancer, William called John's wife and offered to help her. Kalench, whose books had inspired countless MLMers, was not in a network marketing organization himself. William pointed out the benefits for the Kalenches of having thousands of distributors in countries around the world. The Kalenches listened and then decided that both the opportunity and their situation—as well as their relationship with the Todds—made it timely for them to sign up. Since then, the growth of the Kalench organization has been remarkable, with Kalench himself becoming a Diamond in record time in December 1998.

As for the book and tape business, Jan was pleased with its performance, but as soon as they had an offer, they sold it.

Working together on Nikken, "We did whatever it took to build the business," recalls William. For two years, they worked more or less around the clock.

Mastery over Their Lives

Today the Todds have gone a long way toward gaining mastery over the rhythms of their lives. Technology helps in this regard, as they need not leave home to spend time with many of the members of their group. In the Todd's office is a powerful tool for their business— a state-of-the-art teleconferencing unit. During a single day William conducted meetings in Florida, New York, New Jersey, Ohio, and Oregon. Like many other leaders in the business, the Todds are making use of technology to stay off planes and remain at home.

Somewhat ironically, all their success has left them "totally unemployable," they agree. "We would need to be guaranteed a seven-figure income, and be able to work four days a week—from 10 A.M. to 1 P.M.," says William. "The company would have to pay for my Porsche Cabriolet, pay the mortgage on my $1.6 million home, tolerate long lunches, and promise us that we could have six months vacation each year. Then I could hold a job," says William, with Jan laughing at his side.

A Great 'Play Ethic'

Jan agrees with her husband and says, "We're unemployable, but we have a great play ethic."

"For the uninitiated, that's similar to a work ethic, except that it is much more fun. Nobody can hold a candle to our work ethic and nobody can hold a candle to our play ethic either. When we run, we run hard. When we play, nobody can find us," says William.

William and Jan believe in a checks and balance system between work and play. They just recently finished a fourteen-day road trip. When they got back, they cleared up things at their home office and were off for five days of fun with no phones and no faxes.

The list of play events that they have scheduled would astound most wage earners: yearly Hawaii trips, sailing cruises every six months, Europe once a year, and conventions in Japan. They believe that they are really living life the way it is meant to be lived.

While Jan was working her career, they moved around and lived in Hawaii. They now prefer to vacation there rather than live there, and they like the island of Kauai best. There the Todds can enjoy intimate seclusion on such retreats as a thirty-acre estate that can be reached only through private roads, with no phone, no fax, and no cell service. They love to romp by themselves on the mile-long private beach, taking in the blue ocean, gorgeous sands, and fragrant flowers.

A Premium on Personal Time

Also factored into their play ethic is jealously guarded personal time with friends. That twice-a-year sailing cruise is with a special couple from another Nikken organization. They journey down to the Bahamas, board a fifty-foot sailboat, and stay out for a week, cruising the open water and diving for lobster. "We snorkel and swim too. We love to have fun," adds Jan.

"If you're not having fun then it isn't worth it, because stress is the number one killer in this world today," says William, sounding slightly pontifical about living a healthy life now that his is in balance.

On one of his road trips to Pittsburgh, William read a billboard that hit home with him. It said one in three people will be diagnosed with cancer by the year 2000. The message underscored for him the importance of adding value to other people's lives on a daily basis. "That's the whole purpose as to why we've been put on this Earth. You have to reach out, add value, teach balance, and have fun."

William has a peculiar if effective method for reminding himself to feel gratitude for having gotten out of the rat race: "I go to the Marriott Hotel in Irvine and rent a room on the fourteenth floor. Then I sit on the balcony overlooking the 405 Freeway and watch the thousands upon thousands of people who are driving off to do things they don't like. They are spending an eighth of their life on that concrete."

In 1998, the Todds celebrated their fourth year with Nikken. Williams recalls starting with the hopes of being able to make $5,000 dollars a month. Today, their monthly income is about equivalent to what their combined yearly income was in their previous careers. When asked if she really believed William would succeed when they first started, Jan got very quiet. She then confessed that she didn't think so.

Abilities That Have Grown Remarkably

"Wow," said William. "That's the first I ever heard that." He is grateful that he wasn't aware of her doubts. Today, though, they are both confident in his abilities, which have grown remarkably since joining Nikken.

"William has changed," Jan says teasingly. "Before getting into network marketing I wasn't sure he read. I thought he just looked at the pictures." In fact, William has three large shelves of self-help books that he has read since getting into Nikken, and Jan marvels at how different he is today. "He couldn't stand in front of five people without breaking into a cold sweat. Now he can speak before thousands," she says. "It's been incredible to watch him grow and help others."

Jan doesn't think the people he knew before network marketing would even know William today. "Now he is a natural. So talented! I never knew it would be this big or be so great."

"And one of the greatest things," adds William, "is helping those little children."

8

Cultivators

Success rarely happens suddenly. Those occasions when it appears to occur "overnight" are usually illusions of one sort or another; either the rewards do not endure, or the achievement is in fact the outcome of long but unseen effort. Cultivators aren't less desirous of success than those who race headlong after it at breakneck speed, but they often understand more about what it takes to be successful and may waste less effort in the long run. As one cultivator put it, "You tend your garden steadily; pouring gallons of water and fertilizer on it all at once won't make it bear fruit faster."

Many Friends, Simple Pleasures

Ann and Steve Padover live north of San Francisco, in suburban San Rafael, a twenty-minute drive from the Golden Gate Bridge, in a beautiful house that has a courtyard where you can often find Steve gardening while Ann reads, swims, or just relaxes.

Day by day, steady improvement. Ann and Steve Padover found the secrets of building a business where success would be enduring.

Ann loves her lifestyle because "I can read a mystery book in the pool raft. I can talk to people, take the dog for a walk, or go on a trip, all according to my own time schedule, no one else's." And if Ann decides to extend the trip a few days longer than she'd planned, there's usually no pressing reason that she has to return. Ann cherishes the freedom. And all the while "I know that day by day our financial situation and income will continue to steadily improve—no matter where we are, or what we are doing."

Regular, Consistent Growth

Steady reliable improvement is just what the Padovers want. As Ann puts it, "We are not one of your fast-growing ones, going like a meteor through the sky."

On the other hand, there is nothing casual or indifferent about their approach to network marketing or about their dedication to Envion and its products and services. Both Ann and Steve bring to their work just the sort of professional pride you would expect from two Ph.D.s in their mid-fifties. Steve, whose degree is in educational psychology, still works full-time as a college counselor. Ann, however, has left behind both academia, where she built a reputation as a dynamic innovator, and the world of management consulting that was her second career.

Ann's Trademark

Strange as it may sound at first, their unique, casual yet conscientious style of networking is perhaps best symbolized by Ann's sneakers.

That's right. Among her networking buddies she's known for her sneakers, which send a signal and are something of a trademark, in a league, say, with General George C. Patton's pearl-handled revolvers.

Now, there's nothing remarkable about wearing sneakers when you are in the garden, but Ann has gone well beyond that. It all started a few years ago at an Envion gathering where she was scheduled to make a presentation. After she prepared her talk, there came the eternal question, "'What to wear?'"

She had been wearing businesslike suits for her presentations. But somehow these outfits didn't feel quite right anymore. This was not corporate America. There were no dress codes, no rules, no disapproving bosses to fear, no critical clients to worry about offending. In fact, a major attraction of being in business for yourself is not worrying about things like that. She'd be among people she sincerely cared about, delivering a message she believed could help them.

A Friendly Signal

So Ann tossed aside her serious shoes and pulled on a pair of sneakers, and they conveyed just what she wanted—a friendly signal that the person addressing you is unpretentious and relaxed and capable of having fun.

Since that watershed day, "I show up at all the presentations in a suit and sneakers," she says. "Once when I'd forgotten to bring my sneakers to a convention, people were so disappointed that I ran out to Nordstroms and got a pair." At an Envion dinner, people practically lined up to peek under her gown to see if she was indeed wearing sneakers with rhinestones, as the gossip had it. As it turns out she wasn't, but the story tends to underscore the power of the symbol she created.

A Few Years Ago—Worries

If the world the Padovers have created for themselves is today filled with numerous friends, simple pleasures, and growing security, the view from their living room looked a lot different just three and a half years ago.

As Ann tells it, "We were treading water. We were not poor. But our net assets were staying the same." Like other management consultants, Ann worried about getting enough business and where she would find her next client. Steve knew he'd receive only limited increases in his income from the college. Beyond the issue of income, Ann regretted all the time she'd missed spending with her husband and son David.

"Is it always going to be like this?" Ann asked Steve one day in April 1995.

Steve said, "Something is going to happen."

Skeptical, Ann just filed away Steve's response. But within a few months, Ann recalls, "We found Envion."

The Path to Health and Prosperity

The story of how the Padovers found Envion is also an account of how a distressing medical emergency led them onto a path of improved health and prosperity. It's enough to make even a hardened skeptic wonder about life's twists and turns, and to muse a bit about that thing called "destiny."

Without saying it in so many words, Ann begins her account with a tone that says: "Listen to our story. It is packed with lessons." And indeed it is.

"Here is how we got involved with Envion," Ann begins. "We are now in our mid-fifties. Over the last few years my husband was not in the best of health. In June 1995, his doctor sent him to a well-known nutritionist, who put him on a high-carbohydrate, low-fat diet. Two weeks later Steve was in the emergency room of the local hospital with symptoms of a heart attack—though they turned out to be caused by his gallbladder."

Steve was told he would need to begin a course of treatment. Before embarking on it he called his cousin, a doctor, to ask for advice. Steve's cousin responded by offering to help, and then added, "But you ought to see how we are eating now." The Padovers paid a visit, and immediately noted that the cousin and his wife both looked healthier than they had ever appeared before. Part of the reason they looked so good was their energy and obvious loss of weight. Soon, the Padovers were receiving an enthusiastic introduction to Envion and its products.

Nothing to Lose by Trying

Ann and Steve needed little convincing. After all, here was a respected M.D. who was also a family member. Beyond that, he was not just recommending a regimen for both of them, he was following it himself—with apparently remarkable results. The Padovers figured they had nothing to lose by trying Envion—which is just what they tell other people today.

After using the products for three weeks, Ann wanted to learn more. Specifically, she wanted to meet the founder of Envion, Matthew Freese. Turning to Steve, she said, "If Matt Freese is half as good as his products, this might be what we've been looking for."

Ann flew to Envion's headquarters in Nashua, New Hampshire. Within a half-hour of meeting Matt, says Ann, "I knew that this was somebody who was really different. He was way better than any of the products, and they were pretty incredible." Ann called Steve and said, "This is it." She told him how Matt Freese was a solid businessman, who represented all the best in integrity, honesty, and ethics. She noted that he was not "just a slick marketing person."

Freese's Vision Was the Key

Meeting Freese and Envion's executive vice president, Cindy Anderson, gave Ann the key to "understanding what they stood for." It was a vision that deeply appealed to her.

Full of belief and enthusiasm, though with little tactical guidance from the fledgling company at first, Ann and Steve flew into action. "We pretty much started building the business on our own, though there was some help from our upline," she says.

The methods she and Steve used came to them as spontaneously as teaching or helping out friends. "We had a natural enthusiasm and credibility" that were based on the results they had with the products. Those results extend past mere weight loss and additional energy. They include the fact Steve's health problems had disappeared.

"It was easy for us because we had significant results. We looked different and we felt different—and it was obvious. We were just sharing with other people who wanted the same thing," says Ann, adding, "We found that we were building our business just by talking to people we knew."

Their Story Stood Out

Their personal story—along with their professionalism, integrity, and sincerity—gave them distinction in a business that is often misunderstood. "We are not traditional salespeople," says Ann. "We don't do the three-foot rule"—that is, pitching to everyone who comes within three feet of you, a technique that is widely employed in network marketing. "That's not who we are," she says.

Both were pleased with the results they were getting. "We were able to build a nice little group fairly quickly. Everybody was building by talking about the products." As for emphasizing the business opportunity, "it was hardly ever mentioned," Ann says.

Implicit in such an approach were some unspoken assumptions on the Padovers' part: If spreading the word about the products was good and a way to help people improve their lives, then pitching the business too aggressively seemed dubious and maybe overly tainted with self-interest. For people like Ann and Steve—whose careers had been largely devoted to positions of trust—there seemed to be a danger of risking their reputations, compromising their ethics, and betraying their very sense of who they were.

But there were other ways of looking at things, they discovered. The values Ann and Steve had absorbed over their careers offered just one perspective. By contrast, people with business backgrounds were not likely to take offense or see any big problem with being told about a new opportunity for making profits.

Ann's attitude toward presenting the business started to change the day in October 1995 that a woman who had been a customer asked for more information on how one could make money in Envion. After hearing about the business opportunity, the woman remarked, "Why didn't you tell me? I'm an entrepreneur."

It made Ann start thinking: Perhaps emphasizing the business wasn't such a bad thing after all.

Strong Medicine

Then in December 1995 came what Ann calls "a big adjustment"— and she and Steve didn't exactly welcome it at first. It occurred when Matt Freese hired a well-known network marketing consultant named Randy Gage, whose mission was to help distributors see the benefits of presenting the business, not just the products.

Along with virtually everyone else who comments on him, Ann describes Gage as someone who "is in your face." He was strong medicine for many of the Envion pioneers, who were accustomed to doing things their own way. Ann tried to keep an open mind, partly because "I always trusted Matt." If Freese had sent him, perhaps his message was worth hearing. What happened was, "Randy forced us to look at what we were doing and why we were doing it."

Gage began attending all the company functions, and "I got to know him. I made a connection and we would talk," Ann says. "He kept hammering home the point about network marketing," she adds. Her approach began to shift "from just talking about the products to talking more about the business." Gage's unrelenting campaign eventually hit home with Ann.

Getting It—The "Aha" Moment

"One day I just got it," she says. Like countless others in network marketing, she suddenly realized that "it isn't just the products." She was now able to see that "even though the products are extremely important, they aren't the whole picture by any means."

All the input she had been receiving coalesced into a unified vision of remarkable power and simplicity. She realized the limitations of pouring all her energies into evangelizing about the products. Ann's "aha" moment came as she was "drawing circles"—a standard network marketing way of presenting the business by using circles to illustrate how a business can grow and multiply. "I was drawing circles one day and I got it. It then became my passion to get others to get it," she says.

Today, Ann is a committed business builder who says, "People don't really 'get it' in this business. My passion is just that they 'get it.'" She shows them how to "connect the dots" as Matt Freese likes to say. "Then, whatever they decide, at least they're making an informed decision," says Ann.

Teach a Few People

"Getting it," says Ann, is absorbing the idea that to build a successful organization you only need to introduce the business and products to a relatively few people and teach them to do what you did: Use the products, produce a relatively small amount of volume, and teach those people you introduced to the business to do the same to a relatively few people who do the same.

The Padovers emphasize "Listening to yourself" to be sure your message is congruent with your values and beliefs.

Ann shows people that "if you only work ten hours a week, and you never produce more than $100 in volume per month, if you duplicate what you did with people who continue the duplication, you will achieve your financial goals." Ann adds that the example of $100 in volume per month— or $3.33 per day—is a "ridiculously low amount when you find out about all our products." She also notes that a vital part of the equation is "to have a dream or goal."

"All you have to do is find six people and teach them to do what you did—that is, find people who are willing to work ten hours per week and each produce $100 in volume per month." Even when she makes the figures more conservative, Ann is able to show people "how they can reach thousands of people with no one producing volume of more than $3.33 per day." She adds, "When people get this and then understand what our products are, they really light up."

Working Ten Hours a Week

Ann goes on to demonstrate the power of leverage when working ten hours a week. She has prospects write "1 = 10 hours," which represents their putting their own ten hours into the business.

Under that she has them write "6 = 60" representing the six people they find who each are willing to work ten hours a week.

And under that she has them write "30 = 300," which represents the thirty people the six people found.

She next has the prospects add up the hours—which come to 370. Finally, she has an impassioned discussion of how incredible it is that the prospect works ten hours a week and yet benefits from 370 hours of work a week. "Even if you take a vacation, you still benefit from 360 hours of work a week," she says.

Fired Up

Fired by her conviction, Ann became forcefully eloquent on the subject of business building. "That is all I want people to ever get—the idea that they themselves have a business, and that all they need to do is take three, six, or ten people and teach them to do exactly what they did, and they will make all the money they have ever wanted to make."

Ann's biggest source of satisfaction is when someone else finally catches on. "You can see it in their eyes when they get it," she says. "I am a teacher. I teach people to break things down. I really want you to get this."

Anyone Can Visualize It

"It is so exciting when they get it," she says, adding, "Almost anyone can visualize themselves producing $100 in volume per month. Then, they can visualize $200 or $300 per month in volume and see what that does for the bottom line."

After learning how to present the business, Ann and Steve became concerned they had gone too far, that they were shortchanging the benefits of selling the products. After all, they truly believed in the products and that's what had gotten them into Envion in the first place. "Steve and I realized we had to find an approach that kept the individual in mind," Ann explains, noting the importance of having your presentation be congruent with your values and beliefs. They teach the people in their organization to listen and to adjust their presentations to what their audience wants. And the two urge others to above all, "Listen to yourself."

Listening to Themselves

For the Padovers, listening to themselves meant highlighting their personal commitment and experience. It meant standing up for what they believed, sometimes in the face of the advice they had received from Randy Gage and others. Some high-powered, big-time business builders will be inclined to dismiss the Padovers' flexible and individualized approaches as well as the use of personal testimonials. But Ann and Steve are convinced that the average individual will find their story packed with relevance.

Just consider that Steve no longer has high blood pressure, his cholesterol is down, and he's lost forty-five pounds. Add that to a comparable weight loss by their son, and the Padovers are able to say, "Our family has gone from a four-person family to a three-person one." Ann, too, is excited by all the energy she has now. "I used to go to bed at 8:30, wake up tired at 7:30 in the morning, and take a nap by early afternoon. Now I even know what late night TV is about. I wake up earlier than before and I'm not tired." The corporation, too, clearly sees the value in such personal accounts: Ann and Steve's before-and-after pictures were recently published in the Envion catalog.

One Step at a Time

The Padovers place an emphasis on putting one foot in front of the other. "It is important for people to understand it could take four, six, ten years. But you are going to be that much older anyway."

The Padovers' approach stands in sharp contrast to the misguided efforts of the get-rich-overnight promoters and their promises of instant success. Yet, the way Ann and Steve do business is also distinct from those examples of superhuman sacrifice and ultra-intense effort aimed at producing major results in a limited period of time. Ann and Steve do not disparage those who work that way. When they meet someone who wants to take a faster road, they will spend time and energy to help that person move along at his or her desired pace. But Ann does say, "I present it as a much longer-term process. I am in this business to build a very secure long-term residual income in a way that others can duplicate. And we want to enjoy the journey along the way."

The Millionaires Next Door

With their focus on building for the future, Ann and Steve avoid the conspicuous trappings of wealth. "We are the millionaire next door types," she says, referring to the current bestselling book that documents the lifestyles of the low-key, unassuming affluent. "We just bought our first car with Envion"—an Acura 3.5 Special Edition. "You're never going to see us in a flashy $80,000 car, but we're excited with what we have. This is who we are. We waited a long time to get to this point."

Today Ann no longer needs to consult. She travels as she sees fit, whether taking a trip to Wisconsin to meet a marketing associate or attending meetings and training sessions across the country, which she treats as a combination of business and pleasure. Both Ann and Steve enjoy traveling, speaking, training, and making presentations. They also make a special effort to help others. This includes counseling individuals with phone and e-mail support, as well as holding social and business get-togethers and conducting cross-line meetings and trainings with other Envion leaders who have similar views.

Reaching Out to Others

Helping others also means extending a hand to the "orphans" who come their way, which in network marketing parlance refers to individuals

> "Some talents, techniques, and methods are great—for sales. But network marketing is really not a sales business—it's a business of teaching and training, a business of duplication. Using sales techniques—which work great on the used car lot—will actually backfire in network marketing."
>
> *—Randy Gage, consultant, author*
> *of* How to Build a Multi-Level
> Money Machine

who don't have an active upline sponsor to work with them. "It doesn't matter if they are not in my line," says Ann. Even though there is no financial payoff for investing time with such a person, Ann will do so because she hopes that she can "say something that will encourage them to continue in their dream, or give them enough courage to get the help they need to build their businesses."

A reporter once irked Ann by suggesting she had abandoned her career as a professional. Setting him straight, she contended that network marketing is also made up of professionals. "How could helping people get healthy, earn the income they want, and have the time they want be any less 'professional' than what traditional professionals do?" she asks. "Why is a lawyer representing criminals considered any more professional? Or a stockbroker? Or a doctor?"

As a highly educated former academic, Ann did not take naturally to the inspirational language found in some corners of network marketing, with its often gushing expressions of love and spirituality and its New Age emotionalism. "I worry about sounding corny," she says. On the other hand, her stories give you the feeling that deep down she is genuinely softhearted—just not softheaded.

"I'm Here for a Reason"

She tells the story of working with a distributor who "was very excited about one product line," recalls Ann. "This woman has told me that she had prayed for years for exactly what Envion is—an opportunity to help people get healthy, to be their own bosses, to have time for their families, to make a difference in the world, and to make a ton of money." Moved by the woman's sincerity and commitment, Ann says, "When I get a phone call from her I know that I am here for a reason and that is to help this woman and others like her get their dream."

Helping others affects Ann deeply, she admits, and then she adds, "It makes me feel humble—and it makes the effort all worthwhile."

Bearing Fruit

"I NEVER COMPLETED high school," says Leon Huisman. "Dairy and poultry farmers didn't need to do that. Joyce has the education. She went to business school for six months."

Joyce and Leon were born and reared on dairy farms in northwest Wisconsin. Their journey from the farmlands of their youth to the rich and rewarding life they lead today as Shaklee Master Coordinators is a tale of distances traveled. The inner journey, however, was more important than the geographic one.

For example, when it came to travel, Leon, now sixty-four, never even imagined he would go abroad. Dairy farmers didn't do such things. Nor did he ever think he'd be able to stand in front of a crowd and speak. The very thought left him in a state of terror. Besides, why would you want to do such a thing? He didn't even like talking to strangers. As for self-help, he rejected the whole idea. Anyone could see that motivators were fakes and phonies who tried to force people to change their personalities. Leon believed in hard work, honesty, and integrity.

That was pretty much the cast of Leon's mind in 1962 when he and Joyce moved to California and Leon became a brick mason. He liked the work, and as anyone could see, laying bricks was the way progress was made: hard steady work, one brick at a time. Then in 1969 his brother-in-law and sister sponsored the Huismans into Shaklee, a company with a wide variety of products and services that was launched in 1956.

They Sized Up the Business

Leon and Joyce looked at the way Shaklee worked. They appraised it with the calm steady gaze of farmers who'd spotted something out in the field that was new and different. Hmmm, they said to themselves, as they watched the business flourish before their very eyes. You don't need a fancy degree to know that this is a giant opportunity. By the end of the following year, Leon was in Shaklee full-time and was reaping the harvest. "We surpassed the six-digit income in our sixth year, and three years later we reached the $200,000 mark."

Thirty years later, Leon still likes to lay bricks. But he does it when he wants to, as a retiree. "Retiring is quitting doing what you have to do so that you can start doing what you want to," he says. As for his income, it's now "up over the $350,000 level." It makes him feel fortunate. "Most of my friends who aren't involved in networking work really hard. They don't have good retirement income."

A Way to Help Others Grow

The Huismans live on a ranch south of Sacramento, California. Because they were so far out in the country they had to find an effective way to develop downline leaders who could be independent. Leon, however, had little taste for self-improvement. He associated it with hype, and with pushy, overbearing people. But now he was forced to think about helping others develop their abilities. He began taking long trips to attend sales training and develop downline sales leaders. On the way he listened to tapes by the master of motivation, Earl Nightingale. The lengthy drives opened his mind a bit to the value of self-development. With the seeds planted, his interest slowly blossomed. "I never believed in sales training until I heard Earl, but it eventually became part of my life," he says.

Today the former Wisconsin farm boy says Dale Carnegie's *How to Win Friends and Influence People* is his favorite self-help book. There's nothing fake or phony about "appreciating people who are polite and kind," he says; nor is there anything wrong with trying to be that way yourself. It's not only right, it's good business, he notes, adding, "Sometimes abrasive people build fast, but then they are

Leon Huisman was a farmer and a brick mason who once looked askance at self-improvement and would not have dreamed of giving a speech. Then he and Joyce joined Shaklee and discovered a new way of working and living. Today, having built a productive business, they lead a life of leisure, traveling the world and doing whatever they please. Here they receive an award at a Shaklee President's Club Trip.

gone. They disappear. They pushed the rope rather than pulled others along." Sound growth is tended and nurtured over time, not forced, he notes.

A Changed Attitude

As a measure of how much his attitude has changed, Leon believes the personal growth that the business makes possible is as valuable as—and inseparable from—the financial opportunity.

Before Shaklee he had never given a public speech. The thought of being in front of a group was paralyzing. Today he gives presentations with skill and confidence, not to mention excitement and enthusiasm. His earnest and well-informed speeches on nutrition would make the legendary Nightingale himself sit up and listen.

Even more important than the skills the Huismans have developed are the relationships they've forged. "I don't believe that there is any career that can give you a wider range of friends and acquaintances," says

Joyce. "In a few years we had thousands of people in our group," she adds. The Huismans became friends with other Master Coordinator couples and made friendships that have endured for nearly thirty years. "We see some of the couples several times a year and have developed really strong, unending relationships. It's a whole new avenue of friendship."

"We have all types of people today," says Leon. "Even doctors, lawyers, teachers, and police." Among the big successes in their downline are a Montana wheat farmer, a bricklayer, and a teacher who was on food stamps.

Travel—From Dream to Reality

When the Huismans first got married, travel was a distant dream. Then in 1973, as a result of being in Shaklee, they went to Hawaii. "I felt like I was walking on air," recalls Leon. They both thought they had landed in paradise. "I felt like it wasn't really true life," says Joyce. "It was like being in a dream come true."

As someone who had lived in "cold country" most of his life, Leon was rhapsodic about standing on the balcony with the warm breeze blowing on his face and the smell of flowers in the air. He listened to the surf pounding against the Waikiki shore with the rhythmic sound of drums in the distance. "I thought I'd died and gone to heaven. It was warm in the middle of winter. We vowed we would never miss a trip, and that we'd go one or two or three times every year," he says.

In 1977 they flew to London for a five-country tour. It was their first time in Europe. "Our family didn't do that—go to Europe! We were Midwestern dairy farmers," he says. Since that trip they've returned many times, both on Shaklee sponsored tours and on their own. As accustomed as they've become to world travel, they're still occasionally stopped short by the thought of how their lives have been transformed. "We never dreamed that we would spend time overseas," says Joyce.

Luxury and Leisure

By almost any standard, Leon and Joyce lead a life of luxury and relative leisure. "We can stay as busy as we want. We plan our business around our life, traveling to visit family and friends or just hunting and fishing." As for vacations, what's important to remember is that they are paid for by the company, notes Leon. The amount they have earned in hotel and travel expenses is in the hundreds of thousands of dollars. That's on top of their $5 million in bonuses and $500,000 in car bonuses. They've had fifteen Shaklee bonus cars, including eleven different Continentals. Today they have a Dodge Ram pickup and they just received a Lexus 400.

"Some people want to be a boss. In this business you need to be a leader, not a boss."

—*Leon Huisman, Shaklee*

While they revel in their good fortune, a chance event can still occasionally drive home to the Huismans just how good they have it. Recently, for example, they met a corporate executive making $700,000 a year who lamented that his job left him with no time for his family.

Speaking of family, Joyce and Leon have six daughters and one son, plus twenty grandchildren and one great grandchild. Three of their daughters are Shaklee supervisors, pointing up the sustained value of the business that they have tended attentively over the years.

Leon laughs with satisfaction at the idea of a business so bountiful that it's still a source of opportunity for his family. And unlike farmland, whose productivity has natural limits, this can keep on expanding indefinitely.

Says Leon: "We are going to do big things in the future!"

9

Fighters

THEY STRUGGLE, MANEUVER, twist, and turn to gain mastery over their lives. Even when they are stymied, or incapacitated, or without resources, they are looking for a way to get back into the game. They may not have all the answers when they begin, but they know that getting started is the most important step, that forward motion is better than passivity, that action conquers fear. They wage a never-ending fight against negativity, both from within and without. Like the sage Seneca, whose words were a spur to courage, they say to themselves, "Let us train our minds to desire what the situation demands."

Her Excitement Made It Happen

VALERIE BARGER SPEAKS with wonder about the past four years, still finding it miraculous that her life has changed so much. She had been struggling, ill, and living with a growing mountain of obligations that cast a darkening shadow over her life. Then one day a spark was lit,

Her life was totally transformed: Valerie Barger, with daughter, Liberty, twenty-seven, and son-in-law, Tim Andis, twenty-eight, in Paris.

a spark that allowed her to concentrate her passion and fighting spirit on a new and exciting mission. From that moment on, her life was totally transformed.

It was as if an amazing chain reaction had begun, a series of events in which she was the catalyst. In short order, it brought into her life wealth, freedom, travel, new friends around the world, health, happiness, and a renewed relationship with her family. It brought the ability to pay cash for everything, to write a check for $30,000 for a family vacation in Europe "without blinking an eye," or to remodel the houses on her property in Washington's Yakima Valley, where she works, plays, and gives thanks for her new life. "Sometimes I say, 'Oh Lord, how did this happen?' It feels like a crazy tornado has come into my life and totally changed everything. It took everything about my life and tossed it up in the air and it's come down all different."

Just four years ago Valerie Barger was a teacher in charge of her school's gifted program. Despite the enthusiasm and love for her students that she poured into her job as a middle school teacher, the system was frustrating and there were always more bills to pay. She keenly felt the challenge and responsibility of keeping her students excited and motivated. But her personal life was full of pressures. "I was literally living from paycheck to paycheck, trying to squeeze out a few hundred dollars a month for myself. I owed on the house."

The Day It All Changed

She remembers with total clarity that day when everything changed. "I was with a friend who was ill. I was trying to help her find something that would aid in her recovery." As a former cancer patient, Valerie was aware of alternative treatments and wanted to discuss them with her friend.

"I was at her house when I discovered a tape she had never listened to. I asked her, 'What is this about?'" The friend told her it had been given to her. The events that came next seem like small occurrences, but they are imprinted indelibly on Valerie's memory. Each little step took Valerie closer to a new destiny. If this were a movie you'd hear dramatic music playing as she picks up the cassette in its blue and yellow packaging, examines it, and feels her curiosity piqued. Carrying the tape outside, "I threw it in my car's tape player, and I got thoroughly jazzed." It wasn't that the tape itself was so extraordinary. In fact, the production was not even that high quality, she recalls. But on listening to it something clicked. "I realized every friend I had needed what they were talking about on the tape." Unsure of how to follow up but determined to do so, she phoned the couple whose names were written on the back of the cassette.

> "You discover the belief in yourself that comes from others. This is enormously powerful. What stops us is doubt and self doubt. But in networking, even if you don't personally believe in yourself, others will encourage you and show you how you can be self-sufficient."
>
> —Scott Kiehn, Mannatech

"I called them and said, 'What is this about?'" They told her about Mannatech, the company that had originated "glyco-nutritionals" and was at the forefront of the business of neutraceuticals, or scientifically-based nutrition products. It went on to become a high-growth international company with proprietary products in the nutritional and skin care fields. As she got a sense of the Mannatech products and opportunity, "I got more excited," recalls Barger. "I said, 'I know a bunch of friends who could use this stuff.'" Years earlier, Valerie had been in Amway, and she quickly grasped the nature of the business being presented. With growing enthusiasm Valerie then all but reversed the normal roles of recruiter and recruitee. "These people"—their names were Steve and Tina Shelley—"lived three hours away from me. I wanted them to overnight product to me," she recalls. "I wanted it right away. I was real aggressive," she says, in a voice that conveys both her ebullience and determination.

She also realized she needed more tapes, and she asked to have ten sets overnighted to her. When they arrived, she gave them to the first ten people she saw.

"Are You Excited Too?"

With each individual she would say, "Do you have time to listen to it?" If they didn't, she didn't give it to them. If they did listen to the tape, afterward she would say, "So what do you think? Are you excited too?"

She urged Steve and Tina to come to her house quickly and explain the opportunity. On Sunday night, they promised to make the trip the next Friday. "Get as many people as you can," they told her.

With her zeal increasing by the moment, Valerie began urging people to show up at her house. She persuaded her cousin to drive for three hours to attend. Valerie knew little at this point. She was simply getting people to agree by the power of her enthusiasm. "They came to the meeting because I seemed excited. When everybody showed up at my house, just seeing all those people, that's what was exciting," she says.

On Friday night, thirty-five people showed up at Valerie's house. "People were all over my living room," says Valerie. They were sitting on the floors and in the doorways and in the halls and up the staircase.

Steve and Tina Shelley traveled three hours to get there. The Shelleys had been in the business for four months, and were then making about $3,000 a month. They were a bit overwhelmed and bewildered at finding thirty-five people waiting for them, all full of excitement and anticipation but with little knowledge.

The meeting had a few false starts. At one point, the Shelleys put a tape on the compensation plan in the VCR. With so many visitors in the room, people had a hard time even seeing the television set, much less concentrating on the tape's content. Eventually Valerie said, "Please turn off the TV and talk to us. We just want to hear the story."

An Explosion

The pivotal nature of the event is underscored by Valerie's description of what happened next. She calls it "an explosion."

"We listened, and everybody decided to sign up or use the products. Then an explosion happened. People started seeing immediate results. We started seeing wonderful things happen." The physical improvements they perceived fired their zeal about the products and their conviction about the opportunity.

Valerie talked Steve and Tina into coming over several more times. "After the first month, I made $350 and I thought, 'Maybe we are on to something here.' We all started making money together. I was the first person in the valley to do this."

Barger was "used to being in front of middle school kids," she notes. "But to be in front of a bunch of adults was difficult. I made myself do it. I forced myself to go to trainings that were hours away. Over the next few months I took little steps at a time. Then, in January 1995, "I got the vision when I went to the first national conference, my first annual doodah. I scrounged up every penny and then kicked myself all the way to Dallas because of the expense, and because I had to take a day off work without pay to fly down there."

At the conference she met "a gal named Roberta and I sat at a luncheon with her. She was a naturopath with three hundred people in her organization." At one point Valerie asked her, "Do you really think this company is going to go anywhere?" In the years that followed—and as Mannatech soared past the $150 million mark in rev-

"I owned my own hair salon for eight years and I place a big value on being my own boss. But that kind of ownership tied me down. Your customers don't like you going on vacation. Now I'm like, 'Yahoo!' I have more fun. I still have many friendships with my former customers, but I don't have my hands in their hair."

—*Juanita Kiehn, Mannatech*

enues in 1998—her question would be the occasion for a bond of humor between the two.

"If They Can Do It . . ."

That first convention was a turning point. "I watched people," remembers Barger. She saw real people, on stage and off, and took note of how much money they were making. "They were regular people, some of them extremely frumpy. I said, 'I'll be darned. If they can do it, so can I.' When I went to Dallas I was making $1,500 a month. Within nine months I would be making more money than when I was teaching."

Inspired by the conference, and filled with confidence, Barger returned home with the view, "It's you and me, Lord. Let's go for it." She became a whirlwind of activity. "I filled my calendar with appointments. I met with leaders. I held barbecues at my house. By that August I was making $6,500 a month. Then it started leaping. In September it was $8,000 a month. I recall when it passed the $10,000 per month mark. I was hyperventilating when I went to look at my check. That's when I started to make changes in my life. I got debt-free. I paved the drive, built a three-car garage, and remodeled my huge dairy barn. I did remodeling for my daughter, who lives next door. I put up an ornamental iron fence around our little family compound."

By January 1996, one year after the national convention, her monthly check was $17,000. In February it was $23,000, in March $35,000, and by April $40,000 per month. She was now making more in a single month from Mannatech than she'd made in a whole year of teaching.

Life Had Changed

A trip to Europe for one month with her son, Lars Hanson, twenty-eight, her daughter, Liberty Andis, twenty-seven, and her son-in-law Tim, twenty-eight, helped instill in her that her life had fundamentally changed. Rather than scrounging for pennies, she was able to spend nearly the equivalent of a previous year's teaching salary for an experience that was fun, deeply meaningful, and guilt-free. She still recalls the trip with immense pleasure in her voice: "I've never eaten so much wonderful food in my entire life," she begins. Then she recalls highlights of the adventure in a rush of exhilaration—"traveling through the Swiss Alps, going down into Venice, seeing the wine country in France, staying in the lake district of Italy at a resort visited by the kings and queens of Europe, having a breakfast of freshly picked wild raspberries and strawberries, seeing the South of France, the Loire Valley, the wonderful chateaux."

Valerie still laughs with astonishment about "coming home from the trip and there was all that wonderful residual income waiting for me, and it was outrageous. I didn't even have to work, and it just kept on coming and growing. It's just pretty incredible to me that this type of business exists," she says. "All I really feel like I've done is look for people who are open-minded and willing to take a risk. We have a wonderful team. We've helped lots of friends become free. We've helped them get a vision of who they really are, who they were created to be. We go on little trips together. We network and bond. My lifestyle is utterly, completely different than ever before. My time is my own. I do what I want. If I choose to take a month off, I do it."

Profoundly Grateful

Valerie is a dynamo who laughs a lot. But she is also someone profoundly grateful for what life has bestowed on her. "This is totally God-given. God has given me a gift. This opportunity is a gift. Now I try to help other people identify the gift that's been given to them. I help them find their destiny. I have a lot of fun. I tell a lot of crazy things that I have done. I can help others realize that I am a regular person just like them. None of us are any different except for what people do with what they have. The problem is a lot of people do nothing."

Valerie remembers the friend at whose house she found the tape: "She didn't want to have anything to do with the tape or the opportunity. She wouldn't come to the meeting. She simply refused." By contrast, Valerie accidentally picked it up—"except I don't believe there are accidents"—and got hooked.

Ray Gebauer of Mannatech says his business "is about creating miracles in peoples' lives, and about bringing people more freedom." Ray says: "Our mission includes five different levels of freedom: The first is health freedom. That means having vitality, energy, and freedom from disease. The second level is having free products for the rest of your life. Third, there's the freedom from having extra income. Level four is time freedom—to be able to work out of your home, be your own boss, and avoid fighting traffic. Level five is *unlimited freedom*—here you are truly free to do *whatever* you want with your life without having to work or worry about money. You can live your dreams!"

Valerie's story is strikingly different from others in one respect. The initial opportunity was one she recognized and seized upon her own. It wasn't pushed upon her. No one proselytized her. Her drive and tenacity made things happen.

"I didn't try to act like I knew about this. When I first started I photocopied everything myself. We didn't have all the wonderful promotional material that we do now. I would pay the school for the paper. I gave them a few cents for using the copy machine. The excitement is what carries it. The tape itself wasn't even very good." In fact, she no longer uses it. But it was the catalyst that got her going. Her experience calls to mind the words of a renowned turn-of-the-century self-help writer, Orison Swett Marden, who wrote, "Don't wait for extraordinary opportunities. Seize ordinary ones and make them great."

"We Just Jumped In"

"I kept saying, 'Wouldn't it be great if it works the way it says on this tape. I told my cousin, who drove three hours for that first meeting,

'What if this thing really does something? We could each make four grand a month.' I didn't know anything. We all just jumped in—and we've all become close friends."

Valerie is thrilled that her friends have freed themselves from jobs and businesses that were not satisfying. "I like to see people be the best that they can be," she says. She recalls the teacher that taught down the hall from her and attended the first meeting at her house. "It took an entire year to get her on board. Now she's at the head of my biggest group."

Valerie also recalls with a laugh the way she breezed past the jealousy or skepticism of others. During her first year a feature story on her budding Mannatech business appeared in a magazine that got posted in the faculty lounge. As if to mock the opportunity, one of her colleagues drew a mustache on her photograph. Undaunted, Valerie treated the put-down as a joke.

Harking back to that first week when she gathered thirty-five people to attend a session on something she knew little about, she recalls just one individual who reacted with scorn. "He said, 'Valerie, you're nuts. This is a scam.' I just said, 'Give me back the tape,' and I went on to the next person."

Of her penchant for action, Valerie says, "When I am on the trail of something I follow it to the end." She adds: "I do know that if I am really excited about something—if for example there is a book I think others should read, I will buy copies and send one to everybody I know."

Encouraging Leaders to Step Forward

But Valerie also wants others to step forward. She likes the saying by Chinese philosopher Lao-tse: "When the great leader's work is done, the people say, 'We did it ourselves.'" With every group, she is always eager to reach that stage where she can move into the background and let a new leader take charge. "I really push people to be all that they can be. I will push as long as it takes—until a leader emerges. I help people become leaders and do it themselves."

In addition to daughter Liberty and her husband Tim (who are the parents of four-year-old Tucker), Valerie's son Lars works in the business, which is headquartered in Valerie's huge house. Periodically, her father drives his motor home up and stays on the property. In contrast to her teaching days, visitors now present no problem because "My life has changed. My time is my own."

She looks forward to her trips as a way to mix business and pleasure, as with her recent trip to Australia. Whether she works or plays, she knows the income will keep growing.

She recalls once returning from a trip after UPS had delivered checks to her home in her absence. One check had blown free, and she didn't see it. A few days later she looked out on the porch "and I saw this funny looking thing, all rain damaged, and I went out to see what it was. It was an envelope and it had a check in it. It was just a little check. I never even missed it. It was only $4,000."

Comeback from Pain

"PLEASE, DEAR GOD, give me strength."

"It hurts so much."

"Please help me."

Countless people have uttered such heartrending pleas as they sought desperately to ease their physical or mental anguish.

For Mike Williams, there were layers of unbearable pain. First came the agony of his shattered knees. It was a terrible, wrenching pain. But Mike's physical hurts were nothing compared to the psychic pain he was enduring as a husband and father who had to witness the suffering of his loved ones.

The head-on collision with a drunk driver had crushed the pelvis and legs of his wife, Julie, who was left with chronic arthritis in her hips. Mike's daughter, Amy, suffered severe head trauma with progressively worsening nerve damage. Mike knew they hurt, and his heart bled for them.

But another layer of even more excruciating pain existed for Mike in the post-traumatic doubts that made him writhe in torment. He was wracked with guilt and ceaselessly plagued with questions about his own actions: "Could I have done anything different? Should I have run off the road into the ditch?" Though he was blameless, the doubts tortured his soul as the conditions of his wife and daughter continued to deteriorate.

Self-Doubt Due to Failures

The heavy burden on Mike's mind and body was all the harder to bear because of the depressing fog of self-doubt in which he had been living due to his business failures. "I failed in three businesses. I never worked so hard in my life, only to lose money," says Williams.

Mike had failed first in his attempt to sell jewelry to convention-goers. He then failed in his try at selling mechanisms designed to save customers money on their utility bills. Mike's last failure was as the proprietor of four clock shops in different shopping malls. Despite working morning till night seven days a week, he could never earn much above the overhead. Squeezed beyond his limits, Mike became overextended and lost his credit. "In 1988 and 1989, I lost my retail shops, my home, and everything," he recalls. "I remember the day I lost that third business. I lived one and a half hours from the mall in Illinois and had to drive back home to Missouri."

> "For a business to grow, we all have to help each other. We have to share stories and paint the picture of what can happen. You can see the tears in their eyes when they see it, when they get it."
>
> —*Betty Wolf, Reliv*

"We're Losing Everything"

It was a long ride for Mike that day. He recalls how filled with desperation he was. "I believed success was never going to be for me. I had to go back home and tell them, 'Hey, we're losing everything, but don't worry.' I had done that twice before. I couldn't say it to them again. This time I lost all hope. I was really depressed."

Today Mike's heart goes out to anyone in a situation like the one he faced. Pain and depression had robbed him of his confidence to the point that he was unable to face the day. The worst agony was the fear he felt for his family. He and Julie and their four children were living in a tiny apartment, and the thought of being evicted and having nowhere to go filled him with a deep despair. Life seemed to have closed off its options to him. Without funds and without hope, he found it hard even to imagine a way out.

Soon, though, opportunity would knock on his door.

The Story of Reliv and Dr. Kalogris

AS A PARATROOPER during World War II, Theodore P. Kalogris received back injuries that continued to bother him years later. After earning his Ph.D. in microbiology, Dr. Kalogris worked as a researcher at the National Institutes of Health and as a consultant to the World Health Organization. All the time he was building his career, Dr. Kalogris suffered from chronic back pain. In searching for relief, he developed a nutritional supplement made from vitamins, minerals, and proteins—a formula that included the essential amino acids the human body is unable to synthesize and must be obtained through dietary sources. Encouraged by the effects the supplement had on him, Dr. Kalogris began eagerly giving it away.

Among the people to whom Kalogris gave his supplement was a successful businessman, Robert L. Montgomery, after the two met in 1982 in Kansas City, Missouri. Immediately, Montgomery noticed the effect it had on him. His energy increased dramatically. His sinus problems and headaches disappeared. His days became more productive and he was thinking more clearly. Montgomery used the product for the next several years, as did his family.

While having coffee together in 1982, Kalogris quoted a phrase to Montgomery: "Be ashamed to die until you have scored a victory for mankind." As a boy in Greece, Kalogris had heard that advice from his father.

"When you get into a business with people who are really excited, it is fun," says Betty Wolf of Reliv. "You want to be part of a group that is excited about their future. I looked at Reliv's conventions, with their excitement and enthusiasm, and contrasted them with a corporation's boring office parties with their alcohol and politics," she says. "At our conference there was so much noise that the speakers could barely break in. They didn't need little tricks and ice breakers, like in corporate America."

The Words Inspired a Company

The words struck a chord in Montgomery, who continued to think of them over the next few years. They eventually helped inspire the creation of a new company that was the brainchild of the two men.

Over the course of his career, Montgomery had bought and sold two multimillion dollar companies, including a food research and manufacturing firm. He had also become increasingly aware of the potential of network marketing. With his passion for achievement now awakened by Kalogris and his product, Montgomery set aside the idea of retirement. Two other factors also played a role in that decision. The first was his remarkably fast recovery from brain surgery for a nonmalignant tumor. He was convinced that Kalogris's product had helped speed his recovery. The second was his growing conviction that network marketing was going to become the most powerful method of reaching consumers in the 1990s and beyond.

Montgomery moved to put his dreams into action in 1985. The product was christened Reliv, thanks to an associate of his who told him the word was French for "return to youth."

Mike's Comeback

MIKE WILLIAMS'S LIFE was deteriorating on every front. Most pressing, his rent was due. That posed a problem as Mike had only $56 in his pocket. To compound the problem, he was unemployed, and Julie had never worked out of the house. "I wanted my wife to be able to stay at home if she wanted," said Mike. "I wanted my kids to have what I never had, a home that was a sanctuary, so they would feel safe and secure."

"If you enjoy people and want to help them, this is the natural vehicle," says Phil Wolf of Reliv. "The fact is that you can help others, and be rewarded for helping others become successful. Self-centered people don't last long."

But now they seemed to be trapped, without resources. Could it have been a mistake for Julie to stay out of the job market? "She didn't know what to do and I didn't know what to do either. And I couldn't find a job," he remembers. Only much later would he view their situation as having been a blessing in disguise.

It was at that time that someone told Mike about a rapidly growing company in the area called Reliv International. Before long Mike had heard someone present the Reliv story.

Just how badly Mike's spirit had been broken is revealed by his reaction to seeing the presentation. What did he think when he saw it? "I thought that this guy could probably do the business but that I would fail."

What did capture his interest was the product. "I was an avid weight lifter and runner before the accident. Then I got that furniture disease—all my weight went into the drawers," he joked. The agonizingly slow rehabilitation of his knees coupled with his depression left him listless, without energy or enthusiasm.

Their Health and Spirits Revived

"I started taking the product and within weeks I got back the feeling of well-being. My daughter, who couldn't hold down food if and when she ate, started taking it too. Then she started eating again. Within ninety days you couldn't tell that we had been in an accident. Even my wife had less pain."

With both his spirits and health rapidly reviving, Mike decided to take a close look at Reliv. His investigation convinced him that here was an extraordinary product and a superb business opportunity. While he always carefully avoids making medical claims, he knew that his belief in the product—his total conviction in the powerful effect it had had on him and his family—would make him unstoppable.

Surging with newfound energy: On discovering Reliv, Mike Williams developed a new level of confidence; Julie regained her health.

Mike followed two simple rules. The first was that "I wouldn't sell the product unless the customer promised to take it consistently for thirty days." On following up, he was usually pleased to find that people had become "emotionally attached to the product." It was a key part of his philosophy, based on his belief that "people need to connect emotionally to be able to sell."

Before presenting the opportunity, "I would warn them that if this stuff is as good as I said, then we could both become wealthy." In all that he did, says Mike, "I was setting them up to succeed."

"The second thing I did," he says, "was to be picky about who I would work with. I wanted people with a desire to succeed. I wanted people whose most developed muscle wasn't the one in their thumb that controls the remote for the TV."

Running with the Opportunity

Mike ran with the opportunity, becoming more confident, disciplined, and mentally tougher every day. Feeling an exciting new vigor rising within him, he leapt over obstacles that would have defeated him just a short time earlier. He hustled through meetings in thirty minutes, with his car running all the while—because he knew if he turned it off it wouldn't restart. Facing repeated rejections in Missouri, where his previous businesses had failed, he headed out of state, where he could build a new credibility.

Mike still had plenty of adversity facing him in the days ahead, but now he was powered by a deep faith in Reliv and a growing belief in himself. Determined to be a part of Reliv's future success, he was not about to let small matters stand in his way. "Once when I was out of town doing a meeting I'd had nothing to eat the entire day. I didn't even have the money to buy a sandwich. If I bought food, I wouldn't have had enough money to pay for the hotel. Somebody pushed their food tray out into the hall. Half the hamburger was left and thank God they had cut it with a knife. I had it for lunch."

Once a problem arose when Mike was in Chicago showing the plan. A guy at the meeting decided he was running a scam and called the police. Williams had to show the program to some officers. If it happened today, he notes, he would try to sign them up.

"I worked hard but it became fun when I set people up to win. I let them know I was going to win and they could come with me. There is nothing better than when people look you in the eye and they know that you know where you are going," he says.

> "If you focus your mind on your business and the other people who are involved in it, you can succeed. There are people out there who need what you have."
>
> —Phil Wolf, Reliv

Rebound

The company suffered a blow in 1993 when Midwestern floods inundated the Chesterfield, Missouri, manufacturing facility, frightening away some distributors who were faint of heart. The company rebounded, however, and today Mike has fifty thousand distributors in his organization (including Tom Pinnock of Missouri, who was profiled in chapter 6).

"I am the epitome of 'anybody can do it,'" says Mike. "I am not a public speaker. I murder the business," he laughs. His downline put together a list of "Mikeletts"—words he uses all the time and mispronounces. It turned out to be a selling point. As he became successful, people said of the opportunity, "Wow, if that guy could do it, it must be good."

Retirement—and Rising Income

Mike retired for a time when his income hit $50,000 a month. He stopped all activity, focusing only on servicing his existing customers. After no work for four years his income had risen to $70,000 a month. "I started getting up at the crack of nine and watched TV till later in the day when it would hit me that I wanted lunch."

Julie told him to go back to work. Mike wasn't keen on the idea at first, but he realized that his four children would inherit his business. Mike figured that he could quadruple his income for them. This time it was easier. "You do the exact same thing to make $5,000 or $50,000 a month. The more one does, and the longer he does it, the bigger it gets."

"This is a simple business," he reminds us, adding: "People fail only because they quit."

The simple lesson is, he says: "Keep fighting. Don't quit."

10

Trailblazers

T HEY CREATE THEIR own paths. They explore new lands and
new concepts. In their willingness to change, to leave behind
what is old and familiar and embrace what is new and untried, they
display a courage that inspires their followers.

The Business Elite

GARY AND VICKI Morgan are trailblazers whose accomplishments
have made life easier for those who came after them. He was a resourceful entrepreneur. She had a successful career in international
business. Both had the skills and expertise to make their way in the
world. The details of their story are illuminating—but first, an
overview:

Gary, born in England, was a young entrepreneur intent on seeking out and exploiting the best opportunities, wherever he found
them. "My dream was to have my own business," he says. In 1988, at

the age of twenty-four, he came to the United States as part of a two-year, round-the-world trip. His goal: to travel through India, Thailand, and other countries, checking out business opportunities while playing professional rugby along the way.

Confident and Savvy

Gary epitomized a breed of young opportunity seekers who were capable of crossing borders and mastering new situations. His background as an athlete and London bobby helped equip him with the confidence and street-savvy that typify the breed. But all his strategizing hadn't prepared Gary for meeting Vicki. After spending time with her in Boston, he suddenly saw the United States zoom to the top of his list of attractive destinations. He sold his plane ticket and began exploring ventures on American soil, successfully leaping over a host of obstacles posed by his foreign citizenship and the country's tough new immigration laws. Four years later the two moved to Los Angeles and were married. Along the way, Gary sized up the fitness market, ran his own operation selling exercise equipment, and got early wind of a hot new company called Envion. Impressed by its nutrition and performance products, he first began retailing them, and over time became a highly successful distributor. Today the Morgans live in a dream house in lushly beautiful Palos Verdes Estates south of Los Angeles.

For her part, Vicki was also part of the young international business elite. After earning her M.B.A. at Miami University of Ohio, she worked with the French government in the area of international business development. "If a U.S. company was looking to set up a manufacturing plant or sales office, I would work with them," she says. She met with presidents and vice presidents of major Fortune 500 companies and "learned a tremendous amount."

"I Came, I Saw, I Conquered"

Gary and Vicki speak of their achievements in modest terms. But it is clear that they belonged to that small population of businesspeople capable of entering a new industry, a new market, or a new country, and in short order being able to proclaim, "I came, I saw, I conquered." On the one hand, they possessed more self-reliance and competence than many people entering network marketing. On the other, their very sophistication at times created roadblocks that kept them from capitalizing on the network marketing opportunity as rapidly as they might have—though, fortunately, all worked out for the best.

They climbed the heights quickly—once they understood the principles of network marketing success. Gary and Vicki Morgan live in beautiful Palos Verdes Estates.

By nature, neither Gary nor Vicki were inclined to dive into a business on the basis of someone else's assurances. Anecdotes and examples of other people's successes left them unpersuaded. Before allowing themselves to be convinced, they sought to gain their own bottom-line understanding.

The ancient Chinese strategist Sun Tzu, in his classic, *The Art of War,* describes several types or levels of understanding. The highest level involves thoroughly grasping the situation yourself. At times, however, the so-called second level of understanding can be preferable. It's marked by recognizing the expertise of others and accepting their guidance.

Not many people in network marketing had the "right stuff" to impress Gary and Vicki, or to win their confidence. One person did. He was Randy Gage, who'd been hired by Envion's founder and CEO, Matthew Freese. In the face of Gage's forceful and unrelenting reiteration of the dynamics of network marketing, the Morgans began to open their minds. One might say Gary and Vicki downshifted into

Sun Tzu's second level of understanding, allowing themselves to put a measure of trust in Gage's expertise. The first step—as is often the case when setting out to learn a new body of knowledge—was adopting the right mindset and attitudes. Getting to this stage is more important than learning any specific skills or knowledge. Once your mindset is "tuned in," you can often learn the specifics with astonishing speed.

Gage had spent years refining the science of creating "a self-perpetuating, multilevel money machine." Gary and Vicki listened to his reasoning. Each worked out and thought through the logic separately, at different times. But in both their cases, it seems, any teacher less insistent and commanding than Gage would have failed to win their respect and attention. Both had to undergo an enormous change in outlook.

A Tough Transition

Looking back, Gary speaks of the importance of personal growth. For him, that meant relinquishing the fierce independence and near-truculence of the traditional entrepreneur and adopting a mindset more appropriate to network marketing, a new form of entrepreneurship. It was a tough transition. He sees himself as having been "stubborn, strong-willed, aggressive, insecure, and resistant to learning." He's probably being harsh on himself to say all those traits were symptoms of "immaturity," for they represent attitudes that are characteristic of entrepreneurs. Being alert to the point of suspicion or having a stubborn conviction about your own ideas is often just what you need to succeed in a high-risk situation. As for being "resistant to learning," that's known as not being gullible. An entrepreneur planning to set down in India or Thailand—or anywhere, for that matter—would be well advised to be wary, lest he lose his shirt. Gary also criticizes himself for being "selfish," noting how he had to overcome his antagonism toward helping others and his reluctance toward sharing information—two crucial components of network marketing. Yet, being selfish is no weakness of character for high-risk capitalists, who generally guard their company secrets with a ferocity unparalleled outside defense establishments.

So when Gary says, "I have mellowed from the insecure and aggressive and very stubborn person I was," what he's actually revealing is that being pleasant, friendly, and congenial—while suicidal for the old-style entrepreneur and those in many occupations—is a fitting state of mind for a network marketer. And that's great news, for most of us would much prefer to earn a living while being agreeably mellow—as long as we knew we weren't taking the primrose path to the poorhouse. That it's possible to achieve the level of success the Morgans have while also having the luxury of mellowness seems almost too desirable to be true. And yet it is.

Vicki Was Skeptical

One more brushstroke in our overview: If Gary was tough to convince, Vicki was all but impossible, by normal standards. She remained steadfastly "skeptical, if not hostile" to network marketing—even *after* the financial rewards were rolling in.

While some spouses lag behind in supporting a mate, in the Morgans' case, "Gary had reached Diamond level before I had even attended an event," says Vicki.

When Gary invited Vicki to a meeting of the top distributors in the company, she was reluctant to go. "I did not want to go to the meeting of Diamond Directors because it meant taking two or three days out of the week," she explains. But, "I went anyway," she adds.

Now, conventions were nothing new for Vicki, but the Envion event in Las Vegas was something different indeed. "I was going through the MGM Grand on my own," Vicki recalls. "I heard music and realized it was coming from the room where I was headed." The spectacle she came upon was "definitely not what you would call a corporate event"—at least not one resembling any she had ever seen. "I went in and there was music playing and people

> "I believe with every fiber of my being that personal development is the stealth ingredient of network marketing."
>
> —Randy Gage,
> network marketing consultant

were on the chairs dancing," she says, noting that the sight did nothing to put her at ease. "I sat down with my arms crossed, reminding myself that I was here to be open-minded—even though I wasn't."

The speakers included Envion's CEO. Recalls Vicki, "I had met Matthew Freese once before. I listened to him speak, and his sincerity does come across." Vicki's next statement is a good measure of her lack of receptiveness. Even though, eventually, "he won me over," Vicki concedes that at the time, "I probably saw that sincerity as naive."

Randy Gage's Business Principles

The next speaker was Randy Gage. Now here at least was someone who appeared to be in touch with business reality as Vicki understood it. "He was talking about business principles that made sense to me," she says. "He really touched on the psychology of business," adds Vicki, whose undergraduate degree is in psychology. "I uncrossed my arms and leaned forward. This was an eye-opening experience. I was actually still uncomfortable most of the weekend. It still wasn't for me. But I understood why it was for Gary. I began attending major events. I went to local meetings." In time Vicki got to the point where "the more you hear the more it starts to make sense. I saw that I was going to work every day and spending all these hours—and Gary's paycheck was not just meeting mine, it was exceeding mine." When she took a look at the hours she spent working and traveling, "I realized I was missing out on the lifestyle issue. A year and a half ago I left my job."

Dream House

Today the Morgans' lifestyle centers around their home in its paradise-like setting. "This was a dream house," says Vicki. "We walked through the front door and I just as soon knew we were buying. I loved it because it is charming, nicely landscaped, with rosebushes, and a beautiful stone wall, and stained glass windows, and an ocean view." As they talk, a wild peacock screeches in the garden. "This is prettier than Beverly Hills," says Gary. "There are beautiful flowers everywhere. There are pine and eucalyptus trees, and you can smell the scent of eucalyptus in the air. You're nearly surrounded by an ocean view, and we can sometimes see Santa Catalina Island. We get cool ocean breezes."

Gary adds, "People want to know how we in our early thirties could afford to be up here." That is a good question, and "up here" is a good choice of words. In more ways than one, the Morgans live their lives at an impressive elevation. They climbed the heights relatively quickly, compared to the struggles of others. But their success was far from overnight or automatic. In order to get where they are today, both had to struggle with and overcome past preconceptions.

To succeed in network marketing, everyone needs to accept that "learning to grow and expand is okay," says Gary. Many people assume that if you desire personal growth you are admitting you are deficient. It's an inherently negative viewpoint that assumes only those viewed as "inadequate" would want to change. So one of the most fundamental messages that network marketing leaders need to convey is that a desire to improve "doesn't mean there is anything wrong with you," says Gary.

Start with the premise that everyone and everything can change and improve, and that growing is an "integral part of success," advises Gary. He adds, "Personal development is integral to the business." If you don't embrace it, "chances are you aren't going to make it," he says. "In network marketing you deal with a lot of people who haven't had success and don't understand how personal development is important to succeeding."

But "you have to be careful about how you bring that up," he cautions. "Many people consider the personal development mission to be the 'cult aspect' of network marketing," says Gary. The media, for

> "Network marketing is a radical, unique approach to business. It's about empowering others. It's about going deep into their psyches—locating their innate abilities, talents, and natural success programming—then nurturing them through the unfolding process of bringing these to light."
>
> —*Randy Gage, author of* How to Build a Multi-Level Money Machine

example, may equate the high-spirited conventions held by MLM companies as evidence that the groups engage in indoctrination the way cults do. The comparison seems ridiculously farfetched when you consider that most schools or colleges would not merit the term *cult-like* even though they have pep rallies, slogans, insignias, and fervently devoted members. As for personal growth, its purpose in network marketing is to help the individual achieve his or her own personal goals—precisely the opposite of what cults are seeking.

Build with Care

As the Morgans describe the care needed to build a multilevel money machine, they articulately highlight both the macro and micro perspectives. Like many distributors, they extol the importance of relationships: "What makes this business so powerful and beautiful is the integral part played by personal relationships," says Gary. The Morgans also help you grasp the painstaking care needed to create each such relationship, and how taken together these personal connections can form the basis of a vast and effective network.

The strength of the network is found in the bonding experiences newcomers undergo in the early stages of building their businesses— when they are "in the trenches." By working closely with them at this stage, sponsors help create "lifetime bonds"—the type that get forged only in an intensely shared experience, "like serving in the military." It is based on "your demonstrating to this person right in the first few weeks how you are giving up your time and efforts for them," says Gary. "What you do in the initial weeks creates the bond. People see that you care about more than the paycheck. There is the warmth. There is the sharing of the struggle—a struggle to get free, perhaps from credit card debt, or from a boss." Sponsor and newcomer "have a common cause, and the sharing of a common bond." Remarkable as it may seem, "within

> "Relationships are everything in this business. Sponsor people you like because you will be working with them for the rest of your life."
>
> —*Randy Gage*

weeks they have a relationship that can be stronger than the ones they have with their own brothers," says Gary.

"People are very vulnerable when they first come to this business," notes Gary. By being aware of this, sponsors can use it in positive ways to introduce an entire system. "You are raising very personal questions, including: What are your goals? What do you want to accomplish?" he notes. "Here you are getting into what that person's secret hopes and ambitions are. You are showing empathy. You are making a commitment to help. They are seeing you help, seeing you listen. You are investing in that person and taking the time to care."

Bonding, then, "is what creates the environment"—an environment marked by compassionate individuals willing to help others and committed to doing so. "Beyond the paycheck those personal relationships are what come to be the most rewarding thing," he says.

Fear in the Corporations

Vicki's background gives her insight into MLM's contrast with the corporate experience. One of the major fears in a big organization, she notes, "is the fear of exposing your weaknesses." The corporation is marked by "boundaries and fear," adds Gary. There's the fear of making a mistake, of losing face, of not advancing, or of being fired. In the context of the corporation, these fears are realistic rather than merely neurotic. Internal competition is a fact of life, and people are vulnerable to it.

Says Vicki, "In corporate America, you tend to hide your weaknesses and put out your strengths. In this business you are encouraged to put out your weaknesses and you don't feel you have to hide anything. You can expose those weaknesses to people; you can be open. That is part of the exposure Gary was talking about. Once you have gotten into that territory with others, there is a bond there for life." And these strong personal relationships result in motivated and successful distributors. It is a dynamic that is unique to network marketing, explains Gary.

Gary is keenly aware that network marketing demands more from its leaders. "Unlike traditional managers, you only get to use one part of the carrot and the stick," he notes. "In network marketing, if you don't show up for work, nothing happens. As a leader, you need to inspire people to take action," says Gary, because they are not required to obey you. The entire experience, he notes, "develops you enormously. Your communication skills have to be expanded and enhanced" so that you can give others the support they need.

Leaders also gain effectiveness through the force of their conviction. Here Gary draws a sharp distinction between simply having an opinion, on the one hand, and holding a genuine belief. Such a distinction, he maintains, is crucial to succeeding in the business. "I had an opinion about network marketing," Gary says. By contrast, "Randy Gage had a belief, a deeply held belief. That is much more powerful than a mere opinion," he says, adding, "If you fuel that belief, you eventually will have success." In fact, he adds, the force of your conviction "will draw people to you."

As a measure of both their own and Envion's success, in 1998 Gary and Vicki addressed the annual convention of the Direct Selling Association. It was the same meeting at which Matt Freese was honored as a Legend in the Making. At a social gathering, Gary took the opportunity to probe the minds of CEOs from some of the major member corporations. Specifically, he questioned whether, as corporate executives, they were able to grasp the enormous role that the supportive culture of distributors played in the success of their companies.

A People Business

As executives, asked Gary, could they begin to appreciate a mindset and values so remote from the concerns that drove big organizations? The consensus answer was "Yes, because our bottom line is people. In other businesses, you are trying to get rid of people. They are just one resource—and your aim is to reduce your dependence upon them. By contrast, in network marketing, you always want more, not fewer, people."

For all their understanding of the business, when it comes to their own decisions and actions, the Morgans ultimately express themselves in very personal terms. Prior to putting her efforts into Envion, "I traveled a lot," Vicki says. "My direction was climbing the corporate ladder. I couldn't see any other way. I had to keep working hard. What I didn't realize is that I was making important sacrifices. I was missing out on spending time with my husband, my parents."

She looks back now on a time when "Gary and I went a whole month and saw each other for five days. I kept saying, 'It's okay, it will be better some day.' What this business has given me is time—time that I would normally be spending on an airplane. What I am getting out of it now is relationships."

Now Diamonds, they are aiming to become Double Diamonds, a level at which distributors can earn $40,000 per month or higher. While they agree that "we've done pretty good so far," in Gary's words, they are also thinking about "climbing the next mountain."

"Now, we look at the $10 million houses and say, 'Why not us?'"

However far they advance, the Morgans intend to stay mellow, and to remain grateful that Envion is "a happy, healthy place to be."

She's Number One

AS THE DYNAMIC American woman in her seventies walks into the room, the Japanese audience leaps to its feet with a booming chant: "Ichiban. Mama-san," they shout in unison.

Mama-san is number one.

As anyone can see, Mama-san—or, if you prefer, Mary Lou Wilson, from Granbury, Texas—knows how to build a downline. When her company, Enrich International, an innovator in the field of dietary supplements, opened for business in Japan, she was well prepared—and that's putting it mildly. On arriving in Japan, she flew into action with meetings and trainings that went on more or less nonstop for seventeen days. During that period she put three people on her first level and worked diligently with them to sign up a group of 379. From that base she expanded over the following three months

Friendships are the secret of this business, says dynamic distributor Mary Lou Wilson, who stays in close touch with her organization. A meeting in Utah with some of her top leaders from Japan included: Front row from left: Mr. Hasegawa, Mary Lou, Enrich board member Gary Hollister, Mr. Kashi. Back row from left: Mr. Matsumoto, husband Capt. Bob Wilson, Mr. Nagai.

to a downline of more than 15,000 Japan-based distributors. Eight months later, in March 1999, that number had risen to 40,000.

Thorough Planning

Mary Lou's Japanese initiative was so thoroughly planned it might have been inspired by Napoleon, whose precept was, "Control every element of the situation." In a way, though, what Mary Lou did was more impressive than any offensive by Napoleon, because while he inevitably lost some men in battle, Mary Lou's campaigns always result in her troops growing exponentially in number.

To prepare for entering Japan, she read everything she could find on doing business there, from how to conduct yourself in a late-night meeting to the fine points of a tea ceremony. She learned about Japanese food and practiced endlessly with chopsticks—even to the point of pinching paper clips while she talked on the telephone. She learned about colors—red, for example, signifies success, happiness, and prosperity—so she would know how to send the right messages with her clothes and accoutrements. She refined her understanding of the art of bowing so she would know when to bow, and where, and to what level. She studied business law and the rules and regulations governing imports, and in general drank in information on the culture, society, and economy like a student cramming for a big exam. She also took with her to Japan suitcase upon suitcase full of gifts from Texas for each leader she intended to meet. Considering her disciplined readiness, can anyone be surprised to hear that she was showered with accolades everywhere she went and ended up doing more than $1 million worth of business in Japan in her first month? (As she laid plans for a 10-city Japanese tour in March 1999, her monthly personal volume sales were soaring toward the $3 million level.)

As much as the money, though, what she loved was that after the trip ended, "I could say to myself, 'You did it girl.'" Reflecting on just how well she met the challenge, she says, "I was ready for everything except the heated toilet seats." She adds that it took her a while to stop bowing upon her return to the states.

What motivated her to such a high level of achievement? She wanted to show people that she could open a country, and that being a woman in her seventies was no bar to accomplishment. "Age makes no difference and countries are no barriers," she says. "There are no boundaries. Once you make up your mind to do it, you just go do it." It's an idea that's seconded by her seventy-five-year-old husband, Bob, who describes himself as Mary Lou's "support system" and whose long white beard has earned him the nickname in Japan of "Santa-san."

Her Exacting Standards

Living up to Mary Lou's exacting standards is not easy. The woman known to her American downline as "Mom" is famously strict, hates excuses, and won't condone behavior that undermines success. For example, she is tough about ethics in her group, and avers, "I don't tolerate distributors cheating on their spouses. I expect people to act like ladies and gentlemen." She expects herself, like all her leaders, "to be a role model." She demands proper behavior because she knows that it's important to maintaining an effective, motivated, and harmonious group. "I make decisions that make the whole organization better," she says. Anyone who is not ready to work hard would probably be better off seeking out a sponsor other than Mary Lou.

On the other hand, those who are eager and serious about the business will find Mary Lou willing to work tirelessly with them. As a role model, Mary Lou epitomizes the mom who is always there for her kids, and she speaks with pride of the successes of her "offspring." She tells of "one woman on welfare who had a car that had no reverse and no windshield wipers. Within a year she was earning $10,000 a month. Now her kids go to private school, and there is good food on the table." Mary Lou speaks with great affection of one Japanese leader after another, recalling in remarkable detail their accomplishments and her meetings with them. She stays continuously in touch with Japan via phone, fax, and e-mail, and she returns every eight weeks to support, train, and cultivate her relationships.

Like an attentive mom keeping watch over her vast brood, Mary Lou works ceaselessly to nurture the thousands of distributors in her organization. When she identifies distributors who are eager to grow, she is relentless in helping them build, and spares no pains in the care with which she places people in her downline.

Mary Lou got involved in network marketing twenty years ago. Back then, she was ignorant of how to build an organization and had little upline support. She even dissuaded customers from signing up as distributors, for fear of losing their retail sales.

"Mom" calls her group the Wilson International Networkers— the WIN team. At least a few of the team's members have children named after Mary Lou—including a boy, Martin Luis. In his case, according to Mary Lou, the mother, who had been unable to conceive, finally became pregnant with the help of an Enrich supplement.

Time for Helping Others

Mary Lou, whose own children are adopted, is like many network marketers in that she devotes significant efforts to other activities— especially helping others. She works with terminally ill AIDS patients, and notes that she becomes so involved with their lives that when they die she invariably feels as if she is losing a child. She's also written a book on herbs and sits on the boards of Enrich and several other corporations. She gets a fair share of letters from people who call her their role model, and these give her a special delight.

When people take note of Mary Lou's lifestyle—which includes a $1 million home on five acres overlooking a lake—she hastens to point out that in every way except money she has always been an ordinary person. In her words, "Network marketing allows common people to produce uncommon results." She adds, "The glue is the relationships. You can commit to a company and its products, but it is the friendships that make it grow."

"I do Enrich because I love people and want them to have what I have," she says. That sentiment extends to her distributors abroad, including the devoted Japanese crew. She tells of being moved to tears on a trip to Tokyo, when 1,500 distributors stood and in unison gave her a traditional salute of admiration and respect. Today, Mary Lou has downlines in six countries. Japan, however, stands out as the one where her efforts truly caught fire.

It all just goes to show that it's never too late to become number one.

11

Coaches, Counselors, Tough Cookies

CAROL WAUGH IS a dynamic and impassioned coach, helping people succeed by encouraging them to believe in their highest possibilities. She's a compassionate and understanding counselor, full of empathy thanks to the difficult trials she herself has endured. She's also a self-described "tough cookie"—a top-notch, highly professional, pioneering businesswoman who "didn't come here to piddle around, but to be successful." And successful she is, by anyone's standards.

Just as her corporate career was turning sour in 1991, Carol Waugh discovered sweet success at Arbonne International, a company that for more than nineteen years has been offering high-achieving entrepreneurial women a way to break the glass ceiling. Carol and the other Arbonne women in this chapter are inspiring examples of the company's outstanding performers.

A Positive, Self-Confident Image

ALL TWENTY-THREE ARBONNE vice presidents in Carol's success line present a positive and self-confident image in keeping with Arbonne's Swiss formula product line, which includes skin care, hair care, spa products, cosmetics, and a recently expanded nutrition and longevity line. It's an image nicely enhanced by the white Mercedes-Benzes they all drive. "When we pull up at the Embassy Suites for our Monday night meeting, it looks like the car lot at the Mercedes dealership," says Carol. Arbonne is in fact one of the largest Mercedes customers in the country, and recently half of Carol's team was featured in the Mercedes-Benz magazine, *Momentum.*

Recently Carol was listed as one of the top five businesswomen in Nashville—marking the first time a home-based business had been recognized. As Carol puts it, "I work a big, $6.5 million business—and I do it from my sunroom, looking at my flowers, with squirrels and rabbits running around."

Icons for women and home-based businesses. Leslie Huskins and Carol Waugh became Arbonne International's first mother-daughter Vice President team.

Lest anyone be intimidated by the stunning wealth and success of the Arbonne crew, rest assured that its leaders are keenly aware of the need for nurturance, support, and training. If your education was cut short and your business experience wouldn't impress a twelve-year-old, that's just where some of the company's top performers were when they started. If you've been knocked off your feet and are reeling from the pain and injustice of it all, these women understand. Some of them have been there too.

Corporate Hell

Carol Waugh herself had reached the point where she saw her ten-year stellar career at a major corporation unraveling. It was vivid proof that the most ideal job can quickly turn into corporate hell, and that the most outstanding employees are not immune to devastating change. After eight years of being "on top of the world," Carol was suddenly beset by management changes and felt herself being forced out to make way for younger, lower-paid employees. At the same time, she wanted to spend more time with her new husband, Troy, and her two teenage children. She needed options.

Donna's Story

WHEN DONNA LARSON was nineteen years old she worked as a swimming coach. Because she needed the income, she coached three teams at once—college, high school, and club teams. When the season ended, she became an independent consultant with a direct sales company and stayed with that company for ten years.

During those ten years Donna got married, had three children, and got divorced. She discovered Arbonne at about the same time as she got divorced. Her friends told her to go get a "real job." After all, she was single with three children. But Donna liked Arbonne's products and marketing plan. "I saw the potential for much more," she says. "At the time I only had a few hundred dollars in the bank, but I gave back the car I had earned from the other company and bought an old junker. It was a 'beater' as they say in the Midwest, an old clunker."

True to her word: Donna Larson-Johnson set her sights and achieved her goals. Now she's working to create 100 millionaires in her Arbonne group.

The dilapidated car made Donna's son squirm with embarrassment. One day at the supermarket when the bagger kept staring at the old heap, her son asked painfully, "Mom, when are we getting the Mercedes?"

Donna answered, "In a few months." And then, true to her word, she went out and earned one. In succeeding on schedule, Donna felt she had no choice. Her blue-collar family didn't have the resources to help her if she failed. "So I had to succeed. I had to do it," she explains.

Euphiazene's Story

EUPHIAZENE LINDER'S CAREER was very different from Carol Waugh's. In 1988, Euphiazene had been employed for five years at J. C. Penney. Unlike Carol, who was accustomed to making deals worth half a million dollars, Euphiazene earned $97 a week. She had rarely earned more than that in all the years since leaving school to get married at age fourteen. And where Carol was a privileged, high-profile performer and a member of the corporate sales and negotiating teams, Euphiazene was a diligent worker who says, "I wouldn't even take a bathroom break without asking."

Carol and Euphiazene did, however, have one thing in common: a firsthand knowledge of how swift and arbitrary fate could be inside a corporation. One Friday, Euphiazene was named Employee of the Month, taken out to lunch by her manager, and given a raise. The following Monday, because of a cutback, she was laid off.

That was around the time that Lucion, her husband of thirty-eight years, had his second open-heart surgery. Lucion's doctor told him to stop working, and to accept the fact he was totally disabled. Euphiazene was desperate to make ends meet and replace her $97 a week.

Fortunately, Euphiazene had a major resource in her younger sister, Rita Davenport. Where Euphiazene speaks with a rich country accent and had always preferred being a homemaker and avoiding

Euphiazene Linder was earning $97 a week when she was laid off from her department store job. It marked the beginning of a host of positive changes in her life. Today she values Arbonne's spirit of kinship and ethos of helping one another and is thankful her $400,000-plus income has helped her become "the person I was meant to be."

the spotlight, Rita had become a public speaker of exceptional skill. Among Rita's clients was Arbonne.

Guiding Her to Success

When Euphiazene's sister, Rita, gave a training session at Arbonne, she met Donna Larson. Rita saw in her and the other women at the company people who could guide her sister, Euphiazene, to success. Rita urged Euphiazene to sign up. Reluctant and scared but in need of money, Euphiazene started retailing Arbonne products. To her amazement, her first check was for $400. "When I saw that check I went out hollerin' down the street. It was more than I had earned in a month—and I did it in six hours," she recalls.

By 1990, Euphiazene was told she needed to sponsor others in order to get to the next bonus level. But Euphiazene objected. "I wasn't having anything to do with sponsoring," she says. "I knew I couldn't recruit. I knew I didn't have the pizzazz to do it."

> Rita told Carol about the success that her sister Euphiazene was having at Arbonne International. Carol was skeptical. But when Euphiazene called, Carol listened because she needed a new option. Then Carol took a trip and prayed for guidance.

Donna asked Rita to help persuade Euphiazene to recruit other distributors. Finally Euphiazene turned to her older sister and said, "Rita, let me just recruit you."

Rita agreed and signed up as a distributor. "She was fabulous and went right to the top," recalls Euphiazene. "She went from consultant to vice president in six months. Later she was asked to run the company and was named president of Arbonne!"

Rita Davenport had many acquaintances who were high-achievers, but one in particular stood out. From the age of thirteen, she had been best friends with Carol Waugh, who was now seeking to escape from corporate turmoil.

Rita told Carol about Euphiazene's success. Carol at first was skeptical. Compared to her big ticket sales at her current position, she doubted she could make money selling cleansing cream. But when Euphiazene called, Carol listened. She needed an option.

Carol's Decision

CAROL NEXT TOOK a short vacation to Cancun. She read a book entitled *The Power of Your Subconscious Mind.* She prayed for guidance. Carol then made a crucial decision—to get herself back on track. "I realized that if I could see it, I could be it. If you can see yourself being successful, your mind will go to work to prove it true." As part of Carol's quest for success, "I focused on getting myself emotionally well." Back in the vicious atmosphere of the corporate world, facing the loss of all she had worked for over the years, Carol had found herself crying spontaneously in the elevator on her way into the office. Now she was bouncing back, strengthened by the knowledge that she would choose never again to be so vulnerable. "I knew that the best revenge was living well." Then Carol made the decision to go full-time with Arbonne.

Today, after eight years, Carol's income at Arbonne has soared far beyond what her old corporate colleagues and superiors can dream of making—though she counts the benefits she has reaped in much more than dollars. Looking back at her period of burnout and despair, she now knows why she had to go through it: "God had a whole new plan but I couldn't see it." What that plan did for her, though, is clear. "I had to learn to be compassionate before I could counsel people and build this business," she says. "I couldn't have done this business twenty years ago. I wasn't compassionate enough. You have to develop your heart as well as your brain to be able to do network marketing."

Carol emphasizes, however, that she doesn't let people forget that the purpose is to build a business. "I don't let people sit and wallow in their misery," she says. She cautions that when most people join they are struggling, or are in what she calls survival mode—just as she was. "I went from survival mode to success mode. Get out of survival mode as quickly as you can. Get yourself feeling good and seeing the achievements," she says. "That's success mode," she notes. "If you want to grow, learn, and develop, I am here to help you do that," she says, adding: "I'll spend five minutes listening to the whining, but then people have to give me equal time for my positive ideas." To underscore her position, she has a sign in her office that reads, "The Eleventh Commandment: Thou shalt not whine."

Dynamic leaders are often imaginative performers with a knack for dramatizing their lessons in memorable ways. At Carol's training sessions she and her vice presidents do a colorful, full-dress rendition of *The Wizard of Oz*. It's a motivational tour de force in which the protagonists do battle with the Wicked Witch. The evil one, mirroring all the negativists you meet in real life, spews her demotivating propaganda, telling the heroes to "Get a real job. You will never be successful in this business!" Carol, playing the Good Witch who believes in others' highest possibilities, reveals who the Wizard really is: You!

You are all the wizards of your own businesses. You pull the switches. You make the choices. Arbonne gives you the opportunity to be the somebody you were meant to be.

Bring Out the Best in People

Carol Waugh does all she can to bring out the best in people. She counsels them to identify and change whatever limiting beliefs they harbor—beliefs that prevent them from becoming successful. She's committed to helping them succeed because, unlike the corporate world, where anyone can get cut loose at any time, here people's lives are truly bound up with one another's for the long run. "I have an emotional rope tied around my people," says Carol. "I use that rope to pull them toward success." And speaking of emotions, this is also a business where "you have to be passionate," says Carol. "You need to go bananas with passion and attract people to you." At the same time, Carol doesn't let people forget that having a successful business is what makes it all possible. "I am a pretty tough cookie, and I don't let them give me a bunch of excuses. There are always reasons why they didn't make the call. There is always an unmade bed and somebody who needs to be run somewhere."

The highs of the business include the recognition people receive. Carol has been keenly aware of its importance at least since her second convention, when she was the number one distributor in the Parade of Champions. "I could see my husband's eyes glistening with tears as he beamed with pride for his wife," she says. "I have never forgotten that look on his face."

She surely speaks for many women when she says, "We want our families to see us in a respectful manner and be real contributors. This business has given me that with my family."

Involving her family also meant taking three generations on the Cruise of a Lifetime, where Arbonne leased an entire ship and Carol, as the number one point earner, won the presidential suite for her and her husband. Her mother and father and son Chris were there, and

Carol says, "To see the pride in the faces of my family was worth the entire effort."

Carol's daughter, Leslie Huskins, and son-in-law, Jeff, were on-board also, as distributors. Leslie finally left her job with Ralph Lauren to do Arbonne full-time, though she'd had no interest prior to attending a Mercedes presentation. Now she's a vice president herself—with a mercedes. Carol's husband, who is her CPA, not only enjoys the fruits of her labors in the Arbonne arena, he jokingly calls himself Mr. Carol Waugh. Troy says, "A successful wife is a blessing to any family's financial peace. She has taken tremendous pressure off me as the sole breadwinner, and what man would not love that?" Fortunately, both Carol and Troy feel equally blessed.

"I prayed, and God told me I would be so successful," Carol recalls. "God was working on me by getting me into this business. I did my part to be successful, but God piloted my business."

Being Who You Were Meant to Be

WHAT'S REMARKABLE IS that at Arbonne "the somebody you were meant to be" can be a unique individual, different from all the other somebodies in your group—a powerful reminder that this is a business of real people, not corporate clones. Take Euphiazene, who has no doubt she is now living the life of the person she was meant to be. "My secret is I'm still a homemaker and I love to cook. I love the simple things, like being able to pay my bills." Before Arbonne she never dreamed she'd have more than one telephone. Now she has phone lines, faxes, computers, and an assistant to type for her.

Arbonne, Euphiazene explains, has enabled her to live her philosophy of helping others, a philosophy she sums up in the words: "Helpin' people is the key to gettin' where you want to get." No one could doubt her sincerity, or the fact she has helped a lot of people. In addition to her heartfelt faith in God, her other secret to success is to sponsor a lot of "tens." "I am a two who found some tens," she says.

"I've always felt that if I put the other man first I will come out okay. I have never been able to push myself ahead of anybody." After reminding you she has an eighth-grade education, she notes that her group includes teachers, professionals, nurses, and people with college degrees. "It's ironic the downline I've got," she says.

Euphiazene is now an executive national vice president. Arbonnè did a film on her life and her family when she went national. It included video footage from her childhood and ended with "The Wind Beneath My Wings." "I was just sobbing," she says, her voice cracking. "The whole audience was crying too."

Recalling that all the positive changes in her life came about after getting laid off, Euphiazene notes that last year she made over $400,000. The money, though, clearly does not excite her as much as the spirit of kinship. "We're family," she says. "When one of us gets cut, we all bleed."

A View of Money and Relationships

DONNA LARSON-JOHNSON HAS her own perspective on the money and the relationships made possible by Arbonne. After she had been with Arbonne several years, one of her sales associates started urging Donna to meet her brother, Gary. "He would be perfect for you," the associate kept saying.

"She would bug me at the meetings and tell me about this perfect person," Donna recalls. But Donna was striving for financial independence and was not ready for any man, perfect or otherwise. Yet, thanks to her associate's persistence and matchmaking abilities, four years later Donna and Gary Johnson were married. Gary's family added two children to Donna's three, and together they had twins, for a total of seven. Now Donna says, "This business is great for referring life partners—not just business partners." Though she says it with a laugh, it's obviously true.

When they got married, Gary was a medical perfusionist who assisted at open-heart surgery. Just as the overwork and understaffing were becoming intolerable, Donna was able to retire her husband to being a full-time dad and fully qualified Mr. Mom. "It's almost like having a wife to come home to," says Donna. "These little twins have their mom in a home-based business and their dad home full-time. It's been a wonderful environment for these two little girls to grow up in." As for the teenagers, all are involved in sports and Gary gets to attend most of their competitions.

Persuading Husbands to Retire

Before she could get Gary to retire, Donna had to show him on paper that it was feasible. She outlined her plans, then swiftly put them into action. By last year she was an executive national vice president making nearly a half million dollars annually.

Donna was at first driven by her own family's financial concerns. She pushed her income up to the $50,000 a month level—and then she got stuck. Not a bad place to be stuck, you might say.

> When Donna's income got stuck, she set out to shape goals that gave her an exciting vision of the future. Now that she had taken care of her family she could concentrate on helping others. Her new aim is to create what she terms "3D millionaires."

But Donna missed the feeling of ongoing improvement. She was in a "neutral vision" state, to use the term of Richard Brooke, CEO of the network marketing company Oxyfresh, and someone whose teachings have inspired Donna. *Neutral vision* means your view of the future is about the same as your view of the present—in other words, you anticipate things staying the same rather than improving. Positive vision refers to a state in which your future appears brighter than the present. Negative vision is a state in which you see the future as worse than the present.

"You either have a positive, neutral, or negative vision," says Donna. "People with a positive vision are excited and motivated. People with a neutral vision are stuck in a rut." At $50,000 a month, she did not know how to motivate herself to do better. "Who are you to deserve gangster money, I kept asking myself," she now laughs. Donna did not want to be greedy. Surely, her cup was full. Yet she yearned to be inspired with a positive, exciting vision of the future. Finally she realized that she needed a new type of goal.

Creating a Hundred Millionaires

Now that she'd met her objectives, and taken care of her family, she was free to start thinking about others. She set a goal of making $100,000 a month by creating a hundred millionaires in her group.

"For the people in my group to make what I'm making, I had to make more," she recalls with relish. "I raised the bar for myself by focusing on what other people needed." She also came to realize, "Helping others succeed is more fulfilling than working to put bread on the table." Donna enjoys training people, and her enjoyment is reflected in the size of her group, which now has more than twenty thousand distributors.

Donna is now writing a book, *Creating Millionaires into the Millennium,* that describes the process that she calls three-dimensional success. "It's not just being a millionaire, because I know millionaires who are not happy. I want to create 3D millionaires."

Three-dimensional for Donna means:

- Living a balanced life

- Knowing that what you are doing is making a difference

- Having financial "peace"

For Donna, *peace* does not necessarily mean wealth, because some people can gain financial peace with an extra $500 a month. Donna's book will share with readers the three major breakthroughs she's had in her own thinking: The first is that everybody has a vision, be it negative, neutral, or positive. "That idea blew me away, because I used to think that only motivated people had a vision," she says. Donna asks her distributors to close their eyes and envision the contrast between the present and future. "If it is really the same you are a 'rut rider' and will have no motivation to change. There is no contrast in a neutral vision." She then has them write a "millennium statement"—a description of where they aim to be when the year 2000 comes. To make sure her distributors read it every day, the former swimming coach instituted a buddy system in which everyone affirms her statement with her buddy within forty-eight hours of writing it. Almost everyone writes and affirms the statement.

Donna's second breakthrough was realizing that "the universe doesn't care what you want. It only gives you what you envision." Grasping this truth prompted her to start controlling what she was seeing in her imagination. By consciously managing her view of the future, she was able to gain mastery over it.

The third breakthrough was seeing that "motivation and the fruits of motivation—i.e., enthusiasm, energy, perseverance, creativity, and physical energy—are directly sourced from your vision to the degree that there is a contrast between your present situation and the future." In other words, if there is a large positive contrast between now and the future, you will have enthusiasm.

Donna's life since joining Arbonne is itself a terrific story of large positive contrasts. She's gone from a struggling single mom with a broken-down car to a woman who receives great satisfaction from helping others become millionaires.

12

Legends

B IGGER THAN LIFE, these achievers help us all expand our vision. They show us what is possible when we strive to get the very best out of ourselves. But what may be most astounding about these giants in the field of network marketing is that when they started their careers they were not all that different from the rest of us.

Dreams Fulfilled

DON AND JAN Held's Amway organization is large—so large it would be easy for them to retire and never again do anything resembling work. Don and Jan could travel, or just hang out at their estate in Stuart, Florida, spending their days sport fishing and their nights relaxing, all the while brushing aside any thoughts about the cares and concerns of others.

Friend and counselor: Don Held, right, has long relied on the support and guidance of Dexter Yager. Jan was a Diamond before she and Don were married.

But Don and Jan live a very different kind of life, and that raises a provocative question— a question Don himself framed nicely when he asked: "Why do people continue on in Amway even after they've attained the income, lifestyle, and freedom that they dreamed about?" Indeed, why after decades in the business do the Helds stay so active?

An insight may be evident in a recent event: Don and Jan were counseling a young couple. After a while, the grateful woman asked Don if he regretted spending so many hours helping them. Don recalls his reply: "I told her I was in the Big Brothers, the Lions Club, the YMCA, the volunteer advisory board at the orphanage, Foster Parents, Little League football, and the church board. I was the most 'Board' person you'd ever want to meet—and Amway is my ministry."

A Mission to Help Others

For Don and Jan, Amway is a vehicle for solving life's problems. Their mission is to use that vehicle to help others, and for that reason the Helds are remarkably accessible. They give their voicemail number out to those seeking help. They take their calls unscreened. They put the needs of others above their own privacy. So part of the answer as to why their lives are so active is simply that they've got so much to do, and so many people are counting on them.

But anyone wanting to know more about the source of Don's dedication may need to go back many years—to a time when Don was the one receiving the counseling. The story has more than a few surprises, especially regarding the person Don sought out to counsel him—none other than the legendary Amway Diamond Dexter Yager, who has since become a Crown Ambassador. In fact, the pivotal role that Dexter played in Don's career may serve to confound those cynics who always suspect a selfish motive in everyone's behavior.

Don discovered Amway when he was a corporate employee whose financial and emotional life was, in his words, "a nightmare." He had been with the corporation ten years, advancing in status and workload, but his financial status and outlook for the future had not changed.

Don's initial Amway goals were modest—to obtain six pairs of new shoes, for his four boys and two foster daughters, and an automatic dishwasher. But he worked hard, and the rewards were more than he had expected. Soon he decided to leave his employer, IBM, to pursue Amway full-time—a tough decision to make even today, but a shocking one twenty-nine years ago. His parents were all but traumatized that a father of four would even consider such a step. Don tried to explain to them that the security offered by a corporation was false security. He told them of the need "to take risks in order to be different from the norm." Then, to put the finishing flourish on his farewell to IBM, "I gave the company a gold watch when I left. I wanted to make sure I burned my bridges. I wanted to leave no room for going back, no leeway for failure."

It was during these early days in Amway that Don met Dexter. They became friends, and during Don's tough divorce, Dexter was there for support. Don would fly to Charlotte and drive around with Dexter so he could " pick his brain." On these trips Don got counseled by the man who was becoming Amway's most successful megadistributor, someone who has since built on his phenomenal Amway success to also become a heavyweight investor and entrepreneur. Don calls Dexter "my rich dad," and says the long hours he spent with him "taught me about building an organization with the depth needed to create ongoing income even in the trying times that were to follow."

Dexter's Helping Hand

But Don would soon need more than mere advice. As it turned out, the hand that Dexter extended to him would change his life forever. The story is one that has long been cited in Amway circles as a sterling example of loyalty among friends, and it begins as follows: While he was achieving financial success with Dexter's help, Don married a second time. The marriage was a mistake, however, and its collapse devastated Don emotionally. Adding to his pain was grief over the deaths of his father and sister within three months of each other.

Too ashamed to talk to Dexter, Don pulled away from his mentor and from the business. Fortunately, Dexter grasped what was happening and reached out to encourage Don and to support his organization. He stayed in touch with Don's leaders, motivating them and offering them assistance. For all the months Don was out of the loop, or unable to function, the system Dexter had developed helped his business keep growing. The bolstering helped make Don's group today one of the biggest organizations in Amway.

One Crucial Fact

A nice story, to be sure—but you're missing the essence of it without one key fact: Don Held is not in Dexter's line of sponsorship. So Dexter did not stand to earn Amway commissions from his significant efforts on behalf of Don. Those experienced in network marketing will have a keen appreciation of the episode based on their awareness of the following points: First, achieving anything worthy of note requires a measure of single-minded dedication. Second, building a large network marketing organization demands exceptional single-mindedness. Third, famously ambitious distributors who are on their way to becoming megadistributors don't have time to devote to other people's organizations—unless they make it a priority to do so. Fourth, Dexter must have made helping Don a very big priority. All of which is just another way of saying that what Dexter did was no small favor.

To this day, Don and Jan make their number one priority helping others. Even family tragedies have not deterred them from attending meetings when they have made a commitment to be there. "We believe this business brings so much hidden good to people that we can't allow ourselves excuses," says Jan. "We have to set the example," she says, adding, "The meeting may be some people's only chance for a future in this business."

The Helds say their own grief has made them more acutely aware of how much others may need their help. Last year, Don's son Alan, a single father with two children, died of a brain tumor after suffering for several years. "Because of this business," says Don, "I could promise Alan that his children, Charlie and Amber, would be provided for. He knew they would never need or want for anything. More important, he knew I would have the free time to spend with them."

Spending time with youngsters is one activity at which Don excels—and he's had a lot of practice at it. When Alan, Rick, Ron, and Denny were children, Don tried to keep life exciting. The boys didn't just learn about the United States from TV and textbooks. They traveled the highways and byways in a luxurious motor coach seeing the country with their own eyes and having adventures of every sort along the way.

Ron remembers the time they went to see the movie *Jaws,* then a national sensation. After the movie Don went off to a meeting, but not before sending Denny and Rick out on a nighttime charter boat to go fishing—for shark. Denny came through by catching one, purported to be huge. Don showed up at the dock after the Amway meeting with a large group of gawking distributors eager to see the monster. The incident is still the source of stories, laughter, and vivid memories of the beast's immense proportions.

A "Perfect Match" Foreseen

Brotherly as they may be, there's one event for which Ron, thirty-two, Rick, thirty-six, and Denny, thirty-seven, still compete ferociously for credit. Rick claims it was he who first noticed Jan Hawk at a function and alerted his dad that there was someone in his downline he needed to meet. In fact, says Rick, "I called Jan and told her that Dad was available. I could see she was a perfect match." Ron and Denny concede nothing to Rick regarding the prime importance of the roles they each played—roles that perhaps have been inflated with the passing years. Says Ron, "She was so much like Dad that I knew they would be a great match."

The facts that are not in dispute are that Jan was a Diamond herself, fourteen levels deep in the organization, very successful, and running her own functions quite apart from Don.

Jan had been in Amway for fifteen years. Also divorced, she was living in Arkansas. She had met the Held boys years earlier and hit it off with them. One day she stopped by their hometown of Columbus, Ohio. "I didn't come to meet Don," she says pointedly. "I came to take care of an investment."

But they did meet. "Two weeks later Don called me for our first date," Jan recalls. Then they followed up by doing something that came easy to Diamonds with worldwide organizations: They started dating long-distance. One thing led to another and they were married in 1989.

Today Don and Jan's work counseling distributors on all aspects of the business—and all aspects of life—has become legendary. Working with Don and Jan, distributors learn to identify their bad habits and replace them with success habits. Both Jan and Don emphasize that what causes people to stumble in Amway will cause them to stumble in other pursuits as well. "You have to help them overcome their low self-esteem or whatever the issue is—if not, they will take that stuff and fail somewhere else," says Don.

Lifting Your Self-Esteem

Don wants people to know that he himself struggled to raise his self-esteem. In fact, says Don, whenever personal problems caused his self-esteem to falter, his income would hit a plateau. It would remain stuck until he had resolved his problems. In one case he hit a plateau at a quarter of a million dollars annually; but whatever the level at which you get stuck, the principle is the same: You need to believe that you are deserving of more. "Most people don't think that they are worthy," he says. "Twenty-nine years ago I wouldn't have believed it if you told me I would have everything I have today." Says Jan, "Most people don't believe in themselves or their self-worth. It is hard to learn these things alone."

Fortunately, no one need be alone. Being part of a vast organization gives people access to a wealth of resources that is hard to imagine. Don even believes those resources are what helped him recover from cancer several years ago. Thanks to Amvox—the internal Amway voicemail that enables distributors to stay in contact—Don was alerted to specialists and alternative treatments around the world. Today, he says, he is in better, more robust health than ever.

One of the ways he's enjoying that health is spending time with his grandchildren, including a trip last summer to Opryland, and to an Amway "Family Reunion." It's never too early to get youngsters involved in a lifestyle that has shed so many blessings upon the family. Don and Jan believe that prayer, and their belief in God, along with Amway have provided solutions to every one of life's problems that they have faced. It has given them great friends, great wealth, and a vehicle for positively influencing the lives of others.

Nowhere is their enthusiasm for the business more evident than in the delight they express that their children and grandchildren will continue to reap the benefits of the Amway lifestyle. Rick, Ron, and Denny have all joined the business—and no one has any doubts that the opportunity for the members of the third generation will be even greater than it was for Don and Jan when they signed up.

Paradise Found

DON AND RUTH Storms call their magnificent North Carolina estate "Paradise North." Whatever lavish images those words evoke in your mind, chances are your imagination will fall short of the reality. When Paradise North was being built in rural Union County in 1995,

It all started with a grandfather clock. Today Ruth and Don Storms own an island in New Hampshire, a mansion in North Carolina, a penthouse condo in Florida, and a jet plane and yacht. But a clock was their first Amway goal.

local folks were staggered by what they saw, and press reports excitedly called the spread "unbelievable" and "wildly spectacular." The person who summed it up best, however, might have been the veteran appraiser who said, "I think you've gone beyond 'mansion' into some other category that hasn't been defined."

In a sense, that's just what the Stormses have done with their lives—gone into undefined territory. Their glorious estate seems to celebrate unlimited potential, while their success makes us question the restrictions we so often put on our lives.

Spectacular from any vantage point, the seventeen acres of Paradise North are best comprehended when seen from the air—perhaps while you are being flown over in Don's private Hawker jet. Circling the grounds, you see the fields where the Stormses grow peaches, apples, tomatoes, eggplant, corn, peppers, and asparagus. You see a lawn that is better kept than Yankee Stadium. You see the sides of the sprawling house glistening in the sun and glimpse the blue of the pool sparkling in contrast to the gardens and stone driveway.

Don is not one to crow about his physical possessions, but the details of the house always leave observers a bit stunned. Not counting the garage, the mansion's 19,000 square feet make it more than nine times the size of the average house—pointing up the fact that there is not much about the Stormses that is average. Inside you'll find a movie theater, a pool, some six hundred electrical outlets, and a grand piano in an atrium of a foyer that's bigger than many entire houses.

The garage, at 6,000 square feet, is three times the size of an average house. And then there's the modest guest house—twice the size of the typical homeowner's dwelling.

For Family and Fun

The Stormses wanted a place where their four children and twelve grandchildren could spend time and have fun, where Ruth's mother could make her home, and where everyone could share family time together. To that end, the kitchen is world class, well suited for Ruth's famous baking. The Stormses often entertain their friends at Paradise North, and the house has plenty of room for guests to sleep over.

"When I sit in my library late at night and read," says Don, "I sometimes think about the cars driving by outside. The passing stranger looking at my estate probably asks the question, 'Who lives in that home? What do they do?' A person would have to be dull indeed not to ask such questions while driving beside the stone and wrought iron fence that's longer than three football fields. The statement made by the grandeur of it all helps make the answer unforgettable: The people inside are Amway Diamonds.

The Stormses have been building their Amway distributorship for nineteen years, beginning after their move to Charlotte from New Jersey in 1976. Back then Don was working for a TV ministry, and was also on a church board with Amway distributors Dexter and Birdie Yager. Don found himself dissatisfied with the money he was making at his job and asked Dexter if he could do "that business" with him. Though he liked working in the ministry, Don wanted life to be more comfortable. "I could afford a new car every couple of years, but that was about it." What began as a way to supplement his income in two years became a full-time pursuit.

Don confesses he had hoped his stature as a television notable would lead Dexter to build the business for him. "I thought Dexter would do it for me," he laughs, wryly mocking just how little he knew of what was to unfold. Dexter helped him and encouraged him in ways that were invaluable—but he didn't do it for him. Of course,

Don has no regrets, to put it mildly. "Getting into Amway was the best decision, after accepting the Lord and marrying my wife, that I ever made," says Don.

A Modest First Goal

While the level of Don's success today seems flabbergasting, what's more amazing is the modest size of his objective when he started in the business. "Ruth wanted a grandfather clock with cabinets on the side. I wanted to get that for her. It was our first goal," says Don. The example highlights a lesson that Don learned early on from Dexter: Motivate people by helping them focus on attainable goals. If beginners spend all their time dreaming of the distant future, they'll get discouraged and quit.

The Stormses have used the business as a tool for teaching their children how to set and achieve goals, something that's now as natural to son Lee and daughters Gail and Brenda as getting up in the morning. A case in point is how they acquired their home in New Hampshire. Each summer the Stormses vacationed by the crystal clear waters of Lake Winnipesaukee. They were drawn to the area because Don and Ruth had spent their honeymoon at the lakefront resort town of Wolfeboro, and because their Amway business had grown in New Hampshire.

Acquiring Their Own Island

As a boy, Don had vacationed on a little island of his grandfather's in Ontario, and ever since then owning an island had been a dream. At Wolfeboro, surrounded by breathtaking views of mountains covered with hardwood forests, the Stormses carried out a practical lesson in dreaming. "While on vacation each summer over the years, we would look at cottages," says Don. "One day we saw a picture of our island. We went out to look around and have a picnic lunch. It was a 3 1/2-acre island with nothing but a small A-frame. The kids carved their names in a big birch tree," recalls Don. In short order the children informed their parents that this was "our island."

Owning the island instantly became a family project. The Stormses approached the owner and asked to test it out. He agreed to let them stay on the island for two weeks for free, to see if they liked it. Then they made an offer that was one-third the asking price. The owner accepted and took a small down payment. Together the three children and parents chipped in $125 each, a total of $500 a month, and made payments.

Don explains, "The kids were just getting married at the time and couldn't afford a large payment. We made a lot of money in the business and then paid the whole thing off in a couple of years." The A-frame house that was standing on newly named Storms Island in time became unsuitable as one grandchild after another joined the ranks of vacationers. The family then made a project of building a larger house, along with a boat house, a gazebo, a water slide, and a dock for all the boats. The lake, set amid pristine beauty, is seventy-three square miles, and in places as deep as 200 feet. The Stormses draw their drinking water from the lake, then filter it through their Amway water purification system.

Paradise South

In addition to Storms Island and Paradise North, the family also spends time at Paradise South, their 3,500-square foot condominium penthouse on the Gulf shore in Naples, Florida. It overlooks the sparkling white sands of the beach and the warm blue waters where the family often cruises about in their fifty-five-foot Sun Seeker yacht.

Reflecting on all the fun his family has had over the years, Don notes how much shorter their time together would be were they coping with typical careers and businesses. "Most families today can't do much together," he says. As for ordinary family businesses, they rarely have desirable positions available for all the kids, much less the grandchildren. Even more disconcerting is the large number that fail after the founder stops working. By contrast, the Stormses know their businesses will continue to grow and create opportunities. Don and Ruth's daughters, Brenda and Gail, got into the business when they turned eighteen years old. Their son, Lee, got in when he was twenty-one years old.

Three Things They Wanted

After Don and Ruth got that first grandfather clock they realized that they could build Amway together and get the three things that they wanted most out of a business: First, they wanted to have fun doing it. Second, they wanted to "make money now." And finally, they wanted to buy back their free time so they could be together more often.

One way Don adds to his spare time is by using his own jet, which has its own hangar and a private office for the pilot. It's a business tool that allows him to fly home and be in his own bed at night. Among his frequent destinations is the Caribbean.

Last year the children, their spouses, and Don and Ruth took a Caribbean vacation. Don and Ruth chartered a 115-foot Broward Lady Hawke yacht. "On that vacation I spent more in eight days than I used to make in two years before Amway," says Don, turning his thoughts to the early struggles of being in the business. "Ruth has been a part of it all the way through," says Don. "She believed in me," he notes, even when no one else did—no one, he adds, except Dexter and Birdie Yager. When asked about the power of a sponsor's belief, Don recalled the influence of the Yagers. "Dexter said over and over again he believed I could do it. Whenever I didn't believe I could do it, or was doubting it, Dexter would say, 'You can do it.'"

Today, even though he has a worldwide business that extends to Athens, Barcelona, Vienna, Madrid, and Rome, Don still meets people who tell him that it won't work. "Recently someone told me that the company must have set me up in this huge home so that I would be able to sponsor people into the business," he says with amusement.

It's Easier to Succeed Today

Looking to the future, Don notes one trend that is clear to him: "The business is easier than when I got in, and it keeps getting easier. I was in Amway before it was cool. I became a millionaire with products in my garage. Now the marketing plan is more lucrative and the distribution is simpler."

What does Don Storms have to say to someone who would aspire to achieve what he has? His answer is you get started by asking the following: "When do I want it and how do I go about getting it?" Then he adds, "That makes it a real dream. A dream without a date and a plan is a fantasy, not a dream."

Which all goes to show that real dreams can result in accomplishments that are truly fantastic.

13

Poets and Powerhouses

For network marketers, doing business and celebrating life tend to be closely related pursuits. That's a far cry from the tycoons of yesteryear, whose flinty hearts forbade soft emotions; or from the modern corporation, which by design is soulless; or even from typical small businesses, whose endless burdens often leave their owners too exhausted for joys of any kind. In network marketing, by contrast, greatness of spirit seems to spring naturally from great success—and vice versa.

Wayne and Lori Andersen

"WEIRD," THOUGHT DR. Wayne Andersen. "This seems very weird," he said to himself as he looked at the contents of the box he'd just received. He did not see "anything resembling what was in the typical medical doctor's armamentarium." As chairman of the Department of Anesthesiology and Director of Critical Care at a prominent

Exciting new horizons: Dr. Wayne Andersen, a critical care physician, and his wife, Lori, a nurse anesthetist, revel in the health, wealth, and philosophy of Nikken.

hospital in Dayton, Ohio, Dr. Andersen was about as ensconced in traditional medicine as anyone could be. But there was nothing traditional here. The woman who had called him on the phone and urged him to sample this unfamiliar technology was a fellow doctor with whom he had gone to medical school years ago. She was someone he trusted, someone able to capture his attention for a moment amidst the crushing demands of his daily schedule. She'd begun by complimenting him—suggesting that, as the first in his class in medical school, he'd be likely to want to know about this.

As Dr. Andersen listened to his friend describe the benefits of this new technology, he thought of his wife, Lori, a nurse anesthetist at the same Dayton hospital. Lori had hurt her back severely in a car accident, and trying to bear the unrelenting pain while working up to sixty hours a week had led to ulcers. In seeking help for her, Wayne had exhausted his resources in the world of medicine, but to no avail. Maybe there was hope in this new system. It was from a company named Nikken, and that mildly piqued Wayne's interest as he had gone to high school in Japan when his father was in the military. Though he'd been intrigued by Eastern philosophies at the time, he'd returned to the states for college and medical school and had then trained under the leading practitioners in the field of critical care.

He and Lori began using the Nikken sleeping system, which is based on the emerging field of magnet therapy. What happened next was totally unexpected. "After a week, we knew we were onto something fantastic," he says. The improvement was so dramatic that his entire perspective was altered as he learned more about Nikken and the way of life it offered. He saw that the lives he and Lori were leading were exacting a terrible toll on them both. Day-to-day existence had become a war in which the enemies were not only disease, but a lack of balance and bureaucratic insanity. The technology used to produce the seemingly wondrous weapons of medicine had also become a relentless and dehumanizing power. Perhaps the most insidious aspect of this force was its pitiless reductionism—its splitting of the world of healing and medicine into ever more specialized and separate categories. Under its domination, Wayne found it hard even to feel in touch with himself, much less colleagues and patients. "Technology has isolated us," he realized. "That's why we feel empty."

As Wayne and Lori discussed the amazing benefits of their Nikken system, the words of the ancient and revered Hippocratic oath he had taken so many years earlier came into his mind: "First, do no harm." On hearing the words echoing in his mind, Wayne had an epiphany. Almost shouting out loud to himself, he said, "Yet what we are doing in traditional medicine is killing thousands every year." By contrast, Nikken was "absolutely nonharmful" and offered "wonderful systems on the leading edge of wellness technology." Instead of devastating the human organism with medical armaments, its gentle therapy "allowed the body to take care of itself," explains Dr. Andersen. Exhilarated and rejuvenated, Wayne and Lori began telling others in the medical field about Nikken and they too were quickly able to rejoice in the effects the products had on them. Surging with newfound health and energy, the Andersens experienced a meteoric rise to the Diamond level. Four of the six Diamonds he now has in his organization are medical couples—a radiologist married to a doctor of nuclear medicine, plus an orthopedist married to an internal medicine specialist. In two years, the Andersens doubled Lori's income, allowing her to retire from the hospital and spend time with their two-year-old daughter, Savannah. Now Wayne himself is counting the days until he too leaves the hospital. Doing so will enable him to leave behind an atmosphere that is infected with negativity and step into one that is invariably positive. It will allow him to walk away from a world where people are "driven by the pursuit of status and power" and devote himself wholeheartedly to a network of friends "who are committed and work together." No longer a victim of the technological "progress" that coldly and inexorably divides and compartmentalizes, Wayne now revels in the synergy and interconnectedness that Nikken has brought into his life. "It's an outlook that was foreign to me and is foreign to most Americans. It's an outlook that connects Mind, Body, Family, Society, and Finances. It connects me to others in my organization. We are part of the force that helps people go toward wellness."

> The Andersens know they are on the leading edge of wellness technology. Four of the Diamonds in their organization are medical couples. All are helping to spread the word about Nikken in the world of medicine.

Now that he has looked up and seen the world outside the hospital, Wayne finds it profoundly exciting. His mind and heart have been opened, he says, by bonding with people "from all walks of life." After a recent meeting with members of his Nikken organization, he came away singing the praises of a gas station owner, a hog farmer, and a twenty-three-year-old entrepreneur. "There's no way an incredibly busy forty-six-year-old doctor would have been brought together with them," he says—unless they were on the operating table.

He and Lori might never have gotten to know such people, to have experienced such fulfillment, to have found so much happiness—if he hadn't opened that box.

Jerry and Polly Harteis

THE MEMBERS OF the Harteis family of Dallas, Pennsylvania, include fifteen relatives who are Amway distributors who earn an estimated $75 million a year. The Harteis brothers were from a family of sixteen children whose parents and grandparents were dairy farmers.

Jerry Harteis was an agriculture and science teacher and wrestling coach who was living in a trailer in the Poconos and taking summer courses when his brother, Fred, told him about Amway. Jerry and his wife, Polly, quickly signed up, then sponsored Fred's and Jerry's parents, Ruth and Lawrence; other family members soon followed.

Diamond lifestyle: Jerry Harteis was living in a trailer when he heard about Amway. He and Polly signed up relatives; the clan now earns an estimated $75 milion a year.

The Harteis family business now extends to every continent except Antarctica. Lawrence died in 1994, though Ruth, now eighty, still works the business, as do her children, nieces, nephews, and grandchildren. Ruth has the rank of Founder's Sapphire Direct, and the Australian leg of her distributorship includes a Crown Ambassador, the highest Amway level. In the late 1980s Ruth and her late husband moved the largest volume of commercial products of any Amway distributors.

Jerry and Fred, who both recall nights growing up when there were three kids to a bed, say that having plenty of room to stretch feels good. Fred lives in Harrisburg and has a lodge on 3,000 acres in Colorado. In Pennsylvania, Jerry and Polly have a 125-acre horse farm and live in a large English Tudor with two swimming pools on a private golf course. They also own a New Jersey landmark, the Chateau, a huge 1910 Victorian house in Stone Harbor on the Atlantic Ocean. Jerry says the average individual can hardly imagine the lifestyle of a Diamond. But the essence of it is "you can support your family's dreams. More important, you can be with them as they achieve their dreams."

A case in point is daughter Jenn's horsemanship. In 1994 she won the American Quarter Horse National Rookie of the Year Championship. Jerry and Polly traveled to horse shows for forty weekends as Jenn accumulated enough points for the title.

> Jerry enjoys going to "retirement" parties for young people—some no older than thirty.

Daughter Tara and her husband, Robert Sypniewski, who were married in October 1998, recently signed up as Amway distributors after deciding it was their best career choice. One activity that gives Jerry great pleasure is going to "retirement" parties for young people in Amway—some no more than thirty years old—who are gaining freedom from their regular jobs. "It gives us joy," says Jerry, "to watch these young people create lifestyles with income, health, friends, and the time to enjoy themselves." The best part of these celebrations, he says, is "when they smash their alarm clocks."

Dom and Pat Coniguliaro

BACK WHEN DOMINIC Coniguliaro clashed with his ninth-grade teacher, his father told him: "Stay in school or get a job." Dom quit school and became a cook—and began forming some lifelong opinions about education. He later met Pat, an R.N., and by 1964 the couple had three small children. Dom was working in a hotel in Rome, New York—the town now famous as a breeding ground of Amway success stories—when local (and legendary) Amway distributor Dexter Yager stopped by the house one evening to show the plan. Recalls Pat, "We got into Amway that night." Four months later they had zoomed to Direct Distributors. Dom was ambitious, and had in the past "always worked two or three jobs," says Pat.

"This time it was different," she says. He focused on Amway because, "The company didn't care about his background"—or about his lack of a diploma, an issue that had galled Dom over the years. Pat and Dom built a large business. One massive leg of their organization, headed by MLM titan Bill Britt, accounts for a significant part of Amway's volume worldwide and contains more than 100 Diamond Distributors. Dom and Pat, who now live in Charlotte, North Car-

Positive thinkers and goal setters. Dom and Pat Coniguliaro encourage their fellow Amway distributors to get their children involved in the business. It helps them grow up to be the kind of people who "if you ask them to do something, they get it done," says Pat. Of Dom and Pat's fourteen grandchildren, ten were homeschooled.

olina, have four daughters and a son, and are pleased with the way free enterprise has taught their children to be positive thinkers and goal setters. "We couldn't have had a better environment. They were always surrounded by people with a purpose, who cared about others." Pat and Dom encourage distributors to enlist their children to help with the business. "There are so many ways for children to be involved," says Pat. "Having them set goals with their parents helps the family dream together. When we reach a goal as a family it is terrific. Then the kids learn to develop a good work ethic. They grow up to be the kind of people, who if you ask them to do something, they get it done."

Of the fourteen Coniguliaro grandchildren, ten are home-schooled—a fitting upshot to Dom's run-in with education two generations earlier. Pat says the children have thrived in homeschooling, adding, "There is absolutely no problem with socialization. They just don't waste half the day in school like some children do."

Pat puts a major effort into counseling wives in the business on raising children and maintaining one's marriage and relationships. An annual luncheon she started to deal with these issues now attracts many hundreds of women. Pat's humor can be sharp when she addresses the way the media sow confusion among women regarding the importance of the family. "Magazines ask questions like, 'How do you cope with your children?'" she says, then adds, "The magazines make it sound like children are an inconvenience in a woman's life rather than a gift from God." The answer to the question, says Pat, is clear: "Put down those magazines and pick up the kid."

Sheri Sharman

Sheri Sharman was teaching preschool when she discovered network marketing a decade ago. She's made millions in the business since, and helped her mother, Imo.

"DEVELOPING A LARGE organization is simple," says Sheri Sharman, a presidential team leader in New Vision International who says she sees herself as a talent scout. "I keep a lookout for people who have talent to develop. Then I help them." One of the people Sheri started helping a few years ago was her mother, Imo Sharman, then a sixty-five-year-old secretary making $1,400 a month. "At the time," says Imo, "I did not know how to do sales and therefore I was very scared about my chances of having success." Sheri noticed, however, that her new Mercedes had caught Imo's eye. With Sheri's help, Imo soon developed a large organization. On Imo's birthday, Sheri invited her mother to her house. When she arrived, a crowd of her distributors were standing outside. The garage door opened, balloons came pouring out, and as the crowd sang "Happy Birthday," a new white Mercedes rolled forth. "You should have seen my mom's face," recalls Sheri. "It was pure happiness."

Surprise birthday gift. Hardworking Imo Sharman, a secretary, overcame her fears of being a New Vision distributor and built a large organization. Daughter Sheri threw a birthday party for her and rolled out a new Mercedes. Imo thanks Sheri "for believing in me when I did not believe in myself."

Roland Fox

ROLAND FOX LOOKED at the Air Force promotion roster and realized he was not going to be a lieutenant colonel. After twenty years that included flying in Strategic Air Command bombers carrying nuclear weapons, he left the military and headed for the West Coast in an Airstream with his family to begin a new life in network marketing. It took him twenty-five failures before he found Oxyfresh in 1983 and succeeded in a big way. In Roland's view, however, he wasn't failing so much as learning—replacing the old skills he had learned in the military with new ones. For example, he had to learn to listen to people who could walk away at any time, find out what they wanted, and then help them attain it; and he had to look at everyone as a future leader and prepare them for that role. Though it was an utterly different way of looking at things, "I loved it," he recalls. "I couldn't

Flying high: Roland Fox, far right, now golfs whenever, wherever he wants. At annual Oxyfresh tournament. From left, Chris and Rachel Conerly, Dr. Charles Stockard.

get enough of the motivation and self-improvement." Gradually, he learned to think in terms of being in charge of his own destiny. Today Roland plays golf whenever and wherever he wants, and he and Virginia travel and spend time with their fifteen grandchildren. He notes that for the last eight years he has earned more than the Chairman of the Joint Chiefs of Staff, "and I've never had to fight a war." Roland is now working on earning more than all the Joint Chiefs of Staff combined. To summarize in crisp military style all he's learned, he says, would take a book of two pages:

"Page 1. Start!"

"Page 2. Don't stop—and you'll succeed."

Gary DeRitter

LAST YEAR, BROTHERS Gary and Ed DeRitter were especially proud of one distributor in their Body Wise International business. It was their seventy-seven-year-old mother, Ann, who does at least $100,000 a month in volume. Gary and Ed had looked extensively for the right network marketing company after they grew tired of the difficulties of traditional businesses and sold their computer systems operation. Because their father had died of a heart attack thirteen years earlier, the DeRitters were attracted to Body Wise, with its em-

"The beginning of the business is like going through goo! You have to fight your way through the no's, the quitters, and all the other negatives—the negative in-laws and others. Your sponsor is reaching back through the goo pulling you forward. Not everybody makes it; the goo gets them. If you are strong enough with your vision, and hold on to your relationship with the leaders, you will make it. Success is defined by the number of failures you can get through."

—*Gary DeRitter, Body Wise*

phasis on high quality nutritional products, cholesterol and weight management, and athletic performance.

Ann was in her early seventies when she began taking Body Wise products, and they helped her lose weight and look and feel great. At her fiftieth nursing school reunion, she was voted the most recognizable. Ann had never expected her retirement years to be so full of wealth, fun, and ever-expanding dreams—all of which fit in well with meeting a nice guy named Horace Somes at church and getting married. Today, says Gary, "Mom can say things the normal person wouldn't."

Laughing all the way. The DeRitters in a Body Wise telephone training skit, with Ed in costume, Gary, and their mother, Ann DeRitter Somes.

From the phone in the other room Ann was telling a prospect, "I don't care whether you say no to me, just as long as I get you off my list." Says Gary, "At her age she doesn't have all day, so she ascribes to the get in, get out, but get off my list, philosophy." Then he adds, "For a person who wants to make a change, age doesn't matter. People of any age can change the world."

Paulette Kimura-Shimabukuro

SHORTLY BEFORE THEIR son was born, Paulette Kimura-Shimabukuro sat her husband Chris down and showed him how she was doing with her "hobby" of network marketing. Paulette had learned about network marketing when she attended a meeting with her mother—in order to dissuade her from signing up. "I made my mom promise me that she wouldn't get involved," says Paulette. But, "when I got there I realized that this was something I needed to investigate." Always organized and methodical, Paulette spent two months learning about the industry. Now, to her husband's surprise, Paulette was earning more in a week than he earned in two months. Chris hadn't paid much attention. He'd been working as a cable technician and trying to schedule his vacation and sick leave to be home when the baby arrived. But by the time Devin was born, three weeks overdue, Chris had used up all his time off, though he'd

A great way for kids to grow up. Paulette Kimura-Shimabukuro of Nikken loves the benefits of being in a network marketing family. So do husband Chris and son Devon, four.

been working for the same company in Hawaii for eleven years. Chris resigned the day Devin was born and has been home ever since. Devin is now four, and Paulette—who has a master's degree in child psychology—and Chris have thought long and hard on how different his life growing up will be from theirs. For example, when they were children, their parents would say, "We'll see you when we get home." With Devin, Paulette and Chris will be saying, "We'll see you when *you* get home." Paulette says of network marketing in general, and of her company Nikken in particular, "It's a great way for kids to grow up." She adds, "It allows people to have vision, build confidence, and strive with balance—without having to be a major overachiever."

Paulette is grateful to her parents for instilling in her the basics, which she describes as follows: Hold true to family values and traditions; be courageous enough to explore new ideas. And then, after a pause, this quiet and reserved young woman adds with an excitement she almost cannot contain: "Personal growth is *tremendous!*"

Jeff and Shirley Thorne

SHIRLEY THORNE TOOK her lipstick and wrote on the bathroom mirror: "Jeffrey will be boss-free in twenty-four months." Her husband had to stare at the message every time he walked into the bathroom. Back when Shirley first signed him up for a network marketing company, Jeffrey had been changing the shocks on the Jeep and showed little interest. Then he grasped the power of geometric growth, and he and his wife became an unstoppable team. Jeffrey—now a former air-conditioning tech/mechanic—achieved their goal of quitting work right on the two-year mark, just as his wages hit an all-time high of $26 an hour.

The Thorne's belief in writing out goals has paid off in a way that seems spectacular. And Shirley can show just how she wrote it all out in detail.

Unstoppable team: Shirley and Jeff Thorne learned the power of setting goals, and now teach the skill to others, including daughters Kimberly and Stephanie.

Today, as top distributors for Freelife International—a company founded in 1995 with nutritional and personal care products—Jeff and Shirley believe in writing down goals for themselves and their children, ten-year-old Stephanie and twelve-year-old Kimberly. Four years ago they wanted a Land Cruiser, a Lexus, and a Porsche Carrera, plus a four-car garage to keep them in, which would be part of a new home with dormer windows on an oversized piece of property with room for a pool, sports court, spa, two horses, and a big circular driveway. They also wanted more time to travel and be together as a family.

Today, noting how their dreams have materialized, Shirley can pull out her notes and show how they wrote it all down in detail—though with pen on paper rather than lipstick on glass. Setting goals is one of the skills the Thornes have helped teach others because, "when you are in an industry where you can make more money than doctors and lawyers, then you are going to have to learn things—obviously," says Jeff. "But it's well worth the investment," he adds.

The Thornes have built their group methodically and maintained a high retention rate—making sure each new recruit is in the groove and working smoothly. "We look for people who would be fun and who we would like to work with," says Shirley. Because they both love socializing, "we made sure our new place had plenty of property where we could have a lot of friends, neighbors, and parties in the backyard." While their gatherings are casual and down-to-earth, there's one thing that's as certain as the schedules by which the

Thornes always meet their goals: If you join their group, "you're going to get great success coaching—and have a terrific time."

Joe and Teri Gentle

JOE AND TERI Gentle quickly became successful in Freelife International. Then they set out to help Teri's parents build their business. It would allow her father to quit working and the couple to fulfill their cherished dream of moving to a retirement village. In two years her parents were making $3,000 or more a month. The only problem, recalls Joe, was "they couldn't believe this residual income. They couldn't understand that it would keep coming and growing."

Adds Teri, "Let me tell you about the day they moved from their run-down residential area in Paterson, New Jersey. Mom and Dad had sold the house and agreed to leave a lot of the furnishings behind

Not a fantasy: Joe and Teri Gentle, center, proved that residual income was for real, to the delight of Teri's parents, Mike and Joy Riotto. Here they enjoy their leisure—made possible by Freelife— at Disney World, with Teri's sister, Fran Craft, and her husband, Bruce.

for the new owners. Most of it was really junk. At the very last moment the new owners decided they wanted the house cleared out. The movers arrived. They started throwing things out. But Mom had trouble deciding what to keep. She couldn't throw things away. I took a hammer and started smashing things and making a big pile in the street. Mom would try to cling to something that was really worthless junk. I would smash it and tell her, 'I'm going to buy you a new one.'" Now Teri's parents have all new furniture, a company car, and a new retirement home in the village where they had always dreamed of moving. As they build their own business, they travel around the country seeing their eight children and grandchildren.

One night when Joe and Teri were out at dinner with her parents, "Pop pulled out his wallet and insisted that Joe let him pay," recalls Teri. "He said we had been angels. When Mom and I looked back, the two men had their arms around each other. They were crying in gratitude for what this business had done for us all."

Arlene Geraci

ARLENE GERACI ENJOYED carpentry, landscaping, and general home repairs. She saw in the work a way to finance her retirement. She would buy fixer-uppers, or handyman specials, convert them, rent them out, and live on the cash flow. She worked "really hard" to repair the homes and maintain them, repainting and wallpapering when people moved out, "because I wanted to make sure I had a quality product." Arlene's four children would help their fifty-five-year-old divorced mother with the projects. They were used to working together as a family, and all went well until the economy of the mid-1980s slowed. Then a downward spiral began. Her tenants began to lose their jobs. Rental income dwindled. The bank foreclosed on one property, sold it, and sent a bill

"That's the great thing about MLM. If you want more, just do more."

—*Arlene Geraci, Herbalife*

for $28,000 for past due mortgage payments. Arlene was trapped in a nightmare that led to bankruptcy in June 1992.

The devastation she felt was worse than the divorce. Along with her sweat and equity, she had invested her self-esteem and her identity. Now she had lost it all. One little bright spot remained— though it would have been an easy one to dismiss. As a sideline, Arlene had developed a small Herbalife business and was making about $1,000 a month. Even though she wasn't actively trying to build a large

Conquering the world: Arlene, daughter Toni, son Paul, at Leadership Weekend in San Francisco, October 1998. All four children are in Herbalife— the Geraci Dynasty.

downline, she did attend the meetings, seminars, and trainings. "I enjoyed the atmosphere, the positive attitude. They were fun." It was a nice place to meet like-minded people. Now, "I started going to every Herbalife meeting, just to be around those people. I needed something positive in my life." Though Arlene was about to lose her home, she took the money intended to be used for her move into an apartment house and spent it to fly to Las Vegas for an Herbalife training session, because "I knew I had to get around successful people." Seven months later she was earning $8,000 a month. She then decided to build a large business and aimed at becoming a member of Herbalife's President's Club, with a mid–six figure income. It took her nine months to get there. When she stood up in front of four thousand people to accept the President's Club diamond pin, she says, "It was the happiest day in my life."

Now all four children are in the Herbalife business, and are referred to as the Geraci Dynasty. When daughter Lynda joined the business, Arlene had all nine members of her family picked up in limos and flown to Tempe, Arizona, to visit and celebrate. Arlene loves being generous, and to make sure there are no limits to that generosity, "I have a goal to earn a million dollars a year." She states this in a matter-of-fact tone, and then adds, "It's just a fact. There is no question about it."

Kathleen Deoul

KATHLEEN DEOUL ONCE had to drag herself to the office where she looked and felt tired most of the time. Now that she's with Nikken, she loves to rhapsodize about her working vacations, when she and her family—daughter Shannon and husband Neal, a former physicist and engineer—enjoy themselves while visiting her downline: "We were in Alaska visiting the Portage Glacier. It looked like God had poured pancake batter between two beautiful mountain

Soaring to new heights: The network marketing lifestyle means families together, trips that seem like vacations, and residuals that keep on rising. Kathleen Deoul of Nikken was inspired to heights of poetic rapture in describing her unforgettable travels with husband Neal and daughter Shannon.

ranges. Gigantic chunks of ice were crashing into the icy cold black water. The ice glowed an eerie blue like giant Popsicles. The glacier itself ran for miles and miles between the mountains where it had carved its bed. My little daughter, Shannon, ran all the way down to the lip of the water so she could touch the blue ice flows. We went to Juneau, which was like a frontier western town with its Red Dog Saloon. It looked like a movie set sitting on the base of the mountains right on the water. There were a lot of very interesting, intelligent, and scruffy characters who are more interested in freedom than comfort. From there we went to Hawaii. I went down a water slide, which was thrilling because a few years ago I wouldn't have had the energy to do it. We stayed at a hotel I had seen on *Lifestyles of the Rich and Famous.* My daughter asked me to go parasailing with her because she was too light to do it alone. It was unbelievable, incredible. I was in the sky 800 feet high, next to my daughter. I turned my head sideways to look at her, and the noise of the wind died completely. I was surrounded by peace and silence, looking at my daughter's smiling face. I could see her joy, awe, and wonder. I was filled with gratitude for the time we were spending together. I got tears in my eyes thinking that when we returned, I would still be free to make cookies for her when she came home from school. Neal would be free, too. It was a wonderful feeling of thankfulness. When we did return, my Nikken check had increased by $25,000."

Robbie Dodd

MORE THAN HALF a century ago, a fifteen-year-old girl from Desha, Arkansas, was sent off to Atlantic City to represent her state in the Miss America contest. The crown went to someone else—someone older, perhaps—and Miss Arkansas went to work with a modeling agency in New York City. Over the next few years, Robbie Dodd lived a lifetime, emerging in her early twenties as both a cancer survivor and single mother. Recuperating from illness and shouldering

Powerhouse of inspiration: Robbie Dodd's mission is to "open the door to freedom" for others. She intends to set the pace for dreaming by earning $1 million a month.

the responsibility of feeding and caring for two young children, she renounced any thought of longing for past glory; instead, she adopted a lifelong philosophy that transformed her into the powerhouse she still is today. The core of her simple yet profound outlook is this: "Where I am going is more important than where I have been."

Back on her feet, Robbie flew into action selling custom-fitted bras door to door, displaying a conviction that made people think she had been born for the task. "I would put my little boy Christopher in the stroller and pack the product behind him. Then I would take my daughter Cynthia by the hand and start walking. It took me about eighty-five houses to earn enough to put food on the table." As her business grew, she developed bigger dreams, and four decades ago she discovered network marketing.

Today Robbie brings the same dedication to spreading the word about Tahitian noni juice from Morinda, Inc., a product she fell in love with after learning that native Polynesians have used noni juice for more than two thousand years because of its amazing health and energy benefits. "I have an international organization," she notes. "We are in Germany, Japan, England, Australia, and Taiwan." Someone in her group is opening China, and last year she herself opened Sweden, where her downline is now in the thousands.

Because of her background, some people have a special place in Robbie's heart. They include cancer survivors, single mothers—"and single fathers, too"—as well as senior citizens. "I speak at many seminars, like the American Association of Retired Persons, and open the door to freedom to them." One distributor who has worked with her in all her companies is now ninety-three years old. She also was recently pleased to hear from a twenty-two-year-old whose passion for noni juice took him from unemployment to owning a Porsche. She invites members of her diverse group over to her million-dollar, seventeen-room Mediterranean home where they can nurture their dreams while sitting on the terrace with a view of the Pacific and Coronado Island. Her husband of twenty-five years, J. D., joined her in network marketing a decade ago.

When members of her group try to give Robbie Dodd credit for their success, she says, "I just opened the door for them to succeed financially. I opened a door in their minds that let them dream." Robbie Dodd herself is still dreaming, and her goals are still expanding. For instance, she has never earned $1 million in one month, and now has that as a goal.

Why do it, Robbie? You might as well have asked her: Why break the four-minute mile? Why go to the moon? The answer is obvious: "I do it because it will help others. It will be an inspiration. It will open their minds to what is possible." As for what's possible for her, she says, "I believe that there is no ceiling to life. I am the proverbial student. I am in a constant state of opening my heart, soul, and mind to learn more."

> "Think of what happens when you network. Today I am who I am, and they are who they are, because we networked. That means that I gave them the best that I am, and they gave me the best that they are. So we all rose."
>
> —Robbie Dodd, Morinda, Inc.

Sandy Weathers

SANDY WEATHERS GOT people to join her in Herbalife by telling them how much fun it was being successful and helping others. It took a while, but eventually Sandy got her boyfriend, Tommy Gioiosa, into the spirit, and his business boomed. Then one day when the pair

A vital lesson: Have fun! Sandy Weathers finally got Tommy Gioiosa to understand her secret of success. That inspired Tommy to give his parents a surprise gift.

walked into the home of Tommy's parents in New Bedford, Massachusetts, Tommy was struck by how old some of the furnishings were. He noted the worn carpet, the ancient stove, and the furniture you couldn't give away at a garage sale. That night, Tommy said to Sandy, "We have the money now. Why don't we remodel the home for them?"

It took the pair three days of intense organizing to prepare. They told Tommy's mother they were taking her out to buy a sofa. While she was out, the remodeling teams went to work—tearing up the old carpet and replacing it with a new one, laying new linoleum, installing a new stove and refrigerator. The teams put new floors in the bathroom and redid one of the bedrooms. All the old furniture was thrown out and replaced. When Mom returned at the end of the day, she was ecstatic—even noting that the new furniture perfectly matched the sofa she spent so much time picking out. As a new big-screen TV was being installed, Tommy's father hugged his son's neck, and asked through tear-filled eyes, "How will we ever repay you?"

"It was fun," said Tommy and Sandy together. "We did it because it was fun."

14

The Next Wave

BUILDING ON THE accomplishments of their elders, young people are bringing a fresh excitement to network marketing—and they're doing it their way.

Enthusiasm——and Gratitude

"I'M THIRD-GENERATION AND proud of it," says twenty-five-year-old Jenah Victor, a member of one of the country's most prominent Amway families. In the eyes of many, Jenah and her brother and cousins occupy a position a little like those whose ancestors arrived on the Mayflower—except better, considering her family's ongoing achievements. Her grandparents, Joe and Helyne Victor (whom we profiled in chapter 3), were among the founders of the American Way Association, the organization that spawned Amway. Jenah believes it was she, as a toddler, who gave Joe the enduring nickname of "Papa Amway." But there's nothing smug about Jenah's declaration of pride.

The Victor family's Amway organization is flourishing. Jenah Victor is a third generation distributor; her brother "R. J." is in the wings.

It comes across as pure wholesome enthusiasm, plus a healthy dose of gratitude—and with good reason. As a recent article on family business in *Management Review* put it, "Typically, only one out of three businesses is successfully transferred to the second generation. Survival of a family business into the third generation is a rare occurrence."

For Jenah Victor, one experience helped crystallize the benefits of her family business: "More than anything it was YYLC—the Yager Youth Leadership Conference," she says. A summer camp, the conference is open to the children of all Amway distributors—offspring generically known as AmKids. Jenah calls YYLC "awesome—the greatest thing they could have ever done." The sessions are held in North Carolina in two sessions lasting two weeks each, with attendance limited to some three hundred-plus young men and women between the ages of sixteen and thirty. Some attendees go to both sessions, benefiting from "the same information, different friends." Says Jenah, "It gives us the opportunity to see each other. We are the future generation of America."

"This is where we go to get motivated and fired up," she adds. "We learn goal setting, communications, group dynamics, interpersonal skills. There's a big thick binder you go through in class sessions. There's an Olympics based on team effort and leadership. I learned very, very valuable principles—not just what you can get if you're from the right family."

An anecdote about Jenah's introduction to YYLC will amuse all those with a fuzzy understanding of Amway's ranks and titles. A small incident, it speaks volumes—both about Dexter Yager's impressive youth leadership project and about a well-bred young woman's unaffected behavior. Jenah begins with the background: "They have a saying around the business—that you're a 'Diamond Kid.' But I wasn't brought up to think of myself as a Diamond Kid. I was a Victor."

At YYLC, Diamond Kids are accorded some considerations—"such as eating in a special dining room," says Jenah. But when she arrived, she confesses, "I didn't know all this. I was a rookie at the event." Jenah failed to identify herself as among the privileged; and when the time came for Diamond Kids to go their own way, a fellow AmKid excluded her with the words, "She can't, 'cause she's not Diamond."

That night on the phone with her father, Ron Victor, Jenah learned that "I was a Crown Kid," and as such, eligible for any Diamond privileges. Still not quite grasping it all, Jenah wondered out loud if she would be embarrassed for pushing her way in. "Daddy had to tell me, 'Honey, a Crown is higher than a Diamond.'" (In fact, it's a highly select nobility—one Ron had entered at the age of twenty-nine—representing an organization roughly three times the size of a Diamond.) The next day, Jenah handled it all nicely and without putting on airs. "I never let it be known it affected me. I stayed in the cafeteria with my new friends. I had a lot of fun."

For parents, it's a centuries-old challenge: The children of highly successful families often fail to perceive how good they have it, until some outside experiences open their eyes to their good fortune. Acknowledging as much, Jenah says, "I'm glad I didn't work for Daddy all my life." In various summer and part-time jobs, Jenah has worked for the minimum wage and endured the frustrations of being a manager. She headed a student-run radio station while attending Mississippi University for Women. She also spent eight weeks in Poland in 1996, teaching English using the Bible and gaining an illuminating view of the international presence of the Victor family operation. "I found out this business really is worldwide," she says.

In college, the tribulations of a friend proved to be a valuable lesson. The friend's mother became seriously ill. As so often happens, the illness walloped the family business, creating crises at work and at home. "My friend was forced to quit school, and then the business went under also. What hit me emotionally is that at the same time my little brother was born with a rare metabolic disorder. Yet my family was able to do everything necessary to care for him. I heard wonderful things about my dad being the only father at the Ronald McDonald House. My friend had thought that there was security in a family business. But she didn't have that. Yet here my father's business provided me with a residual that kept me in college with a monthly allowance while allowing him time to give my brother all the emotional support that was needed."

Today, thanks to unstinting time and attention lavished on him by his parents, six-year-old "R. J." is thriving. He even seems to have a grasp of family destiny in that he loudly and enthusiastically proclaims to all his intention of growing up to be "a great leader—just like his grandfather." As everyone in his family would agree, in their kind of business there will be nothing to stop him from doing just that.

Papa Amway's Legacy

It was a suspenseful moment for Stephen Victor. He had decided it was time to be frank with a particular young woman. "I just want you to know," he began, "that what my family does is a little different."

Marcia, a fellow student at Bowling Green State University, looked concerned.

"Have you ever heard of Amway?" asked Stephen.

"Amway? What's that?" replied Marcia.

Stephen was thrilled. "Yes!" he thought. Somebody with no preconceived ideas.

Stephen next faced the prospect of introducing Marcia not only to Amway, but to the world of the Victor family, with its organization extending to eighty-three countries and millions of people. Stephen knew that most families were hard-pressed to think past the next paycheck, let alone have the vision to get passionate about unborn generations. But he was from a clan in which Papa Amway would fire up sons Jody and Ron with statements like, "Let's show more people how

The younger generation of Victors is choosing the same business as their successful parents and pio-neering grandparents. The Victor family at a World Series game: In front row, from left, Terri Victor Fraumann, Joseph (Joe) Edward Victor III, and Stephen, with parents Kathy and Jody.

to have independent wealth." On noting the IRS records showing that only 1 percent of the population made more than $200,000 per year, Joe Victor had said, "Let's change that 1 percent to 4 percent."

Like all the members of the Victor family, Stephen speaks about two distinct ways of living your life—Plan A versus Plan B. Plan A is the norm. It means holding a job. Plan B is building a residual income and having the chance to enhance your own life and that of others. Says Stephen, "I grew up in a Plan B world, being around positive people with an emphasis on dreaming bigger dreams. Marcia's mom and dad both had jobs. So we had two really different backgrounds. Now we're married, and both on the same page."

After graduating in 1992, Stephen considered other career options besides Amway, including law school. Perhaps the main concern he had about going into the family business was matching the record of his father, Jody, who had achieved singular distinction by following in Joe's footsteps and becoming a Crown Direct Distributor. "I knew I wanted to do this business. My only fear was, 'Gosh, can I do that?'" His father and grandfather assured him he could.

Today Stephen works as a vice president in his father Jody's corporation, overseeing domestic and international operations. Marcia works there also, in charge of accounting. Then after work, "we build our own Amway business separately from our parents" under the name of Dream Team Enterprises. "We love it," says Stephen. He feels they are living "the dream of having a business that is generational—that can be passed down from grandfather to grandson. It's the dream of every parent to build an asset that you can leave to the next generation."

Stephen contrasts his situation with that of a friend in a family tool and machine shop. "He is also third-generation. But he comes home and complains about the hours and the stress while I come home all excited and can't wait to get out and show somebody the plan."

Determined to match his father's accomplishments, Stephen says, "I see the opportunity today as greater than ever. Now is the best time to be involved. In my grandfather's day they had one way to profit. Today there are many ways to make money."

Families Like Ours

From an office in her parents' house in Manchester near Akron, Stephen's sister, Terri Sue, twenty-seven, helps plan the functions for the family's Amway activities. A former kindergarten teacher, her duties range from booking hotels and ballrooms to acting as her father's personal assistant. Like her cousin Jenah, Terri Sue attended the Yager Youth Leadership Conference and says, "What I liked about it was that you met kids who grew up in a family like yours. That was neat. At school, kids didn't understand why you were going to a rally on Saturday." Terri Sue had decided well before the conference that she would go into the family business, but attending helped confirm that "I made the right decision." It was there in June 1994 that she met her future husband, Greg Fraumann, twenty-nine, the son of an Amway Diamond from Atlanta. Of Greg, she says, "It's kind of funny. I didn't know him at all. Dad kind of set us up without our even knowing about it." Jody had called Greg's parents and urged that they get their son to attend. The two were introduced at the conference and, "before you know it, we were married," says Terri Sue. If anybody has a background as imbued with the business as Terri Sue does, it is Greg. "He was two years old when his parents went Diamond," she says. The Fraumanns have kept the business Greg developed under his parents and treat it as their number two enterprise. Their focus is on building the business in the Victor organization.

Stephen and Terri Sue's younger brother, Joseph (Joe) Edward Victor III, a senior at Bowling Green, will also go into the business full time upon graduation.

For a business to survive to the third generation is uncommon in itself. For that business to spawn an unlimited number of positions for the new generation is remarkable. But what may be most striking is the positive vision shared by these descendants—the conviction that tomorrow will be even brighter than today.

Says Jenah, "In the year 2060, when I have great grandchildren, the opportunity will be the same. It will still offer financial freedom, the freedom to be whom you want to be, the freedom to work part-time and live full time." And then—perhaps reflecting on those less-than-quality hours spent as a wage earner and employee—Jenah adds a thought appropriate for any twenty-five-year-old: "You only get one chance to go through this life."

Helyne Victor says the outlook for her grandchildren is clear: "Their future could not be brighter."

Health, Friends, Hope, and a Car

WHILE THE NEW generation of Victors is entering a business their grandparents launched half a century ago, the brothers and sisters in the following story are stepping into a business that their mother built only in the past few years.

Siblings, friends, and business associates. When Collette Van Reusen's children compared the benefits of USANA to other opportunities, they decided it had all they were seeking for their varied interests and inclinations—including weekly residual checks. From left: Dax Ross, Chelsea Ross, Sharlie Ross, and Zak Ross.

Sharlie's Speech

With tears in her eyes, Collette Van Reusen watched her daughter Sharlie from the screen backstage.

"I wanted to help Sharlie with her speech," says Collette. "She had to stand up in front of five thousand people at the 1997 USANA national convention, and she was eighteen years old." Sharlie finally said, "Mother, I can tell my own story."

Stepping out on stage before the crowd, Sharlie mentioned four things that USANA had done to improve her life, even as she battled with cystic fibrosis.

"First, my health has improved. I know it is due to USANA products," she said.

"Second, all of you have become such friends. I feel your love and your support."

"Third . . . my car." (Great laughter.)

Her fourth point: "USANA has given me hope."

"Let Them Fly"

The self-reliance displayed by Sharlie, now twenty years old, shouldn't have surprised Collette, for in her own words, "I have always wanted to raise children who are governed by their own sense of responsibility." Collette's philosophy had been "You love them and nurture them and then you kick them out of the nest and let them fly." Collette's children, after doing some flying, saw nothing to match the personal and financial rewards of USANA.

While all of Collette's offspring are now involved with USANA, Sharlie Ross is especially identified with the company and its products. Those who know Sharlie might rush to point out that her story is her own—that it has a profoundly inspiring human value far exceeding any kind of pitch used to sell products or sign someone up for an opportunity. But that is exactly the point: Sharing experiences with others is the heart and soul of the way USANA does business. The method works precisely because those around you are not just professional associates, but people with whom you have the strongest of bonds. Here the younger generation provides the acid test that it all works as promised.

A turning point in the story of this family came in March 1994, when Collette took Sharlie in for her annual pulmonary function test, a regular requirement for sufferers of cystic fibrosis.

"Pulmonary function test day is the worst day of the year. You dread it," explains Collette. "This is a degenerative terminal disease." On the previous test, Sharlie's functioning had dropped to 39 percent. "I thought then that when it got down to 35 percent, you only had a year to live," says Collette. "Now I know never to give up hope," she adds.

And on this day, Sharlie's lung function had improved. The test showed her pulmonary function in the 50 percentile range. "It was remarkable to us—and to the pulmonologist, who did the test three times to see if it was a mistake," says Collette.

For the first time Sharlie was feeling better. "In the women's restroom we were laughing and crying and hugging each other," recalls Collette. "Driving home we couldn't believe it. Sharlie began saying, 'USANA. It has to be USANA.' At that point she had been on the product for six months, and she was really feeling it made a difference."

Collette reminded herself that "we are very much a praying family." She thought, "Maybe this is an opportunity to teach Sharlie a lesson." So, in response to Sharlie's enthusiasm for USANA, Collette said, "Maybe your improvement is the answer to prayer."

Sharlie's answer stunned her mother. "Maybe," said Sharlie, "the answer to our prayers is USANA." Sharlie then expressed herself even more forcefully. "Mother, the only thing I've done different is USANA."

That personal testimonial from her own daughter spurred Collette into action. "That was the night I decided to start my business," says Collette, adding she was now determined to make the transition from being simply a user of the product to a distributor. "I realized that maybe it was the way to get out of a huge financial hole."

In the five years since then, Sharlie "has blossomed," says her mother. At the same time, Collette has been USANA's leading distributor every year since 1995, and is on track to become a four-star diamond by summer 1999. While Collette, who still drives a Nissan Maxima, does not like to reveal her earnings, compensation at that level is known to be approximately $1 million per year.

Making a Commitment

Each of the children admired their mother's amazing success, but it took a trip abroad to cement their commitment to USANA. Collette went with Sharlie and sons Zak and Dax to Australia between January and May 1998, coinciding with USANA's opening of the country.

Sharlie, who had just graduated from high school, recalls, "Mom said, 'Take the year off. Travel with me. We're going to start an organization in Australia.' It was so exciting for me. We all worked together. It exceeded my expectations totally." Sharlie, her health rebounding, especially delighted in the speaking opportunities. "I spoke a lot in Australia—at every meeting I went to. I really love doing it," she says.

"I deal with people who have CF," adds Sharlie. "They are passed on to me, and I work with them personally. Every case of CF is so different, and I love helping all these people. I usually find out what they are doing. I tell them what I am doing. I tell them what I take. It has helped my own health so much."

Sharlie's recent activities include being the closing speaker following a panel of doctors and physicians at a USANA meeting in San Diego. Sharlie and Collette hasten to point out they don't presume to have medical knowledge. But, they say, their efforts can alert those with CF to useful nutritional information that they can discuss with their doctors. It's just that kind of personal testimonial that makes network marketing so effective, said analyst Patricia Negron in an article in *Investor's Business Daily* in June 1998. "With direct selling, you have direct contact with the consumer," said Ms. Negron, of Adams, Harkness & Hill Inc., a brokerage. That's important, she said, because the restrictions on labeling imposed by the FDA make it "difficult to communicate what the products are for." So, she adds, "For USANA, I think this format is a better way to go than traditional retail distribution."

As life-saving as the products are, they are not the only reason Sharlie is drawn to the business. "A huge part of USANA is the friends we have made. They are a part of my life—my lifetime friends." In addition, says Sharlie, "I think the business has totally brought our family together. I think it is something I will do, a way for me to make an income. Because of it I can have any career I want without worrying about finances." For a person with a disease like CF to have such choices is in itself a sort of miracle.

"Building My Own Business"

Sharlie's twenty-five-year-old brother, Zak Ross, also says the trip to Australia is what sealed his commitment to USANA. "Mom presented me with the opportunity of building my own business," he says. "She asked me to go along to Australia." The trip—just after his

December 1997 graduation from Brigham Young University—"was my first taste" of being closely involved with USANA as a business. "For the first time, I got a sense of the opportunity and the fact it is something I want to do," he says. While in Australia, Zak worked in his mother's business and also started his own downline. "I had a blast," he says. "It was so much fun." Now back home and fully involved, Zak says, "I really like working with people. And I like learning from my mother. We do several three-way calls daily."

Zak's calling once seemed to lie outside of business altogether. After his freshman year in college, he went on a mission to Santiago, Chile, for two years with the Mormon Church. Then, in 1997, he taught literacy in rural Mexico. "I loved it. I want to get back down there. My passion is Spanish and helping the Latin people," he says. But he also knows "I can't generate an income" with that kind of work. Now, instead of being forced to abandon the ideals of youth, Zak and his wife, Kelli, who works in special education, will be able to pursue whatever passions they choose.

Like many young people, Zak's impressions of the everyday world of work were less than inspiring. "We had a pizza shop in the 1980s," he recalls. It was his father's store, and "we never saw him," he says. "I remember how hard it was. We were pretty much broke. It was a stressful situation." By contrast, says Zak, "This business is so anti-stress. We have so much fun. We travel together, work together, keep in touch." Of his siblings—Sharlie, Dax, and Chelsea—he says, "We work great together. We're good friends." While it's clear this is a family whose members care deeply for one another, it's worth noting that in conventional family businesses the harsh demands of competition often erode such goodwill. Happily, Collette's children will never have to vie with one another for scarce positions. Nor can anyone take their livelihoods away from them, or tell them how to run their individual businesses.

"Income for Life"

They are also unusual in that few people of any age in any occupation today can say with confidence, as Zak does, "I know there will be a stream of income for the rest of my life for me and my family." And, make no mistake, we're talking about money Zak can put in his pockets today. As he puts it, "The residual checks come in weekly. I like the income."

Dax Ross, twenty-six, Collette's oldest, is a 1999 graduate of the University of California at San Diego, with a degree in philosophy. He, too, says his commitment to USANA was galvanized by the Australia trip. "For me, for the first time, I was really involved in USANA. It felt good to see it grow and to be a part of it." His enthusiasm was sparked by "being in on the beginning of something new. There was the excitement of helping people go from nothing to a large organization." In one year, the size of that organization soared to twenty-five thousand Australians, a telling indication of the company's potential for continued expansion. For financially oriented Dax, that growth helped make a compelling case for him "to start focusing my time in USANA." Any doubts he harbored—such as whether he would find the business suitable or enjoyable—were soon swept away. "Spending time with my mom instills confidence," he says. "Her enthusiasm is contagious."

On the other hand, this oldest child feels no pressure to be a carbon copy of his mother. "I don't have the same kind of charisma as Mom," he says without apology. "I would rather work one-on-one with people." In some family businesses, such a show of individuality might alarm the founder, as well as investors and directors. But here being an individual is no sin; the needs of the business are shaped to the desires of people, rather than vice versa. As Dax rightly points out, "In our kind of business, everyone has something they can do. It's not like the traditional business. I do the Internet, Zak does voicemail, Sharlie goes to meetings. There is more of a variety of opportunities." Dax's varied interests include writing and computer design, as well as investing and financial planning, which he sees as going hand in hand with guiding the recently formed family corporation. Dax's stock investments, says Collette, "have made me a wealthy woman all over again."

The family talent pool includes daughter Chelsea, a twenty-four-year-old student at Brigham Young University who, in addition to her building her own business, is treasurer of the family corporation and pays all the bills. "I e-mail assignments to them all," says Collette. "I say, 'This person needs to be contacted.' We have a tag team approach."

Handing Down a Legacy

Asked to sum up her accomplishments, Collette says, "What a legacy we're passing on to our children." Then she adds, "Personally, I am looking forward to mine taking over the bulk of my day-to-day operations! And the way they're 'getting it,' I don't think that day is too far off."

Judging from their enthusiasm, Collette's children give every indication they plan to pour into USANA the same extraordinary zeal that their mother manifested. Fortunately, that's not a burning issue. Unlike the typical business, this one won't crash and burn if people take a little time to discover their "why"—Collette's term for one's driving purpose in life. Meanwhile Collette's "why"—to be the number one contributor to cystic fibrosis research—burns as brightly as ever.

"I set a goal to give back more than I receive. But I found it was absolutely impossible," says Collette. "I couldn't increase my giving fast enough. The more I give, the more I get."

15

A Parable

Tʜᴇ sᴛᴏʀʏ ᴏғ the Rev. Jonathan Stanley and his family reads like a parable about network marketing. Its moral seems to be the following: If you have the courage to start, and the willingness to persist while placing the needs of others above your own, then you'll overcome the obstacles and reap satisfying rewards. Like Ken Pontious in chapter 4, the Stanleys are more concerned with "being the right person" than they are with "finding the right people." Like Dr. Kathy Bliese in chapter 7, they find that selflessness is the path to success. Taken together, those points come close to summarizing the essential lessons of the entire book.

Pastor in a Small Town

Jᴏɴᴀᴛʜᴀɴ Sᴛᴀɴʟᴇʏ ɪs the pastor of a small Presbyterian Church in Gillett, Pennsylvania. The town itself is so little you may have trouble locating it on a map, which helps explain why Rev. Stanley and his wife Donna found it so appealing. In Gillett the couple discovered people who were friendly, an environment that was unspoiled, and an area they saw as desirable for raising a family. "We wanted to live in a healthy, rural setting," says Jonathan. "We're the type who doesn't move around a lot, so when we got here and liked it, we wanted to stay." What made it all look even better was the open-ended agreement offered him by the members of Sylvania Presbyterian Church. While that agreement includes compensation, of course, it has been some time since Jonathan, now thirty-five, and Donna, thirty-one, have needed this paycheck. That's because their income from network marketing has been more than sufficient to support them.

The Stanleys did not set out to become network marketers. Their involvement began after Donna told a friend about a health problem she was having. The friend, who is a pastor, told Donna about Enrich's wide range of nutritional products and supplements. After four months of taking Enrich products, Donna's problem—a bowel disorder—had cleared up. "I'd also lost twenty pounds without dieting," says Donna. Her enthusiasm for the company was so strong she agreed to start building a business. "I was looking for a way to work at home anyway," she says. Before long, Donna had yet another reason to be thankful for Enrich. The Stanleys had been married eleven years, and Donna had recently mentioned to friends her hopes of someday having children. "I remember that one of the ladies in Enrich recommended a product called ST, which contains Norwegian kelp. I took it, and then I got pregnant." Donna feels positive the product made the difference. In any case, daughter Olivia was born in 1998.

Making Calls—Winning Friends

Jonathan and Donna waited before talking with members of their church about Enrich. Instead, they concentrated their initial efforts on making phone calls to strangers—what's known as working the cold market. Many people shy away from cold calls, but Donna and Jonathan didn't have the luxury of indulging such doubts. They plunged in, and found their efforts highly rewarding. "We started to develop friendships with people across the country who had similar goals, dreams, and desires," says Jonathan. "The people who are in Enrich with us are people who have interests like ours, and that makes for really good friendships," adds Donna. "It's neat how you mix the business and friendship all together," she says.

One striking fact is that Jonathan, who went to the Philadelphia College of Bible, is the third pastor out of four in his Enrich sponsorship line. After he joined, he sponsored his father, who is also a minister.

If the Stanleys had not joined Enrich, they say, they

The Rev. Jonathan Stanley, wife Donna, baby Olivia. He believes learning about personal growth and self-help via Enrich has made him a more effective minister.

would not know most of the people they now count as friends. These friends include individuals who are upline and downline from them; it also includes people who are cross-line, or out of their sponsorship line. While cross-line individuals sometimes see each other as competitors, a more beneficial approach is to view one another as allies and resources—and friends. "We have friends cross-line, and we spur each other on," says Jonathan.

Eventually, as the Stanleys built their business, acquaintances at home in Gillett and in their church also started hearing about Enrich. The couple initially was criticized for being in "one of those businesses."

As it turned out, though, "I have not lost one friend because I am involved with network marketing," says Jonathan, adding, "But I sure have gained a few." Jonathan says he thinks he understands the reason that "I took so much flak from people at church for being in network marketing." It stems from their being "afraid I won't need my paycheck." But Rev. Stanley says he believes the business has made him more resourceful as a minister, and that everyone benefits because "I continue to care for my flock, yet I don't rely on my pastoral income." He also finds great value in the information on personal growth that he has discovered through Enrich and the network marketing community. He's convinced that his extensive use of self-improvement materials "translates directly back to my work in the church." In short, he says, "I am a more effective pastor because of the business." For example, he notes that self-help books and tapes have helped him understand more about people and get to root issues faster. He adds, "I am a better communicator, I know more about people, and I get to those deep issues faster." In working with people on the issues in their lives, he finds that network marketers are often more easily helped than others "because they are more positive."

Counseling His Downline About Happiness

If network marketing has helped Jonathan with his pastoral duties, what impact has his ministry had on his Enrich activities? Jonathan says the impact has been significant. For example, in counseling members of his downline, he cautions people against falling prey to the illusion that happiness is just a matter of obtaining "the next level of success or the next big check." Says Rev. Stanley, "They need to learn to be happy where they are." On the other hand, he quickly agrees that "the money helps, of course." After careful observation and thought, he's concluded that "the people who do the best tend to be very happy," and that their success is the result of caring about others first.

The Stanleys find great satisfaction in working with people in the business on issues of personal development. Jonathan strives "to help people face things in their lives that they may not be ready to face." Donna echoes his view, saying, "When you can be honest with somebody about what they need to change—like telling them, 'You're too negative' or 'You need to change who you are hanging out with'—it makes a big difference."

Donna works to help people in her group get past the obstacles in their lives. She finds the task easier when people have no doubt that her concerns are wholeheartedly for their welfare. Adds Jonathan, "If you are self-centered it will come through. Helping other people has to be your complete focus."

The Stanleys believe that if a distributor is self-centered others will quickly realize it. "When someone puts his own needs first, others will feel they are a pawn in his game and they won't build." On the other hand, he says, "When you are just as happy at someone else's success—and when you are genuinely happy for someone cross-line from you—then you have gotten the idea of friendship that runs through this business."

For Jonathan, one of the greatest pleasures of the business is seeing the spark in people's eyes when their group starts to grow. "When new opportunities bloom they get really excited. I love that," he says.

New Horizons—And Trips to Hawaii

For Donna, one of the ways network marketing has opened new horizons is by providing travel opportunities. The Stanleys took their first Enrich trip when they were awarded an all-expense-paid vacation to Hawaii—now Donna's favorite destination. Since that trip they have gone to all sorts of places they couldn't have afforded on a pastor's salary. "The major corporate events are a wonderful opportunity to see nice places and be away for a few days," says Jonathan.

Not long ago, the thought of mainstream ministers signing up as distributors for network marketing companies—and then sponsoring yet more clergymen—would have seemed outlandish. Today, however, Jonathan Stanley is far from unique. He and other pastors in network marketing are proud of their involvement. They happily point out that the business has made them better ministers. They praise the supportive culture of network marketing and its positive impact on the individuals who are part of it.

They also see their newfound financial freedom as providential. For some it offers the opportunity to fund special projects out of their own pockets. For all, it means they can turn their efforts to taking care of their flock without worrying about putting bread on their own tables. Ultimately, though, there may not be that much distinction between the motivations of the Stanleys and that of other people. As Jonathan put it, "You have to understand that we had absolutely no sales experience, and no network marketing history."

They seem to have stayed involved and succeeded for the same reasons that millions of other network marketers do. In the words of both: "We love people."

Conclusion
The Mindset of Success

A S YOU VISUALIZE your own future, use the stories in this book to open your eyes, your mind, and your heart to what you can achieve. We, the authors, believe these powerful stories will give you hope, courage, energy, and enthusiasm. We believe the network marketing lifestyle of freedom and friendship gives you the opportunity to dream, to grow, to prosper, and to give to others the tools to make *their* dreams come true. We also believe you can get started successfully in network marketing simply by having the right attitudes, which include commitment, determination, and perseverance. As you've already discovered, every story in *Heart to Heart* is imbued with many such attitudes of success, some of which are more subtle than others. We also recommend you emulate the following attitudes and actions:

Develop a knack for breezing past critics and skeptics. As any entrepreneur can attest, being assailed by doubters and scoffers is not peculiar to network marketing. Anyone who sets out on a different path needs the self-confidence to persist in the face of detractors. Valerie Barger recalls giving a tape to someone who responded scornfully, "Valerie, you're nuts. This is a scam." Valerie never lost a beat. "Give me back the tape," she said, and went on to the next person.

Take prudent risks. Making a change in your life always involves some risk. But deciding to take a risk doesn't mean becoming a wild gambler. It doesn't mean displaying a fearless machismo. It certainly doesn't mean plunging ahead and leaving issues like expenses to fate. The most successful risk takers are those who take calculated risks, who identify an opportunity and then work to eliminate as much of the risk as they can. Neta Irwin obtained expert assurance that Arbonne's compensation plan made sense. Debbie and Jerry Campisi made a decision to move forward in a measured way while not depleting their assets or spending their existing income in the business. They were willing to make sacrifices, which are usually necessary when launching any sort of a venture. But as Jerry notes, "Getting over your head in debt is a mistake." In network marketing, it's a mistake that can always be avoided.

Refuse to make excuses. Motivated, enthusiastic people often sail over obstacles that paralyze less committed individuals. Bella Werzberger had a host of reasons for never getting started in network marketing. Even her religion seemed to stand in the way, preventing her from attending Saturday rallies and restricting the number of Herbalife products she and others of her faith could consume. But Bella found a way to get past every difficulty, and she and her husband Nick ended up achieving a resounding victory: The Brooklyn couple spearheaded a change in giant Herbalife that led to the company introducing its own line of Kosher products.

Appreciate that persistent effort pays off. When Bella Werzberger first threw herself into building her business she says she hardly knew what she was doing. But her drive and desire eventually helped her bring the challenge into focus. Motivator Richard Ruffalo, exploding with frustration at his blindness, flailed wildly at a large punching bag. But as he struck out in a frenzy, his efforts became gradually more coordinated and meaningful. Soon, he was engaged in a systematic conditioning that ultimately turned out to be the first stage in his triumph as a world champion athlete. Mike Williams was crippled by despair and doubts. But then he began taking steps to build his Reliv business and discovered an age-old secret: Action conquers fear.

Do what is necessary to stick with your commitment. Pam Lewko learned of an opportunity with New Vision International. She discussed the pros and cons with her husband and son, made the decision to pursue it, and went to work. She didn't just drift into the business, or give it a few desultory attempts. She and her family adjusted their lives and their schedules to make Pam's efforts possible. Having a growing baby who was making increasing demands didn't deter Pam; she juggled her tasks, adjusted her habits, and devised new routines. At times the work seemed grueling. But today Pam's family—now financially secure—looks back with pride and nostalgia on the intense period of building the business and even calls it "a pretty fun journey."

Believe in yourself despite setbacks. Gregory Lagana and his family were devastated, financially and otherwise, by their first experience with network marketing. He admits his mistakes were numerous and often colossal. However, Gregory chose not to view the episode as a failure on his part but as a step along the road to success. Roland Fox failed twenty-five times before finding success with Oxyfresh. But in fact, as Roland points out, he wasn't really failing—he was learning.

Foster a passion for the lifestyle of the business. Bobbie Soetaert had several searing encounters with mismanaged network marketing companies. Yet the positive attractions of the business—both the substantial wealth and the supportive culture—left no doubt in her mind that she would leap back into the business each time. Tom Pinnock's dream of being with his wife and family and experiencing the joys of fatherhood enabled him to keep striving until he had made it. Neta

Irwin wanted a home-based business badly enough to overcome her fears of being without a salaried job.

Start with clear simple objectives. Don Held's first objectives when he joined Amway were new shoes for his children and an automatic dishwasher. Don Storms' first goal was to get his wife Ruth a grandfather clock with cabinets on the side. Says Storms: "Decide what you want, how you're going to get it, and the date you're going to have it. Give your dreams a deadline—otherwise they're just fantasies." Shirley Thorne wrote on the mirror with lipstick that Jeff would be "boss free" in twenty-four months. He made it on schedule. The Thornes also attained the long list of other goals they wrote out—each of which, from the type of car they wanted to the size of their new house, was quite specific.

Nurture the ability to think big. Joe Victor got his sons, Jody and Ron, to pursue in a practical way goals that were immense and visionary in scope. "Let's show more people how to have independent wealth," Joe would say. He urged his sons to set a goal of increasing by two percent the number of people in the country that had incomes of more than $200,000. He told them to think of their impact on generations that were yet unborn. With such noble and majestic objectives in mind, other challenges along the way seemed small by comparison. Robbie Dodd wants to inspire others to lift their sights and think big by setting a record of earning $1 million a month.

Gain confidence by observing others who succeeded. For some, a major turning point occurred when they attended their company's national conventions. Gregory and Sheri Lagana, Valerie Barger, Collette Van Reusen, and Dr. Kathy Bliese looked at those around them and said to themselves, "If they can do it, so can I." After her construction business collapsed and she had declared bankruptcy, Arlene Geraci took the money she planned to use for her move and spent it to attend a company training session. "I knew I had to get around successful people," says Arlene. The tactic worked, and Arlene's new goal is to make $1 million a year.

Derive your greatest satisfaction by helping others reach their goals. Such a thought may at first seem fanciful or idealistic. But consider the experience of Donna Larson-Johnson. When her income reached half a million dollars a year, she began losing the motivation to keep her business growing. She had attained her personal goals and satisfied the material needs of her family; why, she wondered, should she work to earn yet more money? Then Donna realized the pleasure she would gain by working with others in the achievement of their goals. She grasped what the best leaders have always known: In Donna's words, "Helping others succeed is more fulfilling than working to put bread on your own table." Donna's goal is to create 100 millionaires in her group, an objective that will lift her own income to $100,000 per month.

View the future as bright and promising. Donna Larson-Johnson cultivates a "positive vision" that helps her envision a future even brighter than the present. Ann and Steve Padover enjoy looking forward to the increasing comfort and security of their lives, a striking contrast to the days before they found Envion. Robbie Dodd, the former Miss America contestant who entered the direct selling industry four decades ago, nourishes an outlook on life that says, "Where I am going is more important than where I have been." Ann DeRitter Somes, now seventy-seven, is on fire with a vision of the future; a model of efficiency, she moves through her prospect lists with a relentlessness that Henry Ford would envy. Mary Lou Wilson, also in her seventies, built an organization of more than 30,000 distributors in Japan because she wanted to prove that age is no barrier to accomplishment.

Find meaning in a higher purpose. Pam Lewko's success has made possible her support of missionary families in New Guinea and South

Africa. Collette Van Reusen is motivated by being the number one contributor to cystic fibrosis research. Dr. Kathy Bliese, a physician and a minister, was able to fulfill her lifelong dream of building hospitals, founding churches, and broadcasting to millions around the world. Jan and William Todd put on events to support the Make-a-Wish Foundation, which fulfills the dreams of terminally ill children. Don Held launched Restore America, to educate teachers and pastors about the values and legacy of the country's Founding Fathers. Jody Victor has poured his energies into free enterprise education in the United States and abroad. Ken and Shirley Pontious have made substantial contributions to support a variety of causes, from subsidizing the incomes of teachers to supporting Mercy Corps International's efforts in relief and economic development. For the Rev. Jonathan Stanley and his wife Donna, network marketing and the ministry at times seem almost to be one and the same.

Forge enduring relationships. Les Brown maintains that there is one way in which the industry is unique—and that's in the loyalty that people have to one another. "In network marketing you are never in business by yourself," he says. That claim to uniqueness seems to hold true, at least as far as the modern world is concerned. What other kind of business sets the stage for people to voluntarily form such lasting relationships? Gary Morgan notes that within weeks of joining the business people form lifetime bonds that may be "stronger than they have with their own brothers." In case you wonder whether Gary's claim is overstated, you need only turn to Helyne Victor. Looking back a half a century, she notes, "In those early days a lot of us formed very, very strong bonds of friendship. And those friendships continue to this day."

Cultivate a sense of unlimited potential. Ruby Miller-Lyman remembers the effect that working in direct selling right out of high school had on her: "I started believing that I could have anything I wanted if I was willing to pay the price." After a lifetime of success, Ruby today holds onto that belief more strongly than ever. For some, the ultimate in achievement may be embodied in a private island, a jet plane, or a mansion. For others it's traveling the world with friends in your own yacht. Debbie and Jerry Campisi remember their own turning point, the breakthrough day when they had no more payments to make on anything. They stepped out of a world of limited horizons and into one where the possibilities for adventure and fulfillment were boundless. They entered the world the Victors speak of—a "Plan B" world, free of the routines and tedium most people take for granted. As the Victors say, once you are liberated you have a chance to enhance your own life and the lives of others. Roland Fox is reminded of his own breakthrough by the simple thought he is now able to play golf "whenever and wherever" he feels like it. For Kathleen Deoul, the meaning of her new freedom was captured in the exhilaration of parasailing with her daughter and knowing her family would always have all the time together they wanted. For others, the unlimited potential of their new existence hits home when they recall the almost unimaginable distance they have traveled. After years of diligent work, Euphiazene Linder was laid off and found herself desperate to replace her wages of $97 a week. Today, Euphiazene's $400,000 a year in residual income is just a small part of the story of her newfound happiness. Shirley Pontious looks at the beauty of her surroundings and can hardly believe how just a short time ago she was living with her son in someone else's garage and often going hungry. Collette Van Reusen was on the edge of bankruptcy. The Laganas and others went over that edge and declared themselves bankrupt. Ann and Steve Padover felt their life was one of shrinking horizons where it was ever more difficult to think positively about the future. For these people, comparing those grim days with their present good fortune still evokes a sense of wonder. "I can't believe it," says Shirley. "God bless America," says Collette. For almost all these people, a life of unlimited potential means one filled with the adventure of continual learning. As Les Brown and Mark Victor Hansen and Richard Ruffalo never tire of reminding audiences, it is the commitment to ongoing personal growth that epitomizes what is best about network marketing. You can't miss the tone of fresh excitement in Robbie Dodd's voice when she says, "I believe that there is no ceiling to life. I am the proverbial student. I am in a constant state of opening my heart, soul, and mind to learn more."

Afterword

The Network Marketing journey develops passion, balance, and happiness. Create a joyful life filled with passion—and start today.

—PAULETTE KIMURA-SHIMABUKURO

How did it begin? Why did you write it? One way to answer such questions is to revisit a scene with the authors—a psychiatrist and an editor—as they sit one afternoon in the spacious upstairs study of the psychiatrist's Ohio home. It's a quiet setting, though now and then the sounds of children romping indoors and out reverberate softly in the room. On the walls and shelves are the documents and mementos of the doctor's medical education, as well as some remembrances of his work with Mother Theresa.

As the shadows lengthen, the psychiatrist tells a story that leaves the two men silent and respectful. It concerns a person he knew, Carol Kall, who died of cancer in 1996 after a fifteen-year struggle. Carol's death triggered a cascade of thousands upon thousands of cards and letters of condolence. Ultimately, tens of thousands of such messages were sent to comfort the family and Carol's husband, Richard. The mourners told of how Carol had inspired them personally, and in so doing had changed their lives.

How did one woman become the center of such an outpouring of affection? She was not a celebrity, or a public figure, or a newsmaker. To be sure, she was an unfailingly positive presence who put the needs of others before her own. But since when in today's world can a private individual forge so many strong connections? The answer is obvious: She was in network marketing. She and Richard were Hawaiian Blue Diamonds in Nu Skin. They had entered the business in 1979.

As twilight deepens, the psychiatrist becomes impassioned on a subject he knows well—how our society and others treat their ill and dying members. Along with sickness, he notes, often comes isolation from friends and companions. Practical and financial concerns overwhelm both the dying person and the family, and emotional issues get shoved aside. Often, the dying person feels discarded.

The bonds of companionship in our mobile world tend to be weak and short-lived, notes the psychiatrist. When formed for the sake of convenience, they evaporate like snow in the desert. Here the editor gives a knowing nod. He recalls the memorial service for a woman whose office was once down the hall from his; she was the Manhattan-based chief of a national magazine. Her name was once known to millions of women. She attended White House functions, appeared on national television, and sat on boards and committees with prominent opinion makers. Yet by the time of her death several years after retiring she had been forgotten in the professional world she once inhabited. Only two of her old colleagues attended the service; they came away shaken by the lack of mourners, and pained that their friend's decades of energy, ambition, and dedication had left such a fleeting imprint.

I doubt that the bonds of friendship were ever there, said the psychiatrist.

"What? She was connected. Influential. One of an inner circle."

But deep, enduring bonds are forged by cooperation and heart-to-heart communication—not in competitive corporate environments.

"True. There, you're friends one day, competitors the next."

We're built to have trusting relationships in our lives. When our ancestors hunted in little bands or looked for shelter, they were working together to battle nature. They needed those bonds of trust. We still need them. And to be deeply satisfied we need more than just leisure-time friends. We need people with whom we share important goals.

"And when we work in similar conditions today . . . ."

That's right We still quickly form close relationships. But not much work is like that.

"Network marketing may be unique. Here you have huge networks welded together by the personal commitment of individuals."

When you think of a network, picture a heart at every node or intersection, all of them knotting together this vast web.

"Heart to heart. It's both a method of communicating and a supportive culture—an enduring supportive culture."

And the personal stories people tell help strengthen that web.

In such a network, Carol Kall's kindnesses were indelibly imprinted on the memories of her friends; here the web of support grew stronger as she declined. Carol's story also highlighted another feature of network marketing: Richard was at Carol's side all during her medical treatments; and though he spent less time on the business, their income continued to grow.

"I wonder how many examples like this there are."

We'll have to do research—lots of it.

As it turned out, the number of examples was endless—case after case of families with major medical crises where the lifestyle and income of network marketing had proved to be their salvation. One of the cases we looked at early in our research involved the Delisles, a prominent network marketing family. Dennis Delisle's parents, Frank and Rita, were the second couple in Amway to become Diamonds. An especially poignant part of their family saga was when Dennis donated his kidney to his wife, Sharon, when other donors could not be found. (The chance that a husband or other non-blood relative would be a donor was a million to one against.) The striking medical anecdote was a touching story about a devoted couple—though it did not at first seem to illuminate anything about network marketing per se. But its aftermath certainly did: After the kidney was successfully transferred to Sharon, Dennis relaxed, taking two years to return to work full time. During all that time, their business kept on growing. Doctors had cautioned Dennis about the impact the surgery would have on him physically. Dennis wasn't worried because, like Richard Kall, he knew that network marketing would make it possible for him to be there for his wife—and for her to later be there for him—"in sickness and in health."

Another similarity exists between the story of the Kalls and the Delisles. Richard and Carol's daughter Laura—a dynamic entrepreneur—joined Nu Skin herself after graduating from college Magna Cum Laude. She went on to become the youngest Hawaiian Blue Diamond in the company. Sharon and Dennis's children chose to become the third generation of their family in Amway.

"You'd have to call that an enduring business opportunity."

If you only got the psychic satisfaction, it would be bogus. In fact, the emotional rewards and the business success reinforce one another. We need to research them both.

You might wince at the thought of having an editor and a psychiatrist dissect your financial *and* emotional life and probe mercilessly into your background in order to test their hypothesis and sharpen their criteria. We're grateful to the many people who let us or our researchers do just that. Most were like Roland Manny—eager to share their experience in order to help more people understand network marketing. Roland walked out on his job as a prison guard when his supervisor ordered him to work on Christmas Eve. Nothing was going to keep Roland from spending that time with Tori, his daughter. His fellow guards, noting that Roland would be vested in just over a year, called him crazy to quit over such an issue. Today, Roland has left the negative environment of prison far behind and entered the world of MLM—just about the most positive of all environments. And though Tori is only six, Roland's bonuses from Herbalife have already funded her future college education. Roland seems to be speaking for everyone in this business who has discovered new meaning and purpose when he says: *Your life is not a dress rehearsal. If you don't like the part you are playing, it is up to you to change it.*

Another one of our research subjects was Bill Jerrils, a carpenter who lost almost everything following a back injury at work. Bill found that network marketing was a business he could do from bed while recovering. Today, Bill and his family are prospering with New Vision International. They live in a beautifully customized house, the finer points of which Bill always enjoys discussing. He can often be found making phone calls beside his exquisitely tiled free-form swimming pool while friends relax in the Jacuzzi or help themselves to food and refreshments at his capacious bar and outdoor refrigerator—all with a view of the mountains in the background. Bill's words echo those of countless distributors: *We work together as a family, living the American Dream.*

An important step in our research occurred when Valerie Free alerted us to the launch of Legacy USA, the subject of Chapter 1. Legacy's revolutionary product, BioChoice Immune Support, was a powerful example—a product with impressive corporate backing that would be distributed via network marketing and the use of heart-to-heart testimonials. Valerie is editor and publisher of the newsletter *Complementary Healing,* which covers breakthrough alternative health products—the kind often first introduced by network marketing and exemplified throughout this book. Yet health and nutrition is just one area where network marketing is in the vanguard. From cosmetics to computers, it's an industry that is forever renewing itself, and where the best is yet to come.

As Jeff and Shirley Thorne so aptly put it:

This business is for people who want to get in front of an economic tidal wave.

The beauty of it all is that the human dimension is always present. Looking back after more than three decades, Dom and Pat Coniguliaro are able to say with immense satisfaction:

What a blessing! The business is forever new, exciting, and profitable.

Is it any wonder that around the world, 50,000 people a day are signing up with a direct sales or network marketing company?

In expressing what everyone in the business would like to say, Roland Fox—the retired Air Force officer and master of succinctness whom we profiled in chapter 13—may have summarized it best. In Roland's words:

I am convinced that if you knew what I know, you would do what I am doing.

Index

Shoe Glow, Amway, 13
Silk Route, 46
Sims, Davie, 141
Skeptics, 313
Slessor, Mary Mitchell, 165, 168, 181
Smith, Adam, 92
Soetaert, Barbara "Bobbie," 108–114, 315
Soetaert, Jerry, 110
Spondylitis, 20
Stanley, Donna, 308–312
Stanley, Jonathan, 307–312
STAR (Super Top Achiever Award) Cruise, 78
Stevens, Paul, 39–42
Stoll, Cecilia, 100
Stolle, Ralph, 6–7, 8, 14–15
    Adalsteinsson, Örn and, 16
Stolle Immune Milk, 14–15
Stone, W. Clement, ix
Storms, Brenda, 266, 267
Storms, Don, 263–269, 316
Storms, Gail, 266, 267
Storms, Lee, 266, 267
Storms, Ruth, 263–269, 316
Success, ix-xi
Sun Tzu, 229, 230
Swiss Miss, 5
Sypniewski, Robert, 276
Sypniewski, Tara, 276

T

Tapes, listening to, 94, 133
Tartaglia, Barbara, xxi
Tartaglia, Louis, vii, xi-xii, xix-xxii
Taylor, Renee, 45, 46
Thailand, 48
The Evangelical Alliance Relief Program (TEAR), 172
Thinking big, 316
Thompson, Don, 79
Thorne, Jeff, 283–285, 316
Thorne, Shirley, 283–285, 316
Todd, Jan, 183–190, 318
Todd, William, 183–190, 318
Travel, 80–81

Triple Diamonds, Amway, 66
Tuttle, Linda, 9–10, 11–12, 13

U

Ultimate Cookie, 77
Unisys, 185
Upline support, 94–95
USANA, 157–162, 300–306

V

Van Reusen, Collette, 155–162, 300, 301–306, 316, 318, 319
Van Reusen, Gerry, 160, 162
Victor, Debra, 51–52, 61, 63, 67
Victor, Helyne, 53–54, 61, 63–64, 293, 299, 318
Victor, Jennifer-Helyne (Jenah), 70, 293–296, 299
Victor, Jody, 52–53, 55–56, 57, 59, 61–62, 64–66, 67, 68–69, 297, 316, 318
Victor, Joe, 51–52, 53–54, 62, 293, 316
    death of, 56–57
    wisdom of, 58–59
Victor, Joseph Edward, III, 70, 297, 299
Victor, Kathy, 69, 297
Victor, R. J. Paul, II, 63, 70
Victor, Ron, 51–52, 59–61, 64, 70, 295, 316
Victor, Stephen, 59, 70, 296–298
VIP (Values, Integrity, and People) system, 81

W

Walk-away residual income, 101–102
Walters, Barbara, 121
Wars, 86–87
Waugh, Carol, 243–245, 248–251
Waugh, Troy, 245, 251
Wave 3 (Poe), xi
The Wave 3 Way (Poe), xi
Wead, Doug, 94
Weathers, Sandy, 291–292
Weisman, Aileen, 65
Weisman, Theodore, 65–67

Wellness International Network, Ltd. (WIN), 164, 174–176, 180–183
Wentz, Myron, 160
Werzberger, Bella, 128–133, 314
Werzberger, Nick, 128–133, 314
Williams, Julie, 218–220, 222, 225
Williams, Mike, 138, 141, 218–220, 222–225, 315
Wilson, Bob, 238
Wilson, Mary Lou, 237–241, 317
Wilson International Networkers, 240
Wolf, Betty, 219, 221
Wolf, Phil, 222, 224
Working at Home magazine, 133

Y

Yager, Birdie, 265–266, 268
Yager, Dexter, 13, 30, 70, 258, 259–260, 265–266, 268, 276
Yager Youth Leadership Conference, 294–295
You Can Be Rich by Thursday (Pinnock), 142

Z

Ziglar, Zig, 87

Contact Information

To contact the authors for consultations and other information, please visit the following Web sites:

www.Heart2HeartMLM.com

www.ScottDeGarmo.com

www.Tartaglia.com